Passing the Torch

Passing the Torch

Succession, Retirement, and Estate Planning in Family-Owned Businesses

Mike Cohn

Second Edition

McGraw-Hill, Inc.

New York   St. Louis   San Francisco   Auckland   Bogotá
Caracas   Lisbon   London   Madrid   Mexico   Milan
Montreal   New Delhi   Paris   San Juan   São Paulo
Singapore   Sydney   Tokyo   Toronto

Library of Congress Cataloging-in-Publication Data

Cohn, Mike.
    Passing the torch : succession, retirement, and estate planning in
family-owned businesses / Mike Cohn.—2nd ed.
       p.   cm.
    Includes bibliographical references and index.
    ISBN 0-07-011603-2 :   —ISBN 0-07-011604-0 (pbk.) :
    1. Family corporations—United States—Popular works. 2. Business
enterprises—Registration and transfer—United States—Popular
works. 3. Tax planning—United States. I. Title.
KF1466.Z9C6 1992
346.73'0668—dc20
[347.306668]   92-4591
                                CIP

1 2 3 4 5 6 7 8 9 0   DOH/DOH   9 8 7 6 5 4 3 2

ISBN   0-07-011603-2   {HC}
ISBN   0-07-011604-0   {PBK}

*The sponsoring editor for this book was David Conti, the editing supervisor was Jane
Palmieri, and the production supervisor was Donald Schmidt. It was set in Palatino by
McGraw-Hill's Professional Book Group composition unit.*

Printed and bound by R. R. Donnelley & Sons Company.

To the memory of my dad,
Milton H. Cohn (1916–1991)

Contents

Part 5. Tying the Deal Together

Part 6. Estate Planning and Wealth Transfer

Part 7. Conclusion

Acknowledgments

This second edition could not have been written without the unbelievable teamwork and support from the folks at The Cohn Financial Group. There are three in particular who slaved to get this finished: Cherril Madsen is a source of inspiration because of her enthusiasm, energy, and dedication to this project. Her expectations for excellence and professionalism establish a high standard for measuring results. Lee Baumann's creativity has flourished over the past year and is reflected in the visual diagrams in the following pages. Her ability to create "maps" for clients and to visually illustrate complex designs should help the reader wander through this book. Mike Ortinau's computer skills, coupled with his constant willingness to help the team, were invaluable in the final stages of this book's development. Without his help, we never would have finished.

Others in the firm provided support in many ways: Jayne Sassano and Howard Steele helped maintain sanity and stability. Sue Osborne, Dina Lansdell, and Audrey Jendruczak willingly took on extra jobs to keep the company running. Roger Hancock is an inspiration in many ways, but especially for his courage and patience in wanting to help other family business owners. Patty Giacchino helped us develop our corporate vision and worked to build our own infrastructure in the midst of our entrepreneurial chaos.

I want to especially thank Jayne Pearl, who is a godsend. Jayne provided more than independent editorial help—she consistently helped my writing to stay focused and provided the feedback that I wanted and feared at the same time. I believe this book has improved over the first edition. Jayne should get credit for any improvements. Her journalistic background, along with her sincere interest in family businesses, makes her a rare and talented individual.

I also wish to thank the Family Firm Institute (FFI). Some of the members of that organization have helped me and my firm grow professionally over the past few years. Thanks to them I have expanded my knowledge and have been able to better serve family businesses by having access to their skills.

Leslie Isaacs has been especially influential by introducing me to the power of teambuilding with family businesses. For her, a special thank you for her role as the Fairy Godmother. Dennis Jaffe has been invaluable as an adviser and academic mentor. Kathy Wiseman brings an impressive dimension to the planning process through her probing questions and ability to get to the heart of issues.

Tom Spitzer, Eli Morgan, and Dick Schwartz of the M Group have been a lighthouse for us. Their support and sincere interest in family business will raise the skills and professionalism of financial service providers.

David Conti, my editor at McGraw-Hill, believed in this project from inception. Without him, the first and second editions never would have been born. His support has been great.

My thanks to *Family Business* magazine for the permission to use material which originally appeared in several issues of the magazine. This material is included in Chapters 13, 16, 18, and 27.

Finally, I wish to acknowledge all of the clients of The Cohn Financial Group for providing me with the experiences and ideas that are the foundation for this book.

I'm especially grateful to my own family for giving me the experience of growing up in a family business—and the love for it.

Mike Cohn

Introduction

I grew up in a family-owned business started by my great-grandfather in 1873. The business began as a general merchandise store and evolved into retail sales of men's, women's, and children's clothing. When my grandfather died in 1944, my dad took over the business with my mom's cousin. Dad bought the cousin out in 1955, and I don't think they've talked to each other since.

I began working in my dad's business in 1954, when I was six years old, helping to assemble paper boxes, run errands, and ride in the van that delivered packages to customers. Our entire family revolved around the business: My mom worked there every day, and my sister joined her on holidays and during school vacations. More important, all the family meals were planned around when Dad was coming home from "the store." We'd always wait for Dad to arrive before we had lunch and supper. Even though the store was physically distant, it was the subject of most family discussions and always "in" our house. My dad would hire friends to work in the store during the Christmas holidays—wrapping packages, making deliveries, working on "the floor" to make sales. The store was a source of pride for me and a source of revenue for friends. The business grew as Dad expanded it to additional locations. Everything seemed in order.

As I grew older, Dad became increasingly resistant to change. For a clothing store to succeed, it has to stay current with fads and fashions and provide the latest "look" to the consumer. Not to my dad. When neckties narrowed and suit lapels widened, Dad steadfastly believed that wide ties and narrow lapels would come back. Of course they did, but not fast enough.

In 1967, while I was in college, Dad closed the store. He didn't sell it, he liquidated it—the worst of all possible conclusions to a family business. During a liquidation, no value is paid for goodwill, no consideration given for reputation or commitment to community. People buy assets for pennies on the dollar. And finally, when there are only a few pieces left, a liquidator arrives, loads it all onto a truck, and carts it away. What's left is an empty building. And sometimes an empty family.

When the store closed, a large part of our family heritage was lost. For more than three generations the store had been the primary focus of the family's activities. All of a sudden, the store was no longer there. Years later, I understood the dynamics that drove my father's business decisions.

When I went to college, I studied psychology and ultimately earned a master's degree in a unique discipline known as humanistic psychology. Abraham Maslow, one of the fathers of humanistic psychology, explored human motivations and concluded that our inner nature—our basic human capacities—is generally good. Basic needs for life, safety and security, belonging and affection, respect and self-respect, and self-actualization are what motivate all of us. Our baser impulses—destructiveness, sadism, cruelty—are reactions to the frustrations we experience when our fundamental needs cannot be realized (actualized). Maslow concluded that when we encourage our inner nature and allow it to guide our lives, we become healthy, productive, and happy.

The tenets of humanistic psychology—security, growth in the human experience, and a systems approach to understanding decision making—are instructive for family business systems.

Most tax experts—whether they are accountants, attorneys, or financial professionals—focus on the technical aspects of financial planning. That is, how do we minimize corporate or personal income or estate taxes? How do we plan for the transfer of the business in a tax-efficient manner? How do we pass the assets of the estate through to the next generation so as to minimize unnecessary transfer taxes? Technical considerations are significant and certainly important in the financial planning process. Yet humanistic issues cannot be ignored: The client's needs, desires, fears, wants, and goals are as crucial to financial planning as are tax and investment codes. To ignore these humanistic issues is to ignore basic needs—for safety and security, belonging and affection, respect and self-respect, and self-actualization.

It is this needs-based, client-centered approach, coupled with extensive technical skills, that forms the foundation for my company, and the thesis for this book on business transfer planning. The first part of the book explores the many reasons that business owners are reluctant to "pass the torch." By understanding and addressing these issues, business owners and successors can get themselves in a position to apply the practical solutions that make up the remainder of the book.

The problems inherent in a business transfer cannot be oversimplified. The emotional and psychological trauma that accompanies the transfer of a family business will cause even the strongest business owner to wrestle with doubts: "Have I made the right decision?" "Should I take an easier way out and sell to a large conglomerate?"

Maslow understood this trauma when he depicted a hierarchy of human needs. Growth toward higher levels of accomplishment causes many people to walk away from the challenge. Business owners succeed against over-whelming odds, and the challenge of transferring the family business cannot be considered lightly. But the rewards, if understood in the context of human growth, can be the greatest accomplishment of all.

Business owners reach a stage in life where they think about and (possibly) begin to plan the orderly transition of their family business and their retirement. Maybe they will sell the business, or transfer ownership to a competent family member or key employee(s). Having worked hard for decades to see their company prosper and grow, they now wrestle with questions about how best to protect the "golden goose" that has supported their family and employees for so many years.

It will be up to the next generation, the son or daughter or key employee, to build the business further. What qualities of leadership and business acumen must the successor possess in order to ensure the survival and profitability of the family business? What strategies should be used to achieve smooth transition of ownership? What choices must be made now in order to promote a succession of leadership that will leave the company running in the black perhaps for several generations to come?

These are the questions addressed in this book. The answers will not rely only on numbers or clearly definable business terminology; human and emotional issues surrounding a business transfer are also tackled, to help the family make the right decisions. What the current business owner is contemplating is a major life change, fraught with financial and emotional risks. My goal in this book is to reduce that anxiety by carefully mapping out the territory that must be covered in order to make informed, calculated decisions based on facts.

Many current owners may not even know what decisions they need to make. However, those who follow this book's guidelines and advice step by step should find at least one strategy for successful business transition that factors in their own unique family and business issues. Decisions will therefore be much less difficult to make and implement. This book will:

- Show how to avoid unnecessary taxation on transferring the business so that the family keeps more of the wealth that has been created

- Help develop a transfer strategy that suits everyone's needs and goals

- Highlight and discuss most of the issues and potential conflicts that arise out of the participant's current "life cycle"

- Detail a strategy to cope successfully with the relevant issues concerning family business transfer of ownership and control

- Help anticipate contingencies and problems that might arise out of decisions

In my experience, many business owners who are superb at implementing their own decisions are often unable to communicate clearly with their family and employees about important business plans and ideas. Although many family business situations are unusual or even unique, they all share a number of concerns. I will identify these common issues and show how to deal with them most effectively.

Part 1 of the book focuses on how to resolve conflicts common to all owner-managers of family businesses. Millions of businesspeople have already gone through these experiences. I discuss those experiences in the light of current life situations. Both owners and successors need to formulate realistic and effective goals, and develop an acceptable "risk tolerance" level. The business transition period can be very confusing and complex, emotionally as well as financially. But there are guidelines to follow that will ease the transition and maximize the current owner's financial independence and security.

Some variables can be controlled, and some cannot. I also outline alternative solutions and provide guidelines to determine what plan is right, taking into account family emotions, business realities, and the complex issues that accompany relinquishing control and letting go.

Part 2 presents formulas for determining the company's value and how to engineer that value in various ways. Creating a new corporation or selling the business to a key employee or outside party will all be explored. These various strategies have been researched and tested thoroughly, and I present details as they apply to particular situations.

Parts 3 through 5 examine options and techniques of ownership transfer and outline various transfer strategies that have been used successfully in hundreds of business and family situations throughout the United States. These sections detail techniques and show how to apply them to any given situation.

Successfully implementing a business transfer strategy requires creativity, flexibility, and above all *commitment*. Effective transfer strategies are based on where owners and successors are *now* in their business and family life. The strategies presented in this book are flexible and open-ended: Each can be set up so that if conditions change at any time, the plan may be altered and even abandoned, depending on specific contingencies.

It is important, however, to realize that there are some "points of no return." The plan should be prepared so that participants will not have to take any unnecessary risks or cross the point of no return until everyone is prepared, and all players and proper conditions are in place. Up to the point of no turning back, there are "abort" procedures to change the timing or the whole structure of the succession plan.

With proper planning, after the point of no turning back, people will usually experience a sense of euphoria, of confidence that they are doing the right thing to protect the business, the family, and the future. I have heard many exclamations of delight and relief at this point in the plan, such as "I feel a tremendous burden has been lifted off my shoulders." Good planning and informed decisions are the best insurance for peace of mind.

The owners will have to consider a wide variety of input in making a succession plan. The spouse may want to run the business after the owner's death, or may encourage the owner to divide up the estate equally, but the current owner may know that the outcome of such a plan would prohibit the chances of the business surviving after the owner's death or retirement. Some key people have been employed for 20 or 30 years and play a large part in the success of the business. These are the "adopted family members," and the current and future owners will want to consider their roles and futures carefully in structuring an equitable and effective plan, especially if key people are expected to work for the spouse, son, or daughter.

The key employee who has devoted 15 or 20 years to making the business more profitable may be much more deserving than the son or daughter who seems bent on destroying the business with bickering and greed. Owners must think carefully about the key players in the plan. Maybe the son would make a wonderful company president in a few years, and the goal may be to protect his succession interest in the firm. Perhaps there are in-laws who are competent and wish to join the firm as managers. There are ways to accomplish these goals without endangering either the future of the company or the security of any deserving employees. In this book I share my experiences concerning how to determine who is ready to handle the business responsibilities of running a company.

Part 6 explores the ways in which careful estate planning will guarantee security to a spouse in the event of the current owner's death without the spouse having to run the business. You will also learn how recent legislation may require the family to change existing estate plans. Most important, you will discover how estate planning and business transfer planning can be coordinated to keep the family together and reduce estate taxation for heirs.

Family business participants are not alone. This book presents numerous case studies of business and family people who have successfully gone through a transition. With their experience and my guidance, I hope that by the time you finish this book, any anxiety you may feel about "passing the torch" will be vastly diminished. As you begin developing a game plan, I hope you will face the challenge with optimism, excitement, and confidence. If this book provides new insights, can guide you through difficult obstacles, and creates a vision of positive alternatives for you and your family business, then it will have accomplished its purpose.

PART 1

Overcoming Personal Hurdles to a Successful Business Transfer

1
The American Dream Machine

The success story behind the founder of a family business often reads like a modern epic. The founder struggles and perseveres in the face of overwhelming odds. In so doing, he or she becomes a hero in a world that needs heroes, a central figure who inspires others, and the catalyst for family ideals and traditions. As a result of the founder's vision, leadership, and bravery, the family achieves economic prosperity; the founder gains power and recognition; and the community is enriched by the creation of jobs. Ideally, the epic ends here and stories are then written about the hero's accomplishments.

Reality, however, is usually quite different. At the height of the business founder's success and power, someone inevitably comes along—a family member, a trusted adviser, even a key employee—and suggests that the founder relinquish the reins of the business to others. At this point, the heroic epic frequently turns to tragedy. The founder doesn't want to relinquish power and the business becomes fragmented as those involved choose sides. As the hero becomes defensive, power is consolidated and battles begin. Often the tragedy ends with a vanquished and shrunken hero and the loss of a power base.

This drama unfortunately is enacted daily in offices, plants, and courtrooms throughout the United States. Family businesses permeate our economy; yet for many businesses, ownership succession has not been resolved.

Family businesses make up 90 percent of the 15 million businesses in the United States. They account for 50 percent of all wages paid and 40 percent of the gross national product.[1] One-third of the Fortune 500 companies are either family owned or family controlled. Well-known names like Tyson Foods, Herman Miller, Hallmark, Bechtel, Marriott, Wal-Mart, Johnson Wax, Cargill, Mars Candy, Estee Lauder, Levi-Strauss, Forbes, Dow-Jones, and Anheuser-Busch are part of a long list of family-controlled businesses.

Family businesses are recognized as special types of companies. Their unique qualities can provide substantial competitive advantages. Family members who work together generally care for one another, their employees, and their customers. Employees are often more dedicated; owners tend to be more approachable. Respect, job security, responsibility, emphasis on quality, long-term goals and thinking, and empowering are attributes I have encountered when researching and discussing family businesses. Books such as *The 100 Best Companies to Work for in America, In Search of Excellence,* and *The Fifth Discipline* extol values and cultures associated with family businesses.

Futurist Alvin Toffler noted in 1990 that giant firms are too slow and maladaptive for today's high-speed business world. In contrast, he noted that family firms

> can make quick decisions. They often are willing to take daring entrepreneurial risks. Family firms can change faster, and adapt better to new market needs. Communication through constant face-to-face interaction and even pillow talk is swift and rich, conveying much with only a grunt or a grimace. Family members typically enjoy a deep sense of "ownership" in the firm, evince high motivation, are strongly loyal and often work superhuman hours.[2]

But there's a dark side that haunts many family businesses. Family enterprises are also known for their feuds. Passion, commitment, sacrifice, and other intense feelings can be virtues or vices of family firms, depending on the perspective of the observer. Stories about infighting among members of the Schoen family of Phoenix (the U-Haul Company), the Bingham family of Louisville (owners of the *Louisville Courier Journal*), and the Beaman family of Nashville (Pepsi-Cola franchisees) have all been exposed in the media.

Another dark-side factor: Aging companies and aging markets require planned change—regeneration, reframing, rethinking—but aging owners are often reluctant to implement the needed actions. Their passionate attachments and resistance to planned change often explain their reluctance to develop well thought-out succession plans.

When a founder-owner ages or dies, the vision which drove the family business often fades or dies as well. Almost 70 percent of family businesses do not survive into the second generation. Many are sold, merged, or liquidated. For every two family businesses that continue into a second generation, four do not. Of those two that succeed, only one survives into a third generation. The typical family business has a life expectancy of only 24 years.[3] Incredibly, then, every 24 years over 10 million businesses will need to be created and survive just to *replace* the goods and services from the 70 percent that do not survive. In other words, we will have to run harder and harder just to stay in the same place. When the business vision is lost, the long-term business prospects may dim. Vision motivates people to take risk, to grow and change, to imagine something better and work toward those goals. Business owners without purpose or direction will ultimately fail.

The health and welfare of a family business have a pervasive influence that extends far beyond the business's physical facilities. All family members are affected by the business owner's success or failure, or how brightly the spark of commitment glows, and in whom it glows. Succession planning in a family business has far-reaching consequences. Ultimately, many who are associated with the family business are affected: suppliers and customers, employees, and the community at large.

Owners and successors frequently encounter problems during the process of transferring the family business. Sometimes these problems can be resolved. At other times, business transfer problems result in tragic outcomes. For example, qualified family members or key employees may become disenfranchised because they never have an opportunity to continue the family business; or children and employees may be ill prepared for leadership roles. The owner may be unaware of the options available or unwilling to relinquish control. Finally, the family may suffer extreme financial loss from estate taxation, much of which could have been avoided with proper planning.

The thesis of this book is that ownership succession can be an exciting and rewarding process, a journey, and an adventure. With the proper navigation instruments, maps, and know-how, current and future owners can reduce potentially tragic outcomes by creating positive alternatives for the family and the business.

The Last Frontier

The family-owned business may be one of the last frontiers of the American Dream. The American pioneers of the mid-nineteenth century followed a vision and discovered new lands. As the end of the twentieth century approaches, America's pioneers are entrepreneurs—tomorrow's family businesses. The following passage, originally written in 1931 to describe pioneers of the last century, sounds strangely modern: "There was zest in their life, adventure in the air, freedom from restraint; men [and women] developed a hardihood which made them insensitive to the hardships and lack of refinements." But there were challenges: "The loneliness that men [and women] endured...must have been such as to crush the soul, provided one did not meet the isolation with an adventurous spirit."[4]

Like the American frontier settler, the American entrepreneur has created new products, new services, and new technologies that have had profound changes on daily life. As families have watched entrepreneurs' visions become reality, jobs have been created and communities developed—all influenced by the business and its owners.

Although entrepreneurs will always be a part of society's fabric, an increasing number of business owners—those who started their companies just after World War II—are approaching retirement. Anticipation of leisure time and activities is too frequently overshadowed by unresolved business ownership and transfer issues. These unresolved issues create a push-pull emotion in many business owners who feel drawn in several opposing directions simultaneously. Inaction and procrastination regarding succession planning are usually the result.

Push-Pull Issues

We're Living Longer

Today more than 30 million Americans—12 percent of the population—are over 65. In the last 20 years, this group has grown more than twice as fast as the rest of the population. The National Institute on Aging, a division of the National Institutes of Health, projects that by 2040 life expectancy will be 86 years for men and 91.5 for women.[5]

Americans are living longer, but they also are leaving the work force earlier—many now retire between ages 61 and 62 rather than at age 65.[6] Fewer and fewer business owners are turning over the reins just as they are about to die. Young retirees in their early sixties (who may live into their eighties) may still have fully one-fourth of their lives ahead of them. The prospect of exiting the family business assumes daunting dimensions when the owner and spouse face 20 years of active retirement.

Concerns about financial security and the retirement dynamics of the family business owner take on greater importance. The issue becomes especially complex when the value of the business is the largest asset on the owner's financial statement and when most of the current income is derived directly or indirectly from the business.

Owners experience a push-pull feeling when they are physically or emotionally ready for a life change but are not ready to contend with financial insecurity, their marital relationship, and their lack of preparedness for something new. These concerns cause owners to avoid planning for succession.

Confusion over Technical Options Available

Advisers to family business owners often have their own biases; instead of listening to clients' needs, they often impose their own views. The estate-planning adviser may attempt to convince an owner that a properly drawn estate plan is the key to succession in the family business—without grasping the fact that many other complex issues need to be solved during a lifetime. The CPA may be preoccupied with current income tax planning and uncomfortable with the idea of accounting for family dynamics.

Our constantly changing income and estate tax laws have become so complex that "generalist" attorney–family business advisers may be out of step with current law while specialists have such mastery over esoteric tax codes that they seem to speak in foreign tongues, incomprehensible at the client level.

Pension and profit-sharing plans, initially established for the owner's benefit as a financial option to coordinate with succession planning, are no longer understandable as retirement benefits are curtailed by legislative changes. Plans are being terminated as administrative and funding costs continue to climb and the owner's share of the benefits package continues to dwindle.

Even when tax-driven succession or estate plans are implemented, the only certainty is that they will need to be changed. Tax laws are enacted, then repealed; planning that was thought to be "grandfathered" (protected under current law) is no longer valid when new regulations are enacted retroactively. It's easier for the family business owner to procrastinate and focus on short-term needs and crises rather than cope with long-range planning.

One of the push-pull issues here is the owner's growing awareness that long-term adviser relationships that have evolved into personal and social relationships as well may need to change. As advisers age (and burn out), they become less interested in listening to their client just at the time when the business owner needs them most.

Selling Out May Not Be So Good After All

Owners are pushed by the knowledge that they can solve financial security concerns with a merger or sale, and pulled by the fear that such a change may permanently alter and disrupt the company and the team of people that they worked so hard to create. When independent owners witness peers selling their businesses to third-party buyers, the aftersale horror stories may discourage them from following that path.

Acquisitions can cause employees who stay with the new owner to feel a loss of control and self-esteem. Several research studies indicate that after an acquisition, employees often experience the stress symptoms associated with a major life change. One study compares the experience to the grieving process triggered when someone close dies. One employee said, "It was like a best friend had died. I felt sad and angry. I did not know what was in store for my future; my productivity dropped off and I eventually left the company."[7]

Sadness, anger, depression, anxiety, apathy, lowered morale and motivation, reduced productivity, and higher turnover can all result among employees who stay on after an acquisition. These effects also extend to former owners who stay on as the acquirer's executives.

Another study identifies two types of mergers: "melting pots" and "pressure cookers." When the acquired firm's employees voluntarily adopt the culture of the acquiring firm, the melting pot occurs. When the acquired firm's employees are coerced, the pressure cooker results.[8]

Both processes, merger and acquisition, also affect the business profoundly. One study of chief executives reported a disruption of the company's management system; managers were severely overextended after the transaction. The sought-after financial security, satisfied by a sale, gets postponed when owners aren't ready to walk away from "their baby" and their adopted family of employees.

The Concept of Family Is Changing

When the owner started the business, the concept of family was simpler. Relatives were often called in to help—because they were "known" and could be trusted. Today the traditional American family has disappeared and been replaced by a variety of hybrid families. Siblings, children, uncles, aunts, and cousins may be physically distant or emotionally estranged; the key employees may seem more like "family" to the current owner.

Fairness to children, caring for aging parents, marriages and remarriages, all add to the business owners' reluctance to address succession planning. Business owners and spouses often find themselves torn—financially and emotionally—between the needs and demands of young children and those of their aging parents.

As divorce rates soar, succession planning becomes exponentially complicated, in both community and noncommunity property states. Negotiations with a former spouse who retains ownership in the business may be a necessary part of a succession plan. Or the succession plan may become stalled until the owner's divorce is finalized. When the family business owner has grown apart from the spouse, keeping the business and ignoring the marital problems may, mistakenly, seem tempting. Letting go of the business and simultaneously confronting marital issues is often too threatening.

As remarriage rates increase (currently 80 percent of those who get divorced remarry), stepfamilies encounter new strains on their new relationships and family business operations. When new extended families are instantly created, equalization and fairness issues centered around family business ownership become more complex.

Summary

If you are like most business families, the business represents most of the family's wealth—and most of the years of the current owner's life. Whether the business is sold outright, transferred within the family, or transferred to key employees, all parties involved in the process will wrestle with many soul-searching decisions. Their decisions should attempt to balance responsibilities to themselves, their family, employees, and the business.

References

1. *Newsweek*, December 12, 1983; also in John Ward's *Keeping the Family Business Healthy* (San Francisco: Jossey-Bass, 1987), p. xv.

2. Alvin Toffler, *Powershift: Knowledge, Wealth and Violence at the Edge of the 21st Century* (New York: Bantam Books, 1990), p. 188.

3. Leon Danco, *Beyond Survival,* 5th ed. (Cleveland: The University Press, Inc., 1979), p. 14.

4. Walter Prescott Webb, *The Great Plains* (New York: Grosset & Dunlap, 1971), pp. 505–506.

5. Ken Dychtwald and Joe Flower, *Age Wave: The Challenges and Opportunities of an Aging America* (New York: Bantam Books, 1990), p. 6.

6. Neal Cutler Boettner, "Financial Gerontology," *CLU Journal,* January 1991.

7. Bruce Brody, "The Coping Styles of High-Performing Employees Involved in a Corporate Acquisition," (unpublished Ph.D. thesis), Saybrook Institute, 1990.

8. Lee Tom Perry, "Merging Successfully: Sending the 'Right' Signals," *Sloan Management Review,* Spring 1986, p. 49.

2
What Succession Planning Is All About

Succession planning involves many diverse areas, including money, financial security, and the transfer of wealth, tax planning, future business strategies, and how family values affect long-term personal goals. Most of all, it involves consensus building.

There are a number of participants involved in transferring ownership and day-to-day operational control of a family business. The current owner (or owners) is contemplating letting go; the current owner's spouse may or may not be active in the business, but is also contemplating significant life changes associated with the succession plan. There are successors who are active in the business: children, in-laws, cousins, and other relatives. Each of them must be considered as an independent participant, since there is no assurance that together they represent any organized group. Even a brother or sister of the owner may be a successor, in which case there are two succession plans to be addressed: the acquisition of the successor's interest by the sibling and simultaneously the sibling successor's own succession plan. Also, the spouses of the successors will have an influential impact—for better or for worse.

There are key, nonfamily executives who will be participating as mentors to the successors, or possible successors themselves. Then there are the advisers: the golf buddy, the family business consultant, the individual therapist, the long-term family or company attorney, the CPA, and perhaps the trust officer. Finally, there are the inactive family members, who must nonetheless be represented in the planning and discussions. Some inactive family members might like to be active if circumstances changed. By the same token, some active family members might prefer to be somewhere else or do something different; only personal or family pressures and fears are keeping them in the business. (More about this in Chapter 4.)

Rules of the Game

Whenever you play an unfamiliar game, one of the first questions is "What are the rules?" In succession planning, there are two critical rules.

Rule 1: There Should Be Only One Team Playing This Game

The "team" should be composed of all the participants described above. That's easier said than done. However, assembling the playing group into a team is the first task in the succession plan. In fact, if you cannot assemble the participants into a team, the odds are that you cannot win the game of internal succession. In that case, external succession—selling to an outside third party—becomes the preferred goal. The next few chapters will explore some of the issues and challenges you face in assembling this disparate group of individuals, including the holdouts and prima donnas, into one playing team.

Rule 2: There Are No Other Rules

Therefore, the first rule becomes extremely important if you and your team expect to succeed.

Some other factors come into play: Knowing when to start is one. The motivation of the participants is another. Third is knowing how much time you have on the succession clock. Fourth is knowing what qualities your participants need to work together on the team. Fifth is recognizing and successfully dealing with the obstacles and challenges you and your participants will face in assembling your team and maintaining it during the transfer process.

Knowing When to Start

Most advisers will tell you that having a succession plan begins at the same time that you receive ownership and control of a business—even if you're 25 years old. While that is true, some of the time it's important to distinguish a contingency plan from a succession plan. A contingency plan covers what happens if the owner is run over by a Mack truck, has a disabling heart attack, breaks a (*you fill in the blank*) in a skiing accident, or dies in an airplane crash. A contingency plan covers death, disability, or unexpected, usually tragic, events. Every business owner should always have a current contingency plan in place.

A succession plan covers what happens when people say, "It's time for a change in ownership or management." A succession plan should not be organized until a certain point in the owner's life. The succession plan differs from the contingency plan primarily in the motivation that accompanies it. The contingency plan is triggered by abnormal, accidental causes. It is the "worst-case scenario," because no one can plan if or when the contingency will occur.

The succession plan is at the other end of the spectrum. It addresses retirement and withdrawal, allows planning for the event to occur, can be triggered by natural causes, and describes a "best-case scenario." Along the spectrum from worst case to best case are many options. As described in the next chapter, succession plans need to consider multiple contingencies and, therefore, have safeguards built into the process.

Motivation

A number of factors can trigger initiation of the succession process. The motivation may come when the owner feels burned out, no longer challenged, or ready for something new and exciting. Abraham Maslow describes this process as a "metamotivation": someone who has already suitably gratified the basic human needs and is now motivated in other, higher ways. Maslow describes metamotivated individuals as having "a feeling of belongingness and rootedness, satisfied in their love needs, having friends and feeling loved and loveworthy, having status and place in life and respect from other people, and having a reasonable feeling of worth and self-respect."[1]

Maslow suggests that metamotivated people are devoted to something greater: values that are personally important, such as the perpetuation of what the family business represents.

On the other hand, if business owners have not satisfied their basic needs—or in Maslow's words, have not "self-actualized"—they may not be motivated to step aside or even consider that it's time to do so. In that case, murmurs and grumbles may begin from the other participants. (Specific symptoms are covered in Chapter 5.) These murmurs and grumbles will generally increase in both intensity and in the number of people participating, until the clamor reaches the awareness of the owner. The earlier an owner becomes aware, the sooner the planning process can begin. Business owners must find a way to understand and address their unsatisfied needs as the cornerstone of any planning. Although the other players can prepare for succession without the owner—by educating themselves, by recognizing their family's values and how these are expressed in the cultural history of the business—the succession plan cannot actually begin until the owner joins the process.

Dennis Jaffe, a family business consultant in San Francisco, has identified several problems that eventually cause murmurs and grumbles:

- The business is a one-trick pony and has not grown beyond its initial product or market.

- The owner denies the need to change and refuses to innovate and adapt to new realities.

- The owner suffers from "burnout," the successor lacks energy or ideas ("we'll do it the way Dad always did it"), and the business is becoming tired and aged along with the founder-owner.

- Family needs overwhelm business realities.

- There's poor communication and an inability to confront issues.

- The organization becomes weakened when "the way we do things" becomes bureaucratized and outmoded.

- The current owner spends more time outside the business than in: "going through the chairs" of his or her trade group or becoming involved with lobbying, local politics, or personal affairs.[2]

Motivating a reluctant owner to join the process can be only one of many challenges. *Keeping* the owner in the process can be especially difficult as the participants begin to encounter the inevitable hurdles and obstacles. Reluctant players in general need to have their hands held. Often their reluctance stems from the fact that personal needs overshadow the needs of the business. In that case, any solution must be constantly defined in light of the personal needs it will satisfy for that participant.

All players should keep their eyes open. Knowing when to start the succession process generally occurs as a window of opportunity. The window may not stay open very long. Here are some examples of when the window has opened for others.

- The current owner has just finished a term as president of his trade association. After months of strategic thinking about the future of the trade group, the day-to-day operations of the family business seem mundane. He misses the speeches, the meetings, the first-class travel.

- The current recession has been longer and tougher than previous ones the owner can recall. Layoffs are painful, and expensive equipment upgrades are required to be competitive. The owner's personal salary needs to be cut to alleviate cashflow problems. She's done this before. Does she have the energy to go through it again?

- Acquisition companies have been buying up competitors. The owner has been a holdout but wonders for how long. A deal similar to those his peers are rumored to have received would give him financial security for life. He could spend more time—at the lake, in Florida, in Arizona.

If any of these sound familiar to successors, then they should act quickly, because the breeze may be blowing through that open window. This is an opportune time to bring up tactfully the subject of retirement or succession planning with the owner.

How Much Time Is on the Succession Clock?

Usually as the participants assemble, owners believe they control the time clock.

Fact: The succession clock should be mutually set by all participants. One owner announced to everyone that he planned to retire at some far distant point in the future. He was shocked to hear the participants boo and hiss at what he believed was an enlightened pronouncement. Another owner erred in the opposite direction when she assembled participants and announced her retirement immediately. In fact, she thought she could leave the game to the participants. She believed she wouldn't even have to stay on the playing field. She, too, was shocked by boos and hisses; the successors claimed they were not prepared to play.

The challenge is to identify and agree on common goals in order to establish a realistic time frame for achieving them. As you will see in the next chapter, as the participants assemble, two processes must be addressed simultaneously: an ownership transfer plan and a management succession plan. These plans are different yet interconnected. They are the yin and yang of succession planning.

The time needed on the succession clock will also depend on how long it takes the participants to become a team. Here are examples of how the succession clock differed for three clients.

Six Months: Two brothers, Roger and David, were ready to retire yesterday. They had two key, nonfamily employees. One had been chief financial officer for 10 years; the other had been general manager for 12 years. The CFO and general manager could run every aspect of the business. In fact, Roger and David were spending less time in the company and more time pursuing personal interests. The succession clock ran for six months. That's how long it took the CFO and general manager to put together a leveraged buyout of Roger and David. Keep in mind that before the ownership transfer began, the management group had spent 10 years becoming a team with Roger and David.

Four Years: Janice and Erica, business partners for 30 years, also wanted to retire yesterday. The only problem was their team wasn't ready. They had four key employees but had never spent time coaching them into more responsible positions. The key people were loyal, and dedicated—workers. They hadn't been invited to learn to think like owners or entrepreneurs. They had not been given opportunities to make mistakes. Janice and Erica ran the show. In this case the succession clock was set for four years, with specific management succession objectives and performance requirements. Janice and Erica agreed to become mentors and coaches instead of always "doing." An ownership transfer plan for the four employees dovetailed into the management succession plan.

Seven Years: George was 53 and looked forward to retiring at 60. His goal was to transfer the business to his son, who had recently joined him after completing his MBA. The son was smart, but had no portfolio of experience. George was just beginning to identify the participants in the succession game. He also needed to put together a nonfamily management team, with some "golden handcuffs," as an interim step. In the meantime, his son could begin to learn the business. In this case, George needed a contingency plan that would give him a foundation for building his succession plan. George needed to train a management group and simultaneously mentor his son into a leadership role.

A short lead time (six months) usually means the transaction will be financed out of future earnings of the company. If the business isn't successful in the future, the earnings to pay the withdrawing owners may not be available. A longer lead-in period gives the company more time to set corporate funds aside, thus guaranteeing payments at a later date.

The longer you wait to assemble the players into a team, the more difficult it becomes, and the fewer options you have on how you handle the succession obstacles.

The longer the lead time, the greater the financial alternatives available, and the smaller the risk for the successors. The greatest number of options for all players occurs when there is plenty of time to experiment, make changes, take risks, develop safeguards. In essence, this is akin to having time to let a team practice before a game. With practice, you can make adjustments in the positions the players hold and "fine tune" the process. If you don't have time for team practice, the risks and the stakes are much higher when you enter the playing field. Owners should begin assembling participants into a team at least three to five years before a transfer of ownership or retirement will occur. Five to seven years is ideal.

Building Your Team

The challenges in assembling players into a team will differ depending on whether the participants are family members active in the business, family members not active in the business, nonfamily key executives, or perhaps all of the above. Whoever the participants, when they share values, power, and mutual respect, and maintain interpersonal boundaries, they are well on their way to putting a team together. The participants can then begin to define, for the good of the team, the succession objectives and how much time is on the succession clock.

Developing and maintaining a successful leadership team (including family and other key executives) is not an easy task. It is the engine that drives the business. A healthy respect for the dynamics of this team, along with "proper maintenance," is essential to the successful transition. Leslie Isaacs and Jack Gibb, both family business consultants, have identified four concepts to illuminate the characteristics of an effective team: trust, openness, realization, and interdependence (TORI).

Members of successful family business teams have tremendous *trust* in one another. They count on one another to be honest, caring, and reliable in meeting commitments. There is a lack of fear in the atmosphere, because of the support that the members come to expect from one another.

The trust contributes to and is based upon the *openness* of team members. Each member contributes a perspective, information, and feedback. Everyone knows where he or she stands. If a problem arises, the players are comfortable knowing that they will be told about it directly, with a minimum amount of "walking on eggshells." Because of this openness, there is virtually no gossip or talking about one another behind backs.

Realization is the opportunity to utilize one's talents and interests to contribute to the effectiveness of the organization. This opportunity is free of the constraints of title, role in the family, age, or gender. When roles on the team allow members to feel respected, actualized, and productive, both the team and the organization wins.

People work together as a team when (1) they have a common goal, (2) they can achieve this goal only through the efforts of all team members, and (3) they recognize this *interdependence.* When it comes to the family business crew guiding the ship through the rocky waters of transition, all hands are needed on deck! Unfortunately, in many cases, team members don't fully appreciate how much they need one another and consequently do not fully involve other members or take care of the relationships. When family businesses truly appreciate the importance of teamwork, they work to maintain the effectiveness of the team.[3]

An example of team building: Four brothers gained ownership of the family's construction-related business through a combination of gifting and leveraged buyout arrangements. The "boys" were not quite ready to manage the business on their own and recognized the importance of several key managers to the long-term success of the business. The family members and key employees who formed the new leadership team recognized that they faced quite a challenge in learning to work together in their new roles. Thus they engaged outside help to facilitate a team-building process.

They recognized that they needed to develop trust in one another, since they truly were interdependent: The brothers needed the key executives' knowledge, credibility at the banks, and relationship with other employees. The nonfamily executives knew that their job security, and that of other employees, depended upon their success as a team and the brothers' commitment to them. They had to gain confidence that each member would contribute his or her best, consistently, toward the achievement of their common goals.

Through the process of team building, all members became increasingly comfortable and open with one another. This openness included discussions of their fears or concerns, and their relative areas of competence and knowledge, and feedback on how they affect one another. As they became more open, they gained greater mutual trust and appreciation.

Each member of the team had an idea about his or her potential and capabilities and desired role on the team. The question arose as to whether they all could realize their dreams, since not everyone could succeed the current leader. The resolution to this issue came as they recognized the important roles they had as owners, and the possibility of structuring the organization in such a fashion that they all would have opportunities to learn, grow, and develop their income through their mutual success.

Over time, this group of "employees" evolved into a committed leadership team, recognizing their interdependence and the need to genuinely work at their relationships. The structure, policies, and procedures they put into place will increase the odds that they will follow through with their commitment to one another, even as outside pressures increase.

Hurdles and Challenges

There are a number of personal and business hurdles and challenges that owners and other players will have to overcome. Some of these occur in the stage of assembling the participants into a team. Some occur after the team is in place and has moved onto the playing field. Successfully negotiating these challenges requires an intense commitment to the succession process. Commitment is evidenced when individual participants are willing to communicate, discuss ideas openly, and come to a resolution about action to be taken. If the players do a lot of talking but fail to take action, they will miss the game because they will never get off the sidelines.

References

1. Abraham Maslow, *The Farther Reaches of Human Nature* (New York: Viking Press, 1971), pp. 299–300.
2. Dennis Jaffe, *Working with the Ones You Love* (Berkeley, CA: Conari Press, 1990).
3. Leslie Isaacs, presentation of unpublished manuscript, Atlanta, Georgia, September 1991.

3
Distinguishing Ownership Succession from Management Succession

What is the greatest cause of conflict in a family business? Is it sibling rivalry? Intergenerational clashes in management styles and goals? Lack of clearly defined job responsibilities? Or is infighting the real culprit—squabbles between active and inactive owners or pressure and meddling from inactive in-laws?

Actually, the answer is none of the above. In my experience, the most common source of family business strife comes from a lack of coordination between ownership succession and management succession. When that happens, the most likely outcome is family conflict—which can be manifested in any one or more of the destructive patterns above.

Ownership succession is the process of deciding, communicating, and implementing a plan to transfer ownership—stock or assets of the family business—to the next generation. Ownership succession focuses on *who:* family members, nonfamily key employees, or a third-party buyer. Ownership succession also focuses on *when* and *how* the transfer will occur. Management succession focuses on *who, what, when,* and *how:* who will run the operating company, what changes will occur, when will "they" be accountable for results, and how results will be realized.

The good news is that sibling rivalry, in-law meddling, and the other conflicts described above are usually symptoms of deeper problems. Why is that good news? Because the underlying problem—most frequently, the lack of coordinated ownership and management succession—is easier to tackle than the symptoms. No one can stop siblings from hating one another, or make conflicting styles mesh. But if everyone's role in the future management and ownership of the family business is clearly defined and a time frame is set, then the issues that set siblings on the warpath can be minimized, and the issues that detonate interpersonal explosions can be avoided.

The point is, both primary issues must be addressed before family business owners can consider a workable succession plan. An ownership succession plan requires future owners of the business to be named. A management succession plan requires figuring out who will manage the day-to-day operations of the business. Although these are separate issues, they must be considered simultaneously. Many internal succession plans fail, with disastrous consequences for the family and the business, when these two processes are not addressed together.

Consider the plight of one prominent midwestern family who used a family business consultant for several years. The consultant focused only on management succession and disregarded the issues surrounding ownership succession.

Independently of this consultant, Dad, who owned the business, developed his estate plan to leave the business equally to his two children. Dad's estate plan *was* his ownership transfer plan. The estate-planning consultant (a well-respected firm) *never inquired* about the management succession plan for the business.

Meanwhile, Dad's college-dropout son decided he couldn't work with or for his MBA-trained sister. The son was as competent as his sister, but their management styles were in conflict. Animosity between the siblings was increasing to an intolerable level. If Dad died, resulting in the estate plan distributing ownership equally to the two children, a feud seemed inevitable. Dad wouldn't be around to act as referee, and a sale of this third-generation business might be the unfortunate and unintended result.

Coordinating ownership and management succession for this family resulted in dividing the company in half. The daughter became owner and manager of her division; the son became owner and manager of his division. In the process of transferring ownership currently to the two children, the family saved more than $8 million in future estate taxes.

Responsibilities Accompany the Process

Before you begin this process, you may already have gifted stock to other family members. Transferring ownership, even in incremental pieces, such as gifting a few shares of family business stock without having a clearly defined ownership and management succession plan, may backfire in unexpected ways.

First, consider the differences between ownership and management succession. Ownership of a family business, even in the form of a few shares of stock, represents a responsibility that is often misunderstood. A responsibility of ownership exists to provide consistent leadership to the company and its employees, and to maintain and enhance the quality of the product or service delivered to customers. Putting family members into an ownership role without transferring an understanding of those responsibilities dilutes the effectiveness of the business and what it represents. Ownership can mean different things to each owner. Without a common understanding of what stock ownership represents, significant problems in the future are sure to emerge when further changes in ownership are being considered.

Parents often transfer stock in the family business to children without conveying to them any responsibility for ownership. There is a power that accompanies ownership rights. By not teaching new owners how to use that power, the current owner runs the risk that the power of ownership will be misused or abused.

Sometimes a transfer of a few shares of stock ownership is motivated by tax planning purposes. Although tax minimization strategies are important tools for preserving wealth, owners should be careful that the short-term, tax-driven decision doesn't create long-term, unpleasant surprises—for the family and the business.

Important to an ownership transfer plan is the commitment to, and development of, a motivated and dedicated management group. A *proper* ownership succession plan, by definition, means also having a management succession plan in place.

Ownership Succession

There are a number of decisions to be made in the ownership succession process; for example, will there be multiple owners or just one in the next generation? If multiple owners, will ownership be equal or disproportionate?

There are several ways that ownership rights can be transferred. Ownership can be "gifted" or given to someone else. Ownership rights can be sold. Typically, a family business is sold to an unaffiliated third party, but there are other options. Later chapters will discuss how to sell the family business to family members or nonfamily key employees. Ownership can also be conveyed through an estate plan. Ownership rights can be retained until death, although this approach can be fraught with many problems. (See Chapter 14.) At death, a preexisting shareholder or partnership agreement—or in its absence, a will or trust—can direct how business ownership will be transferred.

Management Succession

Along with an ownership succession plan must come a plan encompassing management succession. In her work in grooming future managers, Susan Goldstein of Hubler-Swartz in Minneapolis has identified four phases in the management succession process. While these phases are primarily descriptive of the way family members advance through a family business, they are instructive for nonfamily members as well:

Initiation: the period of time when children (or new employees) learn about the family business—how "we" do things

Selection: the process of choosing the leaders for the next generation, on the basis of accomplishments and dedication

Education: the process of developing the skills needed by the successor(s)

Transition: the process of transferring authority and accountability to the successor(s)

These phases of management succession should be integrated into the ownership succession plan. The interrelationships are portrayed in Figure 3-1. Bypassing any of these phases to "save time" can short-circuit plans in the future.

Assuming the pool of potential managers has received appropriate education, outside training, and initiation within the family business, at some point the current owner must select the best candidate or candidates for management succession.

Henry Ford once said that the question "Who ought to be the boss?" is like asking "Who ought to be the tenor in the quartet?" His answer: "Obviously, the man who can sing tenor." Identifying leadership in the next generation may not be that easy. If a future leader has not "emerged" or been designated,

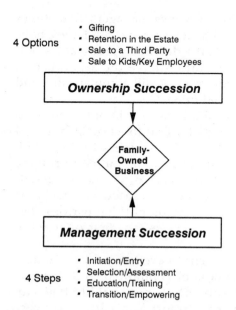

Figure 3-1. The two primary issues—ownership succession and management succession.

he or she may evolve out of activities associated with the management succession plan.

Grooming the next generation to become strategic entrepreneurs involves more than teaching day-to-day management techniques. It requires creating visionary leaders who will have long-term positive influences on the business and the family. Keshavan Nair, in *Beyond Winning,* says, "Leadership is not the gift of genius; it can be learned...through hard work, dedication and commitment....Positive leadership is not complicated in concept, but it is very difficult to practice."[1] One of the roles of the leader is to envision the future. Those involved with management succession should provide the critical thinking and strategic analysis that helps the leader separate the "wild" ideas from the brilliant ones.

Building Safeguards into Your Planning

The succession plan will not always proceed as expected. In fact, more often, it will not. Therefore, it is important to plan for contingencies when things go awry. In order to keep the plan on track, you will need to understand and establish safeguards early in your planning. These safeguards are important for the current owner, the prospective new owners, and the current and future managers. Safeguards protect exiting owners, such as other shareholders, the patriarch, and the matriarch, by establishing performance requirements for the new group—both owners and managers. Safeguards define what happens if mistakes are made, financial or otherwise.

Safeguards also protect the next generation of owner-managers. Sometimes current owners have a change of heart or a change of mind after they have begun the succession-planning process. With defined, preestablished, triggering events, members of the next generation have the assurance of knowing that if they "perform," the succession process will automatically, and contractually, move forward as mutually agreed upon.

In one family situation, Son insisted on assuming ownership of the business and becoming president and believed it was time for Dad to retire. Dad was 64 and agreed to turn over operational control of the business to Son. Dad, however, wasn't sure if Son was "ready" or sufficiently committed to run the company successfully. Before ownership was transferred, mutually agreed-upon accountabilities and performance measures created a three-year "window" for Dad (and Mom) to observe Son. By accomplishing performance benchmarks, Son had the assurance, legally documented, that ownership would be conveyed.

Two years into the plan, it had become evident to everyone, Son included, that he wasn't really interested in the business or committed to it. He was more interested in how the business could support his personal lifestyle. Not surprisingly, the financial requirements to support Son's lifestyle were increasing. His performance, however, did not meet the benchmarks.

Remember that Dad and Mom had retained ownership of the business and, therefore, control over future ownership. They decided at a family meeting that it would be better for the family *and* the business to sell the company to an unaffiliated third party. Both Son and inactive Daughter agreed with the decision. Negotiations with a larger company were consummated, reaping financial and emotional rewards for the entire family.

Keep in mind that this situation could have an entirely different outcome. It might go something like this: Two years into the plan, Son has developed management skills that are doubling (or tripling) the company's profits. Cashflow has improved dramatically and Son wants to use the excess to make long-overdue equipment upgrades, modernize the plant, and reward key, nonfamily members for their loyalty and efforts in achieving company profitability. For their part, Dad and Mom want to withdraw the excess cash to enhance their personal lifestyle. However, because rules and safeguards have been preestablished, Mom and Dad are allowed to withdraw only a predetermined percentage of the extraordinary earnings.

At the end of the third year, the company is even more profitable—and the outlook is very positive for the future. Dad and Mom want to reconsider the ownership transaction with Son. After all, the company is doing so well, maybe they should hold on a while longer. The "deal" established three years earlier now seems underpriced.

Son is protected against this change of heart by triggers, established three years earlier, which define at what point, or date, ownership is to be conveyed, and what the price or consideration is to be. Figure 3-2 illustrates two types of safeguards: ownership and management.

Ownership Safeguards

Action triggers, default provisions, and security devices are the typical ownership safeguards. Action triggers generally protect the next generation of owner-managers. They define *when* a change in ownership or management will occur, subject to the performance measures described below. A typical action trigger occurs when the current owner attains a certain age, such as age 65, or when the prospective heir has successfully demonstrated specific business accomplishments.

Default provisions describe what happens when the future owner-manager group fails to meet a previously agreed-upon level of performance. These are important for an exiting owner-shareholder. After ownership is conveyed, regardless of the method used, there are usually expectations about *how* the company will perform in the future. These expectations can be objectively measured and defined in terms of historical financial ratios, or historical amounts of annual cashflow. Maintaining market share, keeping customers satisfied (according to some acceptable index), and meeting banking covenants are other measures that can be used. Failure to meet future requirements could trigger the new owner group into a default, which would

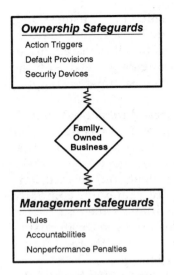

Figure 3-2.   Protecting the two primary issues.

automatically activate prepayment clauses or other "penalty" devices. Keep in mind that the company does *not* have to be in serious financial trouble. A default could be triggered whenever performance falls below a predetermined level.

Security devices protect former owners by defining their interest in collateral they hold, or by defining triggering events that can accelerate payments or cause notes or mortgages to come due. One form of security is placing a salary or bonus "cap" on new owners for a fixed period of time, or defining when bonuses earned can be paid out.

Some security devices do not keep events from happening; they define ramifications or penalties if the defined event does occur. For example, a merger or sale of the business *after* a transfer of ownership can require the new owners to share the proceeds with former owners. Other security devices can preempt future events from happening. These are described more fully in Chapter 21.

Management Safeguards

Exiting owners need safeguards to "unravel" or change a proposed ownership succession plan if the new, prospective owners do not perform management duties as expected. This is an important safety net for current and future owners. Conversely, clearly defined accountabilities and performance measures act as a check-and-balance system by preventing the exiting owner from having a change of heart.

Management safeguards can also address a subtler issue: When the owner makes capricious or arbitrary decisions that undermine or sabotage the successor's efforts, a clear set of policies and procedures—with ongoing training and professional development and performance reviews—will protect the interests of all those involved in the management and ownership succession processes.

The path of management succession for family members begins with clearly defined rules of entry, such as educational, professional, and experiential requirements. Establishing rules in advance can act as a deterrent for the unqualified and as an incentive for those who are committed.

An important question owners should address as part of the management succession process is "What will it take for the business to be viable after the transfer?" The critical thinking required to answer this question will form the foundation for the transfer of management responsibility. The transfer process should define what happens, when, and who is responsible. Those involved in this process should constantly be asking: "What is or is not working?"

Performance requirements that can be objectively measured should be established and maintained both prior to and after a transfer of ownership— and maintained afterward as well.

More to Think About

Attorneys, accountants, and financial advisers often focus exclusively on the tax and legal aspects of transfer strategies. They seldom consider the underlying emotional and psychological issues that are involved. Addressing those issues first can defuse family conflicts at the root of current business problems that are hampering a succession plan. Only after those are resolved can the best transfer strategy (including technical, legal, and tax considerations) be developed. This approach sets the stage for a successful management *and* ownership transfer.

References

1. Keshavan Nair, *Beyond Winning* (Phoenix: Paradox Press, 1990).

4
Hurdle 1:
Goal Setting

Family business owners often consult their attorney or accountant when they begin thinking about succession. Their advisers usually ask, "What are your goals? What do you want to do?" The family business owner leaves the meeting frustrated, thinking, "If I knew what I wanted to do, why would I ask them? They ought to tell me what I should do!"

Confusion over goals and objectives is the norm, because what owners want for themselves and their family may not be consistent with what they want for their business. Leon Danco described this confusion when he identified the four "hats" the business owner wears:

> The reason that he is confused isn't that he's stupid, or that he doesn't understand his business field. It's that each of his roles has different requirements. If he tries to perform well in all of them, he is hopelessly swamped by conflicting claims on his attention.
>
> As a shareholder...he wants to make money with his assets and he also wants his assets to be secure, appreciating, liquid, and useful in his old age, or he wants to convert them into other assets that will be secure—or so he hopes.
>
> As an employee, he wants something worthwhile to do for as long as he wants to work. As chief executive officer, he wants the company to grow, to make more money,...and generate more business. As an aging male, he wants to level off and enjoy the success and contentment he's earned.[1]

It has become commonly accepted that succession planning has an impact on all participants in the process. Each participant may have his or her own objective and opinion of what succession planning means. The problem is that goals are often unclear. For example, financial goals may be identified initially, but soon deeper needs or feelings begin to surface. Small wonder, then, that one of the causes of conflict and dissension is unilateral decision making about the succession plan. The owner decides without consulting the other participants or discussing the impact his or her decisions might have on the business.

Ivan Lansberg, a professor at Yale, has identified four basic constituencies of stakeholders: the family, the owners, the managers, and people external to the firm (such as suppliers, customers, and franchisers). Each constituency has its own goals, concerns, and expectations during a transition of ownership and management.

Family members often view the firm as an important part of the family's identity and heritage as well as a source of financial security that enables them to satisfy their lifestyle expectations. Managers see their careers as tied to the firm and tend to regard the business as a vehicle for professional development and economic achievement. From their perspective, the firm's primary goal is not to look after the needs of family members, but to generate profits and ensure continued career growth. Owners view the business predominantly as an investment from which they want to receive a fair return. Lansberg notes that individuals can belong to more than one group at the same time; therefore, it is possible for the same person to hold conflicting views about the ultimate goals of the firm.[2]

These three systems—family, management, and ownership—are interrelated and support one another to a certain degree. Problems arise when it is unclear which system takes precedence. For example, is the business designed to serve the family's needs, or do management needs come first?

Answering that question will help resolve a number of related questions about the goals and objectives of the succession plan.

When two people who simultaneously belong to more than one system talk to one another about succession planning, it is sometimes not clear from which system's perspective they are speaking. For example, Dad, who owns the business, complains about the company's poor cashflow to Son, the sales manager. Is Dad acting as a father and mentor, as a business owner concerned about the future viability of the company, or as a general manager talking to his sales manager?

Here's an exercise Dennis Jaffe developed that can help clarify and set goals. Look at Figure 4-1. The Family System refers to personal family, children, and spouses. The Management System refers to employees and managers. The Ownership System is all current shareholders, family and nonfamily. The Environment refers to suppliers, customers, advisers, competitors, bankers, and so on.

The area labeled FM consists of family members who also work in the business, but don't have ownership. FO indicates family members who own some of the business, but don't work there. MO refers to nonfamily managers who work in the business and are also owners or shareholders. FMO, the middle space, are those who are owners, managers, and family members. Because this group has three perspectives, members often get particularly confused in their relationships. Boundaries between family, business, and ownership issues may be especially unclear.

Pause for a minute to take a census of the members of your family, the owners of the business, and the key business managers. Write down the group(s) that each one belongs to. Note that there are seven possibilities: FM,

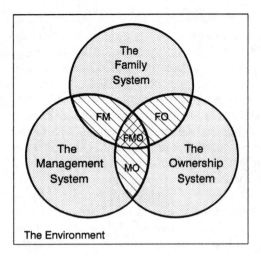

Figure 4-1.   The family firm system.

FO, MO, FM-MO, FO-MO, FM-FO, FMO. Then, looking at the single, dual, or triple memberships, define some of the key interests, needs, and expectations each group of people might have in their respective areas.[3]

Keep in mind there may be *eight* or more perspectives on any or all issues: the seven identified, plus the perspective from advisers, franchisers, suppliers, and others. Building consensus with the eight views may result in modifying some goals.

Issues to Resolve, Goals to Establish

Generally there are a number of important subissues to be resolved in succession planning, depending on whether they are a family matter or a business matter. The "complications" are depicted in Figure 4-2. Family and business are often not clear distinctions, since decisions made in one area usually influence other decisions.

Here is a good example: In the 1970s, when gas lines were three blocks long, Dad installed underground storage tanks at the family business to create a controlled supply of gasoline for the company's cars and trucks. Dad bought reconditioned tanks to hold the gasoline and buried the tanks underground. They haven't been used for many years. A few years ago, Dad considered selling the company; the deal fell through. One of the problems was that financing the deal was contingent on the buyer's presenting a "clean" EPA (Environmental Protection Agency) soil test.

The test determined that gasoline from the tanks had leaked into the surrounding soil. The buyer discussed the problem with Dad, but Dad refused

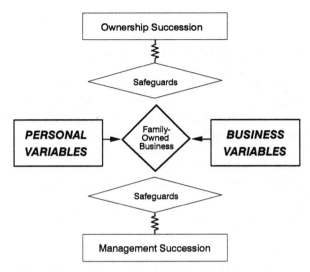

Figure 4-2.   Complications of the two primary issues.

to pay for the cleanup, which was projected to cost more than $200,000. Dad balked and ultimately discussions broke down. The buyer withdrew.

Now Dad is discussing succession plans with the family. The two active children wonder about the "value" of the company in light of this unresolved environmental issue. How will that unresolved matter influence some of the other issues listed below?

Personal variables

Changing concept of "family"

Life cycle of players

"Letting go" issues (power and authority)

Multigenerational family influences (rituals, myths, rites of passage)

Dysfunctional or addictive behaviors

Ego-driven financial needs

Cashflow requirements and income tax planning

Wealth transfer and estate tax planning

Equalization issues

Personal financial security

Business variables

Business valuation issues

Business cashflow and needs for growth

Competition moving in

Market or product changes

Banking covenants

Tying in nonfamily managers

Environmental issues

Economic concerns

Franchisee and "exclusive" distributor relationships

Acquisition potential (from outsiders)

One way to sort through these issues is to develop three plans: a business plan, a family plan, and an ownership plan.

The Business Plan

Leadership training and management development should be included in the business plan, which should address the goals of the business as well as the readiness of the successors. (See Chapter 7.) Does everyone know who the management successors will be? Are they ready for new responsibilities? If not, what will it take for them to be ready? Is there a leader in the successor group?

In one family business the nonfamily general manager, along with an active daughter, created a five-year transition plan to bring the daughter into the general manager's position. The existing general manager was given attractive financial incentives to phase himself out of his job.

The business plan is only the first step in developing a leadership and management training plan. It should address the following issues:

- What business are we in today?

- How are we doing?

- What changes (if any) do we need to make? How can we monitor our results?

- What basic values do we hold collectively as owners and managers? What values do we not unanimously agree upon?

- What do we need to understand from our company's financial statements?

- What investments does our company need to make for its future?

- What is the value of the business and what can we do to enhance that value?

- What risks should we not take?

- What can we learn from business cycles we've gone through? What is our "free" cashflow?

The Family Plan

Those involved in developing the family plan should look at the family from a collective viewpoint. How has "our" family evolved and changed? How have "we" influenced—and been influenced by—our family business? How well do we communicate with one another? What are the "family rules" regarding power, authority, decision making, and personal development? How are our family boundaries established? How does our family respond to crisis? Have "we" grown and adapted as we've aged, or do "we" resist change? Are there unresolved conflicts or struggles from previous generations that are passed on to the next generation to resolve?

Additional questions the family plan must resolve are:

- How have we developed our career choices? Are family members actively encouraged or discouraged from coming into the business?

- Are those who are not currently active in the business allowed to enter? If so, when, and with what experience?

- How does our family view women working in the business? What if daughters are more qualified than sons?

- Is it "okay" to talk about leaving the business if one of us isn't happy?

- How has the history of our family enhanced or hindered us in developing our individual selves?

- How does our family view the wealth that has been created? What income is needed for withdrawing owners?

- Does the business financially support inactive family members? If so, for how long?

Addressing these questions in the context of a family meeting (discussed below) can help establish a future direction for the business and the family.

The Ownership Plan

Decisions regarding the estate, including financial security for a surviving spouse, are part of the ownership plan. Other issues to be resolved include:

- Who will be the future owners of the business? What method or combination of methods will be used to transfer legal ownership to successors? What involvement will withdrawing shareholders have in future decisions?

- When will a transition occur and what will it be contingent upon?

- Is active participation in the business required for ownership? Can nonfamily (key employees) become owners? Can inactive family members hold ownership?

- Will there be a distinction in voting rights for different owners; i.e., some holding nonvoting stock and others owning voting shares? (More about voting rights in Chapter 23.)

- Are there existing shareholder agreements—also known as stock redemption or buy-sell agreements—that influence or restrict the ownership decision? Will those need to be amended? (If so, some of the points covered in Chapter 20 may be helpful.) What other problems can be anticipated?

Figure 4-3 summarizes the dilemmas regarding ownership and management succession by introducing the variability of time. The less time there is, the fewer choices there are.

Realizing Shared Goals Is a Shared Exercise

Goal setting goes beyond subjective beliefs about others; it involves including others to determine their needs and expectations. Recall from Chapter 2 that

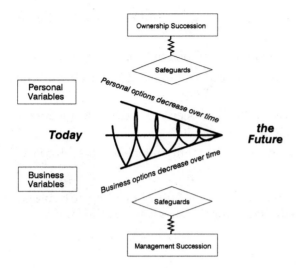

Figure 4-3.   The two primary issues over time.

organizing the participants into a team was Rule 1 in the succession process. Here's where that begins. Determining participants' expectations, concerns, and needs *without bias* is the first step. In my experience, one of the most important benefits of involving all participants from the beginning of the process is that those who "own" the process are more supportive of the process moving forward.

Consensus building—having all participants involved with goal setting—will put some important issues "on the table" early in the game and set the stage for effective family mediation and compromise, if necessary. Excluding participants from goal-setting discussions makes them feel left out, unimportant, and can create resentment later. Those who make assumptions about excluded participants ("They'll go along with Dad") are leaving this important aspect to chance. They risk failure early in the succession-planning process.

Goals should attempt to be set with as little bias as possible. Emotional issues and conflicts should not be addressed in a goal-setting meeting. They should be recognized, but addressed *after* all the business issues and concerns have been expressed. Postponing conflict reduces the emotional intensity of goal-setting meetings, while acknowledging that "open issues" are legitimate and will be resolved later.

Having a Family Meeting

Families often get together on weekends, social occasions, and holidays, but rarely is a formal meeting set to discuss succession planning.

A family meeting is similar to a corporate board meeting. An agenda is prepared in advance, a meeting date and time are established, and someone is

FAMILY MEETINGS

Ground Rules

1. Participants are problem solvers: When we brainstorm solutions, we work together, not against one another.

2. Focus on the problem, not the people: Accept the validity of the other's position.

3. Work toward a win-win solution: Anything less (win-lose) is not acceptable.

4. Satisfy the underlying interests: Personal compromise for the sake of the business may be required.*

Possible Agenda Items

1. Advantages and disadvantages of having a family business.

2. Business history and founder's dreams.

3. Individual dreams, goals, plans.

4. Family mission statement.

5. Codification of family values related to the business.

6. State of business affairs.

7. Family financial need and plans.

8. Communication patterns and teamwork strategies.

9. Conditions under which you'd sell the business.

10. Business role in the community.

---

*Fischer, Robert and William Ury, *Getting to Yes, Negotiating Agreement Without Giving In,* Penguin Books, New York, NY, 1983.

Figure 4-4. Having a mediator conduct family meetings helps to keep the family focused on its agenda (purpose) and to defuse negative emotion (conflict).

appointed as recorder for the meeting. The "minutes" or notes of the family meeting create a record of the discussion and help establish continuity and communication among all family members, including those who cannot be physically present or are not active in the business.

Figure 4-4 outlines four rules that should be in place prior to a family meeting, along with a list of possible agenda items. One of the most difficult rules for people to accept is personal compromise for the sake of the business.[4] The "golden goose" (the business) should be protected if long-term results are everyone's goal.

Dr. Pat Frishkoff at Oregon State University has established eight objectives that a family meeting should begin to address:[5]

■ Take time out to talk about important issues

■ Provide feelings of involvement

- Disseminate information in a fair and formal manner
- Share dreams and concerns
- Provide a forum for discussion and open communication
- Improve business decisions
- Promote family harmony and cooperation
- Create a shared vision

The initial family meeting might take the form of a two-day retreat, giving everyone a chance to get away from the business and to focus on the issues at hand. It is usually advisable to hire a facilitator to conduct the first meeting. The facilitator, an outside, impartial mediator, can keep the meeting focused on its agenda (purpose) and defuse negative emotion (conflict). The facilitator can ask hard questions, especially of the senior generation, and can assist the participants in improving listening skills. If conflict emerges, the facilitator can help manage it.

As a forum for determining the objectives of the participants, the family meeting can serve to resolve some of the confusion about multiple roles mentioned earlier. Most important, the participants in the succession process begin working together rather than independently or even against each other.

Nonfamily key managers can also participate in this process. However, the first few meetings generally are best reserved for family and owners. Once all members begin to work together on family and ownership issues, nonfamily management can be brought in to provide the third perspective.

Should You Keep the Family Business in the Family?

The most important goal to address in succession planning is whether to keep the business or try to sell it. Imagine the following: Leonard's business has been in the family for nearly 100 years. He feels fortunate to have two capable children in management who can take over the business for another generation. Recently, several businesses like Leonard's sold out to large chains. After his peers boasted about their deals, Leonard estimated he could receive $7 million cash if he sold the business. A quick calculation revealed that the interest alone on $7 million would far surpass the annual salary Leonard draws from his business.

Leonard looked at the portraits of his father, grandfather, and great-grandfathers on his office wall and wondered what they would say right now.

Many families find themselves in Leonard's situation. Large companies are often interested in acquiring successful family businesses. These companies can offer significant dollars as well as employment agreements and a variety of other compensation packages. The deal could provide financial freedom for all family members. Is this the best avenue for the current owner? For the family? For the business? What effect would a sale have on the community? What other factors, if any, should be investigated?

Extraordinary commitments and compromises will need to be made to perpetuate the business. If the participants are not willing to make commitments or to compromise on issues, then selling to a third party may be in the best interests of the family *and* the business.

Everyone needs to understand clearly the advantages (and disadvantages) of keeping the family firm independent. Those advantages need to be discussed with the next generation, which should be as excited about opportunities and as committed to the future of the business as the current owners. Or both generations may agree that it's a good idea to sell the company. If there are no family members to succeed the current owner and no cash-rich buyers on the horizon, key employees may be interested in buying the business. Even if these key players do not have the financial resources, owners should not count them out. Part 4 explores strategies for key employee buyouts.

Why should the family business remain independent? What does the family gain? How does the business gain? What does it provide to employees? How does the community benefit?

One survey asked business owners their reasons for passing on the family business.[6] Some respondents indicated an interest in providing an opportunity for their children. Perpetuating the family business can provide freedom, a sense of control over personal destiny, and autonomy. Many indicated that the family business provided an opportunity for personal growth, creativity, and expression. Other business owners were more interested in perpetuating their family heritage, building a tradition, history, and roots for future family members. Some wanted to create a living memorial. Overall, there was a sense that perpetuating the business keeps the family together.

For some, the family business was a way to ensure their own retirement and personal purpose past age 65. But at what costs? Will it help the family work together, strengthen family bonds, and allow more family time together? Keeping the business may generate financial advantages and wealth for current and future generations, but there are other alternatives for creating wealth.

Overall, the survey concluded that most family business owners believe the benefits to the family outweigh the disadvantages. But if this is true, why do almost 85 percent of first- and second-generation family businesses not survive for a third generation?

Are Participants' Goals on a Collision Course?

Perhaps the owner's goals for the business are to husband the company's assets so the assets can be used to buy the owner out. Simultaneously, successors may want to use business assets to expand and grow. Such a potential conflict should be discussed and resolved in light of what the company can afford to do and as part of an overall transfer strategy. The solution may involve scaling back the growth plans while the owner agrees to change the timing on receipt of money from the company.

One client found herself the target of a minority shareholder suit led by her son. The client had been gifting stock to her children, with the intent of using corporate assets to provide a salary continuation agreement for herself at retirement, in lieu of keeping the stock and having the business buy it back. The son, who had other plans for the corporate hoard, threatened to sue. Ultimately the family chose sides. It took years to finally resolve the issues, with a combination of methods described in Parts 2 and 4 of this book.

Achieving goals is a team effort, whether in a business or in a family. Communication is a first step in understanding issues and expectations from all those who will help accomplish the goals.

Other Considerations

There are other important considerations in deciding whether to keep the business in the family. Family financial needs and personal goals and dreams are just as important as maintaining the quality of the company's product or service and continuing to earn the loyalty of its employees. The decision will be influenced by the expectations of the company's customers, and by its reputation in the market and with suppliers. Peers and associates who own other businesses within a company's industry will influence the succession plan.

Will the quality of the business product or service be maintained or enhanced by retaining a family business? Will the successors understand and appreciate the loyalty of the key employees? Will the business maintain a competitive edge by "keeping" the business in the family as opposed to selling it? Will supplier or dealer relationships be maintained or changed? Chapter 22 examines strategic alliances and partnering as an unusual hybrid arrangement.

Another key issue: Are the owner's peers and associates selling out to third parties or transferring their businesses to children or employees? This may be one of the greatest influences on everyone's decision. If someone sells to a conglomerate and has only horror stories to describe the relationship, the commitment to working with family members may be greatly enhanced. On the other hand, if the sale was good for the owner, the business, and the employees, other owners may be influenced to do the same.

Whatever your ultimate decision as an owner or a family business participant, remember that your first hurdle is to set goals and objectives, and a time frame in which to achieve them.

References

1. Leon Danco, *Beyond Survival,* 5th ed. (Cleveland: The University Press, Inc., 1979), p. 23.
2. Ivan Lansberg, "Managing Human Resources in Family Firms," *Organizational Dynamics,* Summer 1983, pp. 39–46.

3. Dennis Jaffe, *Working with the Ones You Love* (Berkeley, CA: Conari Press, 1990), p. 53.

4. Robert Fischer and William Ury, *Getting to Yes: Negotiating Agreement Without Giving In* (New York: Penguin Books, 1983).

5. Pat Frishkoff, presentation at Oregon State University Family Business Forum, March 2, 1991.

6. John Ward, *Keeping the Family Business Healthy* (San Francisco: Jossey-Bass, 1987), p. 16.

5
Hurdle 2: Solving Family Conflicts

One of the biggest hurdles in developing an ownership transfer plan is how to solve existing or potential conflicts that could threaten any plan's success. These conflicts may be between siblings active in the business, between family successors and key employees, between owner and successors, between existing partner-shareholders, or any other configuration that raises doubts about the future working relationship of new owners and senior managers.

The stakes are high: the "family jewels" and continuation of the family business. If conflicts cannot be resolved, selling the business may be the best and last solution. Yet selling the business may be everyone's least desired outcome. Emotions can distort clear thinking just when calm deliberations are most needed; usually, everyone is highly emotional about the fate of the family business.

As noted in Chapter 3, the single most frequent cause of conflict is lack of coordination between ownership succession and management succession. Withholding a succession plan can also be the current owner's way of avoiding problems. The owner's thinking usually goes like this: "It's okay to let my successors run the company and make day-to-day decisions, but by retaining ownership, I have the power to step in as referee when fighting occurs and also the power to make (or veto) the big decisions. That is, I can countermand any decision they make that I don't agree with."

One difficulty with this shortsighted approach is that the owner, by being involved as referee, isn't teaching the successors how to work together, just when "working together" is one of the most important tasks the successors should have. Someday the referee will no longer be around. The fighting may get worse with no one to call "time out."

Family Ties

Triangles and Boundaries

Murray Bowen, a psychiatrist who studied family interactions, recognized that when two emotionally connected people are under stress, they often drag in a third person to form a *triangle*. Generally, the one who is most uncomfortable is the one who recruits the third person. The outsider will likely accept an alliance with one of the original pair, and become part of the problem.

Bowen discovered that the conflict may spread out, activating other triangles and involving more and more people. In fact, as this process is repeated over time, it sets off a chain reaction with predictable stages, especially when the parties face change or stress.

The family is more than a collection of individuals. It is a system with rules, roles, and a power structure, a system with *boundaries*. Each family has its unique forms of communication and problem solving, as well as powerful emotional attachments and loyalties, which often spill over into the family business. Unhealthy boundaries sit at one of two extremes: They can be claustrophobically tight or too loose to maintain the family as a cohesive unit.

Enmeshed versus Disengaged Families

When the family influence is too pervasive (as the children are leaving the family), emotional glue can result in a clinging interdependence. The technical term for this is *enmeshed.* An aging patriarch or matriarch may mistakenly encourage the clinging, believing that it keeps the family close. However, this interdependence also may hurt the family business by discouraging the critical thinking and strategic decision making needed to perpetuate the company. In an enmeshed family, any attempt by one family member to change creates resistance from all other family members.

Family therapists recognize that the family and its individual members are healthier when individual family members maintain a high degree of differentiation. Differentiation is not to be confused with "emotional cutoff." In fact, the opposite occurs. A differentiated person has higher self-esteem and stronger connections and relationship ties.

The enmeshed family frequently expects everyone involved in the business to stay tightly connected to "the family way of doing things." When family boundaries and family rules are extended to business situations, the results are unpredictable and conflicted.

Disengaged families are as unhealthy as enmeshed families. In the disengaged family, there are no strong connections; ties between members may be weak or nonexistent. Ownership transfer may be withheld because the current owners have very little or no communication with the successors. Withholding ownership may be used as a tool to force behavioral changes, without recognizing or acknowledging why the behavior is occurring.

Members of the disengaged family tend to protect their "space," and the emotional glue that binds the family together is missing.

A healthy family is somewhere in the middle of these two extremes. Healthy families grow and evolve. Members leave the family and are allowed to become independent individuals, yet they remain close and connected to their family of origin in a healthy way. Conflict can, and often does, occur in healthy families. In fact, conflict may be a healthy catalyst for making needed changes in a family business. Conflict is not the problem. It is the way in which conflict is managed—acknowledged (or denied) and resolved—that can create problems.

Conflict in the family business is usually more intense than in other relationships because it spills over into personal lives, weekends, holidays, and family outings, and affects children as well as grandchildren. Attending family events can be unpleasant, but avoiding family gatherings heightens conflict because the rest of the family often talks about those who are absent.

Life-cycle issues become confused when adults in business are still viewed by their parents as children in the family setting. Two brothers who are business partners may still relate to each other with the same rivalries or competitiveness that they entertained when they were adolescents.

Healthy families and family businesses manage conflict by developing mechanisms for resolving disputes. In a healthy family personal boundaries are respected, as are business boundaries. Rules, roles, and power can be understood, challenged, and discussed. Communication in a healthy family business can occur in a less threatening environment than when the family is enmeshed or disengaged.

Don't misunderstand. Stress in family businesses is common. In a study of family businesses by Paul Rosenblatt and his associates, 90 percent of the families reported ongoing tension or stress in their relationships because the business was a family one.[1]

In-Laws and Outlaws

Spouses may never feel "part of the family," and in retaliation may enthusiastically join the "outsiders" group, even as they envy those outsiders who eventually make it into the inner circle. One woman, now in her third marriage (no children), was discussing her will with her brother. The woman wanted to name her brother as the sole recipient of the assets of her estate. The brother was surprised and asked, "What about Tom (the third husband)?" His sister's reply: "He's a keeper, but he's not family."

Spouses are frequently blamed for family business problems. In an enmeshed family, the spouse may be blamed for pulling the son or daughter away. In the disengaged family, the spouse may reinforce emotional distancing from other family members. In many ways the spouse provides a mirror on the relationship between parents and children. Spouses often can see through parental intimidation, challenge habitual patterns of behavior, and look with disdain at parents' or siblings' frailties and shortcomings. The result can create a dilemma for the child: to challenge traditional relationships at the risk of creating conflict with parents or siblings, or to preserve the status quo and risk conflict with the spouse.

The stress level can become especially intense when plans are being made for ownership and management succession. The anticipated transition often causes family members to position themselves for a number of significant changes in both the business and the family. When family relationships are realigned, the traditional patterns of family influence often change as well. Succession plans, by definition, require long-standing management and ownership structures to give way to new forms. Changes in the life cycles of family members often do not coincide with changes in the business's markets and products.

Why and When Conflict Occurs

When boundaries between the business and family are not clear, major changes mapped out in the succession plan can detonate emotional conflicts.

If the business employs many family members, they have likely learned to follow certain rules in their day-to-day behavior since they were children, and have carried over these rules into the business. Maybe a clear distinction was never made between business and family rules. What is appropriate or tolerated at home may be inappropriate in business, and should not be allowed at the office. Understanding these differences is an important way to head off conflicts that may be hidden beneath the surface of relationships.

Family rules were established to protect children and teach them how to survive in the world, so they can learn to operate outside of the family system and on their own. If children go to work outside the family business, they will, in all likelihood, be trained in their job and told the rules and procedures of the business. However, if they first come to work in the family firm, they may not understand the philosophical differences between the business and the family.

These two independent systems—the family and the business—overlap in a family enterprise, in a gray area where family boundaries and business boundaries converge. Sometimes the cross-purposes of being involved in both systems create conflict because the rules, values, behavior, communication patterns, and goals of the family system usually conflict with those of the business system.

Yale University's Ivan Lansberg points out that conflict is the result of innate differences between the family's and the organization's purpose: The family's purpose is to care for and nurture family members; the business's purpose is to provide goods and services at a profit.[2]

The areas of operation highlighted in Figure 5-1 have different rules regarding participation, compensation, appraisal of activities, and training

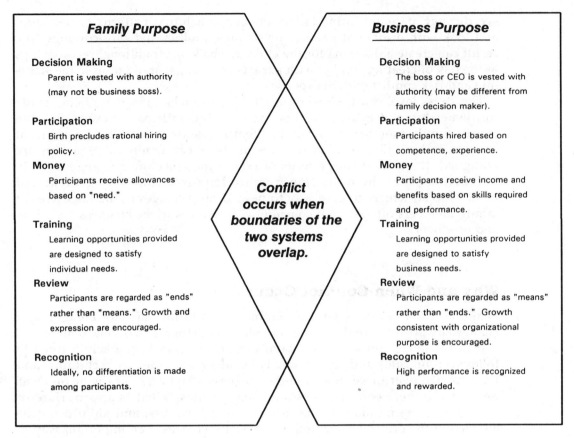

Figure 5-1. System overlap.

given to members of each system. For example, the older generation assigns tasks and responsibilities to a younger member of the family with the objective of developing the individual, instilling positive values, and nurturing personal growth. When the same young person is assigned tasks and responsibilities in the business, the purpose is to serve the business, not to promote individual growth. When that young family member acquires a position of responsibility in the business without understanding this fundamental difference, efficiency in the business is bound to suffer. Confusion and stress for all family members and business associates are the result.

Consider the following consequences when rules are not clearly defined:

One business owner spoiled his son as he grew up. He continued to bail him out whenever he encountered financial difficulties. For instance, in his mid-twenties and thirties, the son launched a series of business ventures, all of which were financial disasters. Dad rescued him each time instead of letting him learn from his own mistakes. Years later, the son was active in the family business as sales manager, getting by with a mediocre performance. As it came time for Dad to seek a business successor, Dad disqualified his son as a candidate, and chose to sell to an outside party. The family rule that operated at home (take care of family members) was not compatible with the business rule. The owner didn't even understand the difference between the rules and, therefore, never explained to his son that when it came to succession, the stakes were too high for the family rule to take precedence. The father never gave his son a chance to learn and play by the business rules.

Symptoms of Distress

Family feuds often simmer for years before they begin to boil. Recognizing symptoms of distress early and dealing with the underlying issues that are causing the distress can keep feuds from developing. Symptoms are often pervasive—within the business and family, outside it, or even back in time to previous generations. For instance, a feud between two people in a current generation may have its genesis in a crisis for which a grandmother blamed her spouse. Members of the current generation may still be replaying unhealthy patterns in their relationships, patterns that their grandparents began.

Here are the telltale signs that conflicts may be simmering beneath the surface of a family and its business.

External	Customer dissatisfaction
	Loss of market share
	Rise of competitors
Internal	Low employee morale
	High employee turnover
	Reasonable increases in sales that fail to translate into increases in profit or cashflow
	Drug or alcohol abuse among family members
	Absenteeism by family members
	Emotional flare-ups
Eternal	Patterns (familial feuds, problems, addictions, divorces, illnesses such as ulcers and insomnia) that can be traced back through previous generations
	Denial that problems exist

Systems—both family and business—require proper maintenance. Wear and tear will take its toll on the business and the family. For example, as plant and equipment age, ignoring repairs will erode productivity. In the family, system aging occurs as family members continually avoid touchy issues. The elaborate ways they find to avoid communicating or confronting even the most intolerable problems will cause anyone to get gray hair.

Family problems are apparent when members are more interested in "being" right than "doing" right. That is, they refuse to compromise their position—whatever it is, and no matter how ridiculous. Delivering pain is more important than solving problems.

Each system (the family and the business) goes through a process of evolution. Habits and patterns of behavior are passed along through each system. Rituals, rules, and traditions are often maintained from one generation to the next. Succession planning requires gaining an historical understanding of the two systems so that current and future participants can decide whether it is best to perpetuate or attempt to change the direction set in motion by family and business history. Attempting to improve the health and well-being of both systems through this historical perspective will influence the design, and usually the chances of success, of any transition plan.

Mediation for Conflict Resolution

Four deficiencies tend to underlie family disputes: poor communication and listening skills; inability to accept change or differences; unwillingness to compromise; and lack of respect for others. Changing such behavior requires a new frame of reference that is focused on the present and the future and directed toward specific goals. Emotional and mental energy that goes into sustaining conflict can be, and must be, redirected in healthier, more positive directions.

Mediation can effectively create this new frame of reference and redirect misguided energy. With the help of an objective third party as mediator, participants can often reach agreements cooperatively. In an adversarial, competitive process, neither party can win. The mediation process attempts to develop acceptable and workable solutions by considering the needs of all participants.

Conflicts, and the resulting stress, often mask deeper emotions such as anger, resentment, rejection, disappointment, helplessness, and pain. Clinical or professional help may be needed to uncover and address underlying issues. Sometimes, all it takes to resolve conflict is a supportive ally. Lawyers are often perceived as a logical (and ultimate) choice for filling this need. Lawyers themselves will second that notion. However, the warring family member who hires an attorney as an advocate is often unaware of how this first move will escalate the competitive struggle. It can extract a devastating financial and emotional price on the family and business.

Litigation is about winning, or conversely, avoiding losing. Finding a way to create a cooperative working relationship is not the focus of the process. Mediation takes quite a different approach to resolving conflicts. A mediator does not solve a problem, like an arbitrator or a judge; a mediator creates a climate for the parties to solve their own problems. There are four basic propositions.

1. The mediator is impartial. Although the mediator plays a central role, he or she remains neutral and does not take sides.

2. Mediation is a voluntary process and is an interim step to avoid a battle. When mediation breaks down, war may erupt. The participants must be willing to discuss issues, and to consider compromise toward mutually agreeable solutions.

3. The mediator maintains confidentiality. Trust in the mediator gives participants an ability to reveal true motives and needs. Important to the process is the mediator's skill in communicating those needs to each participant so that each begins to understand the other's position.

4. The mediator has considerable procedural flexibility. That is, there are no fixed rules. The mediator provides the framework for solving the dispute. The mediation process can evolve to fit the needs of the situation. For example, the mediator may initially meet separately with the parties, avoiding face-to-face confrontation. As emotionally charged issues are clarified and defused, the mediator may move to bring the parties together.

Mediation can be especially effective when children of owners are fighting about their future roles in the business. In some cases, each child tries to influence a parent to make a Solomon-like decision, putting the parent in a lose-lose situation. By triangling parents into the conflict, children ask them to choose one child over the other. The parent may become more passive, and even deny that the conflict exists, creating more frustration for the children who cannot envision a resolution. Or one child may successfully influence Dad, the other Mom, so that the conflict now extends to four people instead of two.

An important role of the mediator is to facilitate communication. In some cases, families have experienced relief just from being able to talk about such previously undiscussable topics as future roles and authority, compensation, competence of family members, equalization, death, and estate planning. The best method of resolving conflict, however, is to establish, early on, healthy ways the family can deal with disagreements and disappointments. John Ward notes in *Keeping the Family Business Healthy:*

> The process of resolving conflicts must be established long before the children arrive in the business. It must begin in the home: in the lessons children are taught, in the way the family conducts itself. It continues with...the children's entry into the business and their preparation for leadership roles....Families find that considering these challenges ahead of time increases the chances of solving them to everyone's satisfaction.[3]

Another approach to resolving conflict is to form a family council, in which family members act as a review board to resolve disputes in a democratic and judicial fashion. A third vehicle is an outside board of directors, empowered to establish and review performance measures, resolve compensation issues, allocate resources, and hold the company's officers accountable for meeting business and family goals. This approach attempts to separate family issues from business needs. An outside board may seem to emphasize and protect the health and well-being of the business at the expense of the family, but individual board members often volunteer to mediate family disputes.

Summary

It is almost impossible for new owners and new managers to handle the responsibilities of a business when conflict is rampant beneath, on, or all over the surface of the family and the business. Before mapping out (let alone implementing) a succession plan, owners and other family and business members need to air and thoroughly wash out all their dirty laundry. Unresolved conflicts may be manageable under the strong leadership and style (positive or negative) of the existing owner. But succession planning sets in motion changes in ownership and management, causing family and business relationships, responsibilities, and systems—with all their constructive and destructive patterns, rules, and conflicts—to endure under intense stress. In short, old patterns that developed to avoid conflict may no longer work. Even the wisest, most well-developed succession plan may be doomed if conflict is not addressed at this point.

References

1. P. C. Rosenblatt et al., *The Family in Business* (San Francisco: Jossey-Bass, 1985).
2. Ivan Lansberg, "The Succession Conspiracy," *Family Business Review,* vol. 1, no. 2 (1988), p. 121.
3. John Ward, *Keeping the Family Business Healthy* (San Francisco: Jossey-Bass, 1987), p. 54.

6

Hurdle 3: Recognizing Stages of Life (And Their Impact on Business Decisions)

In developing a transfer plan, participants will find it helpful to understand that people pass through distinct stages in life. As they do, their business decisions—and values—change along with their needs, their relationships, and their tolerance for risk. Often, the needs of people at one stage conflict with the needs of people at another stage. Examining a potential successor to the family business is like examining one photo out of a sequence of thousands, or like viewing a frozen frame in a videotape.

A lack of perspective can result in a number of conflicts. Understanding general human behavior can provide security to the business owner unsure of his or her younger successors.

Often it is very difficult for 60-year-old business owners to remember how they felt when they were 35. They may believe that today's young people seem even younger than they were at 35, or they may feel that other 60-year-olds seem much older than their years. Similarly, it is difficult for the 35-year-old to understand many of the decisions made (or postponed) by the 60-year-old, particularly when those decisions affect the family-owned business. Age differences can have a significant impact on the successful operation and ownership transfer of family businesses.

Man passes through five major stages in the adult life cycle, the first beginning about age 22, and the last at age 60.[1] In each of these adult stages, an individual acts and feels differently. Business decisions reflect particular life-cycle stages. This fact can be particularly significant when a transfer of ownership occurs from one generation to the next. When different values and natural differences between the generations are not recognized, the transfer can lead to unnecessary conflict and potential failure. Research is now under way to study the life-cycle stages of women. Early findings suggest that life-cycle stages are different for men and women.[2]

Early Adulthood

The first adult life-cycle stage, beginning about age 22 and lasting to age 40, is characterized as "early adulthood." The adolescent stage, characterized by education, preparation, roaming, making big mistakes, being confused, and exploring, evolves into the early adult. During this new phase, the individual goes through an initiation period in which the burdens of childhood are cast aside and the "child" becomes an adult in his or her own way. This novice adult period can be a novice parenthood period as well. It is a time of changing relationships with parents as well as with a spouse.

During this phase, institutional ideas are challenged and solutions are linked to personal experiences. Early adulthood is a time of personal gratification in support of an emerging value system. It is during this period that the individual has the greatest energy, capability, and potential, and challenges the directions of the older generation. It is also a time of contradictions. Pollyannaish illusions begin to fall away. Frequently they are replaced by a new cynicism directed at the traditions and practices of the older generation.

This type of behavior was exemplified recently at a meeting I had with clients and their 24-year-old son. The 24-year-old was very demanding in his relationship with his father. The son wanted immediate ownership of the company, not ownership transferred over five years. The son "needed more income" and "didn't want to work long hours."

As we discussed the situation, the son began to realize that he had limited business credentials and negligible financial strength. Why should his parents transfer the business to him? What skills was he bringing to the table? What proposals did he have? What offers was he making? Why would a 60-year-old sell to a 24-year-old with no net worth?

Gradually, the father-son relationship began to change. The son, instead of demanding and expecting, began to see his father's position. And the father, instead of seeing the son as a demanding child, realized that he had to evaluate his son in a different light. The father recognized that the son was a key employee. As such, the father needed to spend some time preparing that key employee to handle the responsibilities of the business.

This 24-year-old typifies most "early adults" who inherit or acquire a business. They want to grow and expand the business quickly. They seek capital for expansion and will "sacrifice" current earnings for future growth. They have a higher risk tolerance as well as a higher debt tolerance than their elders. Early adults use business assets to leverage the business's growth through either acquisition or forward integration, such as expanding into new markets or territories. Personal retirement planning often is of little interest, because the cash needed to fund a retirement program might jeopardize future expansion opportunities.

Mid-life Transition

The first mid-life transition occurs between the ages of 40 and 45, when major life choices are made. If the 65- or 70-year-old has not turned over the reins of the business, the 40-year-old feels stalled in development.

For counsel and guidance, the 40-year-old may seek a mentor relationship with a nonfamily member. The "child" who, until now, has taken a back seat to a parent's business decisions, begins to exert his or her influence. The parent's challenge, and opportunity, is to recognize the offspring's contributions and give the "child" the leeway to implement his or her own ideas. Alternatively, the parent can neutralize the offspring's contributions by undermining a son's or daughter's efforts, thus risking that the offspring will either leave the business or seize control by force.

If a "child" leaves the business between the ages of 40 and 45, generally there will be hard feelings on both sides. Nothing positive is accomplished. The owner has lost a potential heir at a time when the owner needs to know and feel secure that the heir is in place, however unprepared he or she may be. The heir loses a business opportunity, but may choose freedom and independence over vacillation and insecurity on the part of the current owner-manager.

One client chose the neutralization route when he rendered his active daughter "invisible" by telling her that she had the power and authority to make and implement decisions and then undermined her behind her back. This occurred during a three-year transition period. Because Dad was still active in the business, the older key, nonfamily employees would come to Dad every time Daughter made a decision or a request with which they didn't agree. Dad, reluctant to confront his key employees, would tell them to continue doing things as they always had and to ignore the daughter. When Daughter confronted Dad on these issues, Dad would apologize and promise to stop negating her efforts. Nevertheless, the pattern continued and Daughter eventually became a nonentity in the firm. Her growing sense of worthlessness created tremendous internal conflicts. Although she wanted to continue the family business into the third generation, she wasn't sure how long she (and her husband) could withstand the emotional turmoil. Increasingly, freedom and independence became more attractive alternatives to this particular business opportunity.

Middle Adulthood

During middle adulthood, between ages 45 and 55, the individual builds on the foundations established during early adulthood. With business expansion programs now in place, attention is focused on creating a strong management team and an organizational structure. During this period, day-to-day operational responsibilities for the business should be delegated to the key management group. Sensitivity to key employees' needs is important and additional compensation and recognition programs should be explored. Credit lines become well established and banking relationships mature and solidify.

On the personal side, mental and physical changes associated with "aging" become more noticeable. Physical stamina, endurance, and attention spans begin to lessen. With an increased likelihood of stress- or age-related illnesses, internal messages become all-important. During middle adulthood, family members should understand what, if any, opportunities exist within the business; leadership and lines of authority should be discussed and established.

Late Adult Transition

Near the end of middle adulthood, the individual enters a period of confusion known as the late adult transition. Between the ages of 55 and 60, the phrase "I'm burned out" can be heard repeatedly. Accomplishments are compared (not always favorably) with dreams, and a confusion of purpose exists.

One day the business owner wants to build new branches; the next day, he or she wants to sell the business to the first prospective buyer. During this period of confusion, the business owner wants to keep all options open. This is admirable on the surface but unfortunately, the result is usually a propensity to do nothing. This static state can delay indefinitely a transition to the next generation.

During this period, financial and strategic planning are particularly critical. Yet, this is the time when the owner is most likely to procrastinate making any decision, thus running the risk of entering the next phase with no business plans, no successors, no management team, and eventually, no more options.

One client described the effect of aging on business decisions this way: "You become somewhat apprehensive at the age of 60. You wonder about your health, whether you are still doing a good job, and whether your children agree with what you are doing. You have all these questions and very few answers.

"You begin to lose confidence in yourself. You lose confidence in other people, and you begin to feel more insecure. I feel far less secure this year than I did when I was 50 or even when I was 55 or 57. And I worry that by the time I'm 65, I'm going to feel very insecure and that I won't really know what's happening any more. Then by the time I'm 70, I may be so insecure that I won't be capable of making any arrangements with my children."

Clearly, middle adulthood is a period when strategic thinking and decision making are needed. Unresolved issues create fragmentation and inconsistency that can prevent present and future business owners from reaching their highest potential.

Late Adulthood

Beginning at age 60 and continuing to about age 70, the stage of late adulthood occurs. During this time, the business owner is interested in personal retirement planning. The owner has less interest in expanding the business and sees growth programs from the "not with my dollars" perspective. The owner's interest in building retained earnings is now of tremendous importance, because the owner looks at the business financial statement as a personal savings account. During this period, there is greater cashflow in the business as cash is being accumulated instead of being put to work. There is less risk tolerance and less debt tolerance. The business owner looks forward to paying off the mortgages (if they aren't already paid off) and not encumbering business assets further.

During late adulthood, the heavy responsibilities incurred during middle adulthood should be reduced. Nevertheless, for the unprepared 60-year-old, suddenly leaving center stage can be a traumatic experience. Now is the time that transfer strategies should be in place, or the owner risks the possibility of becoming a tyrannical ruler, stalling his or her successors, and threatening the long-term growth and success of the business.

Business owners who are in their early to mid-seventies are often so comfortable that it's too late for them to let go. They prefer the status quo. They don't like to change and they don't like anything that threatens their concept of security. If change does occur, and if no ownership transfer plan is in place, succession planning is going to be initiated by the younger generation. Business owners in their early seventies may resent the younger generation's ideas, even though they "know" the reasons and "understand" the rationale. Emotionally, it is easier to preserve things as they are and let estate planning take its course.

One 68-year-old client has a 40-year-old active son and two other offspring. When the son asked us to talk to his mother about the importance of transferring ownership, the son was concerned that he would become partners with his inactive brother and sister. Because the business represented the bulk of her estate, Mom had been reluctant to plan any transfer strategies for fear of being unfair to the two inactive children.

As I worked with the family to resolve equalization for the inactive children, we were able to address the more important issue: the necessity of transferring the business before Mom became recalcitrant. Although Mom insisted on having the transfer accomplished over a three-year period, she did agree to enter immediately into purchase options with her son. The son (or the corporation) had an automatic "call" to purchase the stock from Mom.

The transition went smoothly for the first two years. But recently the son called me to say that his mother regrets letting go of the business and is beginning to change her mind. The son has done nothing wrong. "It's just that Mom doesn't like change any more." The son, however, is protected by the purchase options and is therefore able to proceed with the transition and the continuity of the business.

Summary

The five life-cycle stages and their effects on business and personal decisions are summarized in Figure 6-1. When an owner starts a business, he or she assumes risk with energy and perseverance in the face of adversity. Gradually, in spite of overwhelming odds, success arrives and the business survives and grows. Then, as owners confront "passing the torch," new challenges emerge.

| | | EFFECT ON: | |
LIFE CYCLE	AGE	BUSINESS DECISIONS	PERSONAL LIFE
Early Adulthood	25 – 40	* Interest in growing, expanding the business * Increase capital for expansion * Level or reduce retained earnings * Higher risk tolerance * Higher debt tolerance * Low interest in personal retirement planning	* Initiation (burdens of childhood) * Need for personal gratification * "Novice" adult, husband, father * Changing relationships with parents * Full energy, capability, & potential * Contradictions & illusions
Confusion (Mid–Life Transition)	40 – 45	* May make strategic business decisions more difficult	* May seek mentor relationship * Time for major life choices (if not already made) * The "invisible" son? * Ultimatum vs. the "laid–back" heir
Middle Adulthood	45 – 55	* Build on foundations established in early adulthood * Expansion programs in place * More sensitivity to key employees * Need for management team and organizational structure * Credit lines established	* Mental and physical changes: "aging" * Increased likelihood of illness * Importance of internal messages * Senior leadership & authority
Confusion (Late Adult Transition)	55 – 60	* Keeping all options open * Propensity to do nothing	* Compare accomplishments to dreams * Confusion of purpose
Late Adulthood	60 – 70	* Increased interest in retirement planning * Less interest in expanding the business * More interest in retained earnings * Greater cashflow * Lower risk tolerance * Lower debt tolerance	* Must reduce heavy responsibilities of middle adulthood * Moving out of center stage can be traumatic * Part of "grandparent" generation * Give up authority or become tyrannical ruler * Possibility of creativity, wise elder with youthful vitality

Figure 6-1. The effect of life cycles on decision making.

They are more personal in nature. The environment to be "conquered" is internal rather than external. The challenge is mental, not physical or economic. It involves teaching rather than doing, sharing and communicating rather than making unilateral decisions.

If the independent business is to survive and grow into the next generation, extraordinary efforts will be required by all those involved. The wisdom acquired during late adulthood and the energy of early adulthood must work together to ensure a smooth and successful transition. The 60-year-old who understands the life-cycle stages can capitalize on these changes to teach (and share the accomplishments of) the next generation.

References

1. Daniel J. Levinson, *The Seasons of a Man's Life* (New York: Ballantine Books, 1978), p. 18.
2. Cynthia Iannarelli, "Socialization of Leaders in Family Business: A Study of Gender," unpublished doctoral dissertation, University of Pittsburgh, Joseph M. Katz Graduate School of Business, 1992.

7

Hurdle 4: Commitment

Once family and business members have agreed on common goals and have resolved any family conflicts, they must address one more nagging issue before proceeding with a succession plan: All parties need to be committed to succession planning and to each other—in their current and future roles.

Owners frequently wonder whether successors are as committed to the business as they were in their earlier years. Such thoughts may veil deeper fears that may be quite different.

Translation 1: "I'm afraid they won't make it and everything I've worked for will be destroyed."

Translation 2: "I'm afraid they will be so successful they won't need me any more."

Successors frequently entertain their own doubts about whether their parent will really let go and retire. They, too, may be harboring deeper fears:

Translation 1: "I'm afraid the succession plan is an empty promise, a ploy to get me to work harder with no appreciable rewards attached."

Translation 2: "I wish Dad and Mom would teach me how to be an entrepreneur and share their wisdom so I would be less likely to make a huge mistake."

In both cases, what's missing is trust in and commitment to each other. Unless all participants recognize and come to terms with their doubts, the succession process will become muddled. Developing and implementing a succession plan requires many types of commitment, from every imaginable constituent in a family business.

Future successors need to commit to investing huge amounts of time, energy, and passion in the family business, while maintaining a balance between their professional and personal lives. Owners and successors need to commit to a mutually agreeable strategic vision and business plan to implement common goals. Immediate family members must make a commitment to the chosen successors, and in-laws must commit to the time and energy their spouses will have to devote to the business. Commitment is required of all constituents, including key nonfamily employees, to the future successors and the strategic vision of the business. Finally, the current owners must make a commitment to the future owners and managers they select. (Yes, a successful business transfer requires as much commitment from current owners as it does from future successors!)

Many family business owners are surprised by this last entry on the commitment list. They tend to focus on the commitment of others, especially their successors. Yet an owner's commitment is critical to any succession process. Owners who have built a business over 30 or 40 years are obviously committed to the business. However, they must also be completely committed to their successors and the succession process itself, or the chances for a successful transfer—and business—will be slim.

One client asked my firm to intervene between his son and a son-in-law, who had asked for a 50 percent interest in the business in order to stay with the company after Dad retired. The son responded, "If you give him half the business, I'm leaving!" Both son and son-in-law had worked in the company for several years and had become valuable to the business.

After the two successors compromised on the son-in-law's receiving a 25 percent stake, Dad was distraught rather than relieved. It turns out he was counting on us not to resolve the dilemma. He was not committed to any succession plan that would dilute the business's "blood," and secretly hoped his son-in-law would leave. Once my associates and I realized his hidden agenda, we were able to address it by drafting a comprehensive shareholders' agreement that restricted the son-in-law's rights to the stock if he should leave the business, divorce, become disabled, or die. The agreement enabled Dad to put his full commitment behind the stalled succession plan.

Can Commitment Be Measured?

How can owners objectively assess whether the pool of available successors possesses the required degree of commitment? How can successors gauge whether current owners are truly committed to relinquishing control of the business? How can the family determine whether key nonfamily members will back the owners' succession plan?

Let's start with what doesn't measure commitment: the number of hours worked. Commitment requires more than coming to work at 8 a.m. and leaving at 5 p.m. At the other extreme, commitment does not require on-the-spot, round-the-clock involvement. Maintaining a balance between work and personal life is important. If the next generation provides leadership, professional managers can help accomplish some of the tasks and responsibilities; the seven-day week is unnecessary.

The actual time commitment on the part of the next generation is really not the owner's concern. Rather, the concern should focus on the *mental* and *emotional* commitment of the successors to the business. If the current owner is to feel comfortable with the next generation's ownership (including employees who are buying out the owner), the successors often need to exhibit a shift in their priorities. Unfortunately, learning to "think" like an owner usually happens only after successors become owners. Stepping into the current owner's shoes means stepping out of some other shoes; and those empty shoes will now need to be filled as well.

The creativity, sophistication, and competitiveness of most businesses today requires professional management and leadership. When the brain is left in the "on" position at all times, it is easier to take advantage of opportunities that may arise on weekends or on vacations, during social occasions, or simply at home reading the newspaper. Such opportunities cannot be capitalized on when the mind is turned off.

So how can commitment be measured? One group of business owners looking for evidence of commitment and entrepreneurial qualities in their children focused on *vision* and *passion*. Vision is the ability to see the big picture—farsightedness. For one family, vision was the ability of their three active children, who were successors, to create a plan to turn their small machine shop into an industry leader in manufacturing conveyor systems for bottling companies.

Vision does not mean daydreaming; it is not an idle fantasy. It is constructive, inspirational, inventive, original. It may evolve over time or it may occur in a brief creative moment. Family business consultant Leslie Isaacs offers this description:

> So often people blame others, the economy, or bad luck for their lack of success. Yet those who are truly successful accomplish this in spite of challenging circumstances.
> The single most important factor in high achievement or success is VISION: that is, having a personal or professional mission that is articulated through specific goals with concrete objectives, action steps, and time frames. The probability that we will achieve our mission and goals increases to the degree [that] we discipline ourselves to follow the plan we have created.

The second element of commitment is passion—devotion to a task with enough energy to accomplish a personal vision. Passion can be more easily recognized in a successor than vision. It is represented by a willingness to work, an enthusiasm for the task. For most business owners, commitment is more than mere obligation. It requires fire-in-the-belly energy.

As hard as it is to measure commitment in others, most of us don't even know the extent of our own true commitment (or our own strengths and weaknesses) until we are put to the test. Likewise, the best way to gauge commitment in others is to put them to a fair test. There are two effective ways owners and successors can test each other.

First, owners should give potential successors *full* responsibility for an important project, division, or product line well before a succession plan is cemented. This demonstrates to successors that the owner is, in fact, willing to let go. It also allows the owner to see how the successors work together, who is willing to take initiative, and how strongly each person is committed to the business and to others.

It is critical for owners to observe how well successors run this project or division day to day. In many ways, commitment is about extraordinary performance under ordinary circumstances. Successors will undoubtedly encounter a crisis or two as well. This is an opportunity to test whether everyone involved has the qualities that bind families and create traditions that will last for generations. A crisis is a time when new rules are created, new procedures are established, and leadership skills are exhibited. Successors will be forced to take risks—not always successfully, but often with results that change family relationships. Successors "under fire" can prove themselves or, conversely, discover that they are not quite ready for the rigors of entrepreneurship.

Second, owners should ask potential successors to write a business plan. This task gives successors a forum for expressing their creativity, pragmatism, and hope for the business. Owners get a chance to see how realistic, business-wise, and creative the successors are. For owners who hold an installment note and depend on the business's future success for their payments, this test of successor commitment is critical. (See Figure 7-1.)

Enhancing Commitment with a Business Plan

A written business plan is not just a test of commitment. It is also an important means of *building* commitment among owners and heirs. The first draft should be developed by heirs, to give them a forum for presenting their ideas and ideals for the business. Then the owners should work with heirs to factor in their experience and objectives.

Very few family businesses have a written business plan. Usually the parent who acquired or started the business has successfully operated it for so long, in the same fashion, that no formal business plan ever seemed necessary. In reality, a business plan would have helped facilitate strategic business decisions. When opportunities came along, the business plan would have helped the owner respond to a new idea, product, or investment by providing a simple litmus test: Does the new opportunity fit into long-range strategic goals? Without a business plan, there is no easy way to figure this out.

A written business plan can also help owners let go, giving them some formal measures against which to gauge their success. Owners tend to hang on to their businesses long after they should shift responsibilities to others. They strive to achieve still more when they lack a visible measure of their accomplishments. When the time comes to think of transferring ownership, a business plan becomes even more necessary.

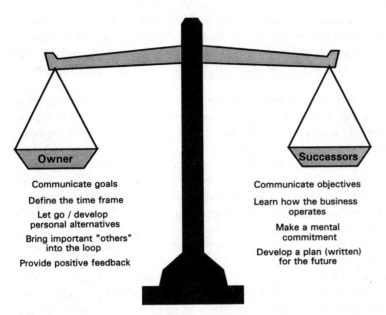

Figure 7-1. Commitment required by the successors.

A business plan should be prepared in conjunction with an ownership transfer plan. Ownership transfer should be contingent on having the written plan presented; otherwise, it is impossible to evaluate the successors' goals and ideas for the business. As a matter of course, I recommend to my clients that the successors prepare a business plan as one of the requirements for ownership transfer. There are eight important reasons for successors to take on this assignment:

1. It forces successors to think critically about strategic issues facing the business and to express logically, and in writing, their solution to the problems and challenges.

2. It gives the current owners an indication of how the successors will run "their" company in the future.

3. The goals and objectives laid out by the successors can establish performance requirements needed by the current owners to achieve personal safeguards and financial security.

4. It requires that successors work together, before the ownership transfer, on roles, responsibilities, and accountabilities.

5. It requires financial forecasts and cashflow projections to be reviewed and discussed.

6. It gives successors an opportunity to evaluate their own strengths and weaknesses objectively; this evaluation often leads to establishing a different time frame for ownership transfer.

7. It enhances cooperation and dialogue between current owners and successors in regard to company history and culture, as well as future challenges the company will face.

8. It requires commitment. When performed properly, this project can be the most effective test for measuring the readiness and devotion of successors.

Summary

Studies indicate that fewer than 5 percent of all start-up family businesses ever appoint a next-generation owner-manager. How can family businesses be successfully transferred when the next generation is never even appointed to take over? Of those owners who do appoint successors, many cloak their decisions in documents that become effective only after the owner's death.

Owners who complain about the younger generation's lack of commitment should realize that it is impossible for successors to be committed to an organization when they are unsure of their status within it. Current owners should make a commitment to their successors by giving them every opportunity to succeed. Then owners will learn if successors can handle the challenges they will surely face.

It is better for owners to find out now if their successors are ready to accept the responsibilities of running the business.

8
Hurdle 5:
How to Let Go

If the participants can get over the first four hurdles, the fifth hurdle, "letting go," may not be as much of an obstacle for the owner as it first seemed. In fact, some of the commitments and requirements established in Chapter 7 will have set the stage for this important transition. It depends to a large extent on what the owner has to "let go toward," as well as what the owner is "letting go of."

In my experience, most business owners in their early sixties are tired of the day-to-day hassles of their business, but they are not tired of "the business" itself. In fact, many 60-year-olds seem to have wonderful ideas for expanding their companies. They just don't have the energy to do it themselves. Therefore, in structuring an ownership transfer plan, it's important to understand what the current owner still likes about the business, and what he or she doesn't like. Three issues are critical:

1. Is a management team in place that can handle day-to-day decisions and crises?
2. Can the current owner leave town for two to four weeks and *not* call in daily?
3. Is the current owner suffering from burnout?

If the answer to any one of the above questions is yes, it's at least time for the owner to consider letting go and moving on in the succession plan.

How do people know they're suffering from burnout? Christina Maslach suggests three major symptoms.[1]

- Emotional exhaustion—feeling drained and tired even before the day begins
- Depersonalization—feeling disconnected from people, negative, and resentful
- Reduced sense of personal accomplishment—feeling ineffective, with no sense of satisfaction from results achieved

Sometimes owners know they are ready to let go of the day-to-day operations, but they want to continue having a hand in the company. How can this be resolved for a successor group? One solution is for the exiting owner to maintain a "voice" in major decisions—such as selling or merging the company, recapitalizing, issuing dividends, and changing any stock voting rights. (See Chapter 21.) It is important for owners to know that there are a number of ways to "have your cake and eat it, too."

Another way for owners to remain involved is to establish a permanent family council. If the initial family meeting on succession evolves into an ongoing process, a formal structure may develop for coordinating family and business interrelationships and for resolving disputes. Dennis Jaffe outlines ways to develop family councils in *Working with the Ones You Love*. A family council may also provide an avenue for satisfying the owner's desire for ongoing involvement and a mechanism for sharing experiences and wisdom with the successors.

The transfer of the business is more than a financial and tax issue. Carole and her husband, Paul, had established financial priorities such as security and wealth but they had never established any priorities for personal happiness. They had started with nothing and worked 40 years to reach their present rut—caused by their inability to let go of the business. Today their personal assets include more than $1 million in cash and investments; notes worth $600,000; the business, valued at $1.7 million; a profit-sharing plan with $400,000 in Paul's account; and miscellaneous other personal assets. Carole and Paul live in a 6000-square-foot house on three acres, including a lake and a boat dock. They haven't used the boat this year, and they used it only once last year.

Paul admits, "We lack direction. We have no capable management in the business, no overall game plan, no strategy." He wants to transfer the business to his son, but is concerned that the son "won't do it my way." In confronting the transfer of power and decision making to the next generation, Paul fears that the next generation will do things differently—and perhaps better—and if he "lets go," he may be forgotten.

It is important to explore some of the emotional bridges to be crossed in business transfers. Many financial advisers spend a great deal of time structuring the financial aspects of business continuity, tax-planning the transfer, and creating retirement and pension plans in favor of the current owner-manager to ensure that he or she is financially secure. The underlying issue of *how* the transition will actually be accomplished on a day-to-day basis is never addressed, and the practical problems of handling everyday crises are ignored.

How will the former owner spend his or her time? Will the owner still "come in," and if so, how often? Will the business continue to provide an office and a secretary?

The issue of letting go may be even harder when the sale is to a third party. One owner recently sold his business to a conglomerate for more money than he ever thought his business was worth. At the seller's request, the transaction included continued active involvement of the present owner. At 56 years old, he was not ready to retire. The first 90 days were the worst three months of his life. The parent corporation didn't respond to his memos, didn't run the business as he had, and didn't express interest in community involvement as he had. My client's problem was that he never mentally let go of the business.

When a business is sold or transferred to family members, employees, or a third party, in all likelihood, the new owners will run it differently. If the new owners are interested in the current owner's ideas, they'll ask; and they may or may not listen to the answers. Letting go is critical to the future success of the business and to the mental health of owners, both past and present.

Practice Letting Go

The current owner can "practice" letting go through sabbaticals and retirement rehearsals. *Sabbaticals* are commonly used in academic environments, and first began at Harvard in 1880. A formal sabbatical is a period of leisure, for personal or professional development, with a job guaranteed at the end. The practice is carrying over to the business community as well. Some companies have begun to offer employees educational, personal, and community-involvement sabbaticals. An owner might explore a work sabbatical—from two months to a year or more—to pursue other interests. Whether for continued education, public service, or recreation, a sabbatical can help owners find out what there is to "let go toward."

Retirement rehearsals—including phased retirement and part-time involvement—provide a way to take some of the stress out of a life-cycle change. Working on a project-oriented basis is another way of phasing out and can dovetail into long-range planning for the company. The project-oriented approach can also be used to provide consulting opportunities with other companies, often coordinated through an existing trade association or local contacts.

Letting Go the Easy Way—But Not the Best Way

There is an easy way an owner can let go: by transferring ownership in stages, over time, so that ultimately the next generation owns up to 49 percent of the business. Potentially adverse income tax or estate-tax consequences of this approach are addressed in other chapters. This chapter focuses on the emotional and psychological consequences.

When considering a transfer over a three-to-five-year period, owners will need to examine their motives to determine if they are making a real commitment. If the ultimate ownership to be transferred is 49 percent, then there is no real commitment or risk as long as the current owner retains that controlling 51 percent. The owner can observe successors and if they make a mistake, sell the business out from under them, as long as there's no contractual commitment to transfer the whole business.

Tom, the 42-year-old son of a client, has worked in his father's business for 20 years. Dad plans to give Tom 49 percent of the business over the next three years, at which point Dad can still sell his controlling interest to someone else or hang on to the controlling interest until he dies. Clearly, Tom is at risk.

The business may be at risk also. Tom may be prevented from implementing needed growth plans because an aging, controlling shareholder is risk averse. If Dad doesn't let go, he may risk Tom leaving the business and the business itself losing value.

Really Letting Go—The Road Less Traveled

The alternative to partial transfer requires a greater emotional and communication risk: opening up and sharing, teaching, and educating. Total transfer means committing now to the future by working with successors, allowing them to make mistakes, guiding them patiently and training them to become successors in more than name only.

The 100 percent business transfer, contractually legalized, can also be spread over a three-to-five year period. In this case, the commitment is both emotional and contractual. One business owner wanted desperately to transfer the business to her daughter. This plan became a rewarding experience as she watched and helped both her daughter and the business grow. To achieve this kind of peace, the owner recognized and accepted her new role as consultant and adviser rather than doer. She became the teacher instead of the boss, and she let her daughter, the "student," make her own decisions. And mistakes. The emotional risks were as great as the emotional rewards for both owner and successor.

Another business transfer solution is to sell the entire business outright and, with it, the management problems and day-to-day decision making. Most business owners can come up with creative reasons for selling the business to a third party. A common thread running through this rationale is that the owners believe their heirs are not ready to receive control of the business.

One of my clients has convinced himself that because his son was divorced three years ago, the son isn't ready to assume control of the business. Because they are disappointed that the son's marriage failed, he and his wife are withholding stock from him.

Interestingly, the son confided that during the 15 years of his marriage, he was depressed and lacked ambition. He lived in his father's shadow and his father never felt threatened. Now that the son is successful in his second marriage and out from under his father, he is more career-oriented and has his own ideas about the family business. Dad doesn't like this "new" son as well.

Transferring the business now makes Dad feel vulnerable. Nobody likes to have decisions, business or personal, challenged.

Control and Identity

The issues of control and identity are important in business ownership. Only one person is ultimately responsible and accountable for day-to-day operations. Frequently, it is through these day-to-day decisions that the owner-manager derives a sense of self-worth and, ultimately, a sense of security and well-being. Often business owners haven't developed lifestyle alternatives outside the business. Some have unhappy marriages and prefer to spend all their time at work. Others truly don't know what to do for relaxation. Work is their security blanket.

The hardest part of transferring the business is relinquishing control. As the spouse of one client noted, "My husband will think twice before he gives up his control of the business. He's always called the shots." The wife compared her husband's control of the business to her role as homemaker. "If I had a full-time housekeeper and had to adjust to the housekeeper's needs for running the home, I would feel as though I had lost what had been mine. I derive my identity from my responsibilities for the home."

Control and identity do not have to be inseparable. One solution lies in achieving a sense of self-worth from more than one source, including family and hobbies as well as business.

Do You Know How to Have Fun?

If owners haven't discovered positive alternatives to work by the time they are 60 or 62 years old, they will have great difficulty leaving the business. One client's dilemma is illustrative. "Nobody is going to drill a hole in your head and pour in fun. I'd like to retire, but I'll admit I haven't developed an alternative to long hours at the office. I'm not sure that my wife and I know how to have fun. I wish we had explored other interests when we were younger."

The potential "black hole" of age 65 can be a beginning rather than an end. Here is how.

The next-generation owner-manager should become president of the firm with responsibility for management of day-to-day activities. The retiring owner-manager can be promoted to chairperson of the board, or consultant emeritus. The former owner should no longer work directly with employees; to do so would undermine the new president's authority and responsibility. As chairperson, the former owner can be responsible for helping establish long-range plans for growth and also for developing an outside board of directors to help the company in the future. Implementation of those plans is the responsibility of the president. The board leader and the president can confer daily, but implementation of activities is always the president's job.

The former owner, current board member, and possible creditor should receive weekly reports from the president and should work with the president to increase revenues and to research demographic and market changes. The retiring owner-manager now has time to become the best spokesperson the firm can have. Maintaining contact with possible acquisition candidates in the community is one way to keep the door open to future business growth as well as to potential sites for expansion. In addition, the former owner can prepare and motivate the president to implement and manage any expansion programs.

One client successfully accomplished his chairman-of-the-board status by moving his office out of the building. Employees could no longer go to him for day-to-day decisions. The new office, a block away from the business, has a "war board" on which is outlined seven or eight long-term business strategies and tactics for achieving those plans. Business responsibility is allocated to each of three children who are active in the business. The three children report to the chairman regularly. All four meet to discuss day-to-day progress and to decide how to achieve long-term business objectives.

Successful business transfers begin with the owner's assessment of the present situation and of decisions that will be in the best interests of the business. The retiring owner needs to relinquish authority and move from center stage, allowing the offspring to assume the business's major responsibilities.

Owners should take a few minutes to answer the following questions in order to assess their own situation:

- Are all participants ready, willing, and able to commit the time and energy necessary for the business to remain successful? Are they willing to compromise in order to reach a workable solution?

- Has a realistic time frame been established with "benchmarks" or mileposts along the way?

- Will a change in control mean a change in ownership?

- Have plans been communicated to all family members (active and inactive)? To all key nonfamily personnel?

- Has the current owner learned how to enjoy leisure time?

References

1. Christina Maslach, *Burnout: The Cost of Caring* (Englewood Cliffs, NJ: Prentice Hall, 1982).

9
Hurdle 6: How Much Does the Owner Need to Retire?

One Michigan business owner who was ready to transfer his business, claimed, "All I need is bait and gas money for the boat." He then proceeded to negotiate selling his business to his children until they agreed to pay him the full fair market value: a cool $3.5 million.

Money is, psychologically, more than a unit of value. What money measures at the grocery store is relatively simple: A 10-dollar bill buys $10 worth of groceries. What it measures in our minds is more complex.

Most owners' largest asset is the business. Its value is usually tied up in equipment and machinery, trucks, inventory, and receivables. The owner, however, may look at the value of the business as a potential pile of money, which can represent many things: freedom, authority and power, security and safety, victory and rewards, personal self-esteem.

People's view of money can be described as their *money personality*. To an entrepreneur, the pile of money (for the value of the company) represents the success of something built—a job well done. The bigger the pile, the greater the sense of accomplishment. To a security-conscious individual, the size of the pile isn't as important as how well protected it is and how long it might last.

Arlene Matthews, writing in the *Washington Post*, used Freudian terms to describe the money personality:

> When we take action with money, we may sometimes be acting on behalf of what our superego deems the Good Self—perhaps the Virtuous Scrimper, the Exceedingly Generous Charitable Donor, the Hypercautious Investor or the Vigilant Bargain Hunter. We may sometimes be acting on behalf of what it deems the Bad Self—perhaps the Unlucky Gambler, the Chronic

Borrower or the Corner-Cutting Petty Cheat. We sometimes act on behalf of the id,...engaging in spur-of-the-moment extravagances...[that later make us] feel like comedian Flip Wilson's mischievous character Geraldine, who plaintively contended, "The *devil* made me buy that dress."[1]

Those who have it need to live sanely with money, especially during a life-cycle transition. A business owner contemplating retirement and successors contemplating the cashflow of the company need to understand what money means on different levels, and to connect feelings about money with changing life cycles.

Determining the Owner's Financial Dependence on the Business

Although most family business owners take enough money out of the business to enjoy a comfortable lifestyle, they often fail to create any other significant assets in their estate. Family business owners with significant assets are frequently beneficiaries of inheritances. A few have been successful in passive real estate or other investment opportunities. Seldom do business owners consciously diversify their net worth by creating outside assets.

There is some rationale to this shortsighted approach. The successful and profitable business may represent the best investment prospect. The owner knows the company and its markets, the officers and employees, and feels confident that the business is assured of future success. Rarely does the owner have time for the same amount of due diligence with other investment opportunities.

A potential problem occurs when the owner begins to consider passing on ownership to successors and realizes that his or her "money" is locked inside the business. Two important questions must be addressed here: How much of the business value is needed for personal support after ownership is transferred? Does (and should) the business provide financial opportunities to children who are not active in it?

In order to determine financial "dependence" on the business, owners must calculate the amount of money they will need from the business after they transfer ownership. It's safe to assume they will want to maintain their present standard of living for the remainder of their lives.

The Impact of Inflation

Figure 9-1 illustrates how the Consumer Price Index, which equaled 100 in 1967, rose to 393.8 by 1990. Because of inflation, goods and services which cost $1.00 in 1967 cost $3.94 in 1990.

If inflation were zero, a $100,000 current annual income would allow a business owner and his or her spouse to maintain the same standard of living for the rest of their lives. Figure 9-2 however, shows what 6.1 percent annual

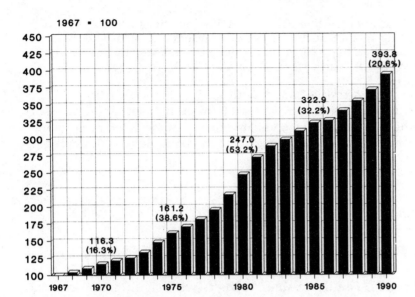

Figure 9-1. Consumer Price Index for all urban consumers. The average annual increase is 6.1 percent. (*Source: Bureau of Labor Statistics*)

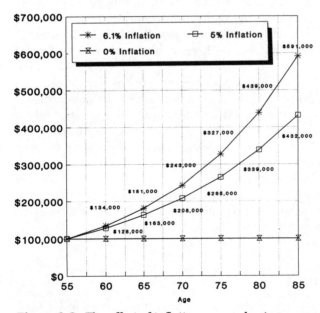

Figure 9-2. The effect of inflation on purchasing power.

inflation will do to a $100,000 income in 20 years. If the business owner is 55 now, and inflation is 6.1 percent per year, in 20 years $327,000 *per year* will be needed to buy the same goods and services that can be bought today for $100,000. At age 85, $591,000 per year will be needed to maintain the $100,000 annual lifestyle.

Why Financial Planning Is So Important

Income during retirement may be affected by several factors besides inflation:

1. The ever-increasing complexity of investment and savings vehicles require more time, effort, and technical expertise than most people can or will devote to managing their funds. The result can be a loss of earning power on investments, which may be important in funding future income requirements.

2. Qualified retirement plans provided by the owner's company are often complex; they may be affected and even cut back by future changes in tax laws. Retirement packages that can provide a greater financial benefit for the owner are often not implemented as part of an overall transfer strategy.

3. People are living longer. To provide inflation-proof income during retirement, owners may feel tempted to stay with the business longer than is appropriate.

4. Owners can no longer assume that they can count on insurance products and companies to provide annuities, retirement funds, and death benefits for estate liquidity or to fund shareholder agreements. With the insurance industry in upheaval, owners now must track the health of their carriers and viability of the products they buy.

5. Constant changes in tax laws makes tax planning confusing for the CPA *and* the client. This year's plan may have to be unraveled next year.

6. Owners must realistically assess the risk of permanent disability, hospitalization, death, or other calamities, and have appropriate contingency plans. Most people tend to believe that they can beat the odds or that statistical information applies only "to the other guy." (See Figure 9-3.)

How Much Is Needed to Retire?

Five key factors should be considered before determining what the owner will need to retire, and how financially dependent the owner is on the business.

1. *At what age does the owner plan to retire?* Although retirement may not mean full withdrawal from the business, it may mean a change in the character of income as the owner currently knows it. In any event, it will be necessary to determine how much the owner will have in investable assets at retirement age.

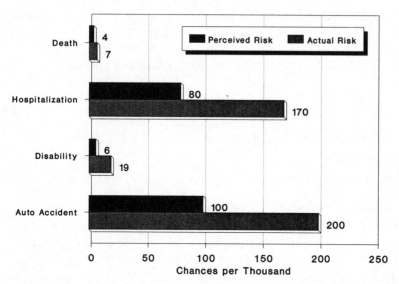

Figure 9-3. Actual versus perceived risk. (*Source: N. A. Sutton, "An Illusion of Control,"* Best's Review: Life/Health Insurance Edition, *July 1987, pp. 54–58)*

2. *What interest rate should be assumed?*   The assets at retirement age will be consumed or paid out over the owner's and spouse's life expectancies. Therefore, it's important to choose a conservative interest rate to avoid outliving the income stream. Throughout the 1980s, Treasury bonds, considered a conservative investment, yielded an average 12.6 percent. As of mid-1992, Treasury bond yields were 7.82 percent. If the plan is to live only on interest from investments, it will be necessary to have a larger amount available to provide an income stream that protects principal. On the other hand, if principal is depleted, as well as interest, there may not be anything left for children who are not active in the business. Chapter 23 explores equalization strategies for inactive children and how they can affect estate planning.

3. *How long do owner and spouse expect to live?*   No one enjoys predicting his or her mortality, but some idea of life expectancy can be obtained by averaging the mortality of parents and spouse's parents. Estimates should be conservative to protect against outliving personal resources.

4. *How much is needed each year to live comfortably?*   If the business is paying for a lot of personal expenses on a deductible basis, it may be difficult for the owner to calculate exactly how much money will be needed to live on. Financial independence requires sufficient income and assets to prevent outliving resources.

Lifestyle changes must also be considered. If the owner has been unaccustomed to traveling or taking long vacations and would like to do so during retirement, he or she will need to identify an amount for annual travel expenses. If buying a condo is in the plans (or selling one), that too must be taken into account. Gifts to grandchildren should be planned, as well as extraordinary purchases of art, antiques, cars, jewelry, and other luxury items.

Although most people don't become spendthrifts after they retire, many have an opportunity to enjoy some of the things they postponed while they built their business. Others maintain the same lifestyle they always enjoyed.

5. *What rate of inflation is projected over the remainder of the owner's life?* Over the past five years inflation has averaged about 5 percent per year. Choosing a higher rate of inflation makes for a more conservative projection, as it will require more funds available at retirement age.

Case Study

John and Anne Smith are each 55 years old. They currently need $100,000 per year *in today's dollars* to support their standard of living. If they both retire in 10 years, when they are 65, they will need an inflation-adjusted $100,000 annually for as long as they both live.

In addition, after one spouse dies, the other will need $75,000 annually (in today's dollars) for as long as he or she lives. Anne and John must also consider the after-tax rate of return (before and after retirement), inflation, and life expectancy.

As illustrated in Figure 9-4, Anne and John's needs continue to increase, even as their income sources decline. Anne and John's sources of income were provided through compensation from the business from ages 55 to 64; after that, Anne and John depend on retirement benefits or income from personal assets throughout their projected life expectancies of age 90. The difference between the "sources" line and the "needs" line represents Anne

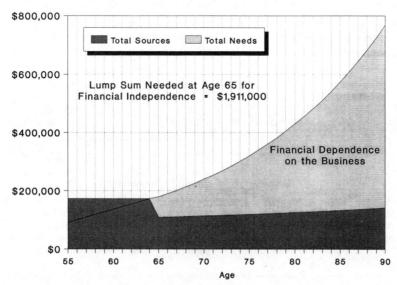

Figure 9-4. John and Anne Smith's sources of income compared to financial needs.

and John's financial "dependence" on the business—the amount, either in a lump sum at age 65 (after taxes) or in a stream of payments, beginning at age 65, that John and Anne need to maintain their current standard of living. Any surplus saved after Anne and John satisfy their annual living requirements will be available to their heirs. If there is a shortfall, Anne and John will run out of money. Anne and John have 10 years, beginning at age 55, to begin accumulating some of the funds they will need during retirement.

Anne and John have three choices if they want to keep the business in the "family." First, they can begin now to accumulate funds in the business. Second, at age 65, they can fund their "dependence" by selling the business to children, key employees, or an outside buyer, and rely on future payments to support retirement. Last, they can use a combination of both.

Instead of being dependent on a future income stream, John and Anne could elect to sell their business for cash (assuming the business or the new owners can raise cash). The lump-sum amount of cash needed to fund the deficit through their ninetieth year is about $2 million, net after taxes.

It is unlikely that internal buyers for Anne's and John's business will be able to afford a cash buyout. Without a buyout, however, a transfer to family members may be jeopardized, because Anne and John cannot afford to let go. John and Anne may be forced to sell the business to an outside party. But if John and Anne can be made financially secure (as we'll explore later), and assured of receiving their payments, an installment transaction from the successors may be acceptable and allow them to keep the family business in the family.

Options to Retirement Needs

As shown in Figure 9-5, John and Anne can change their assumptions about the five key retirement-income factors in order to adjust the amount of money they will need at retirement:

1. *Standard of living.* If John and Anne decide to reduce their standard of living, the amount of money they will need at 65 will, of course, decrease.

2. *Interest rate.* Assuming a higher preretirement and postretirement investment return can significantly decrease the amount of money John and Anne will need to set aside.

	Today's Standard of Living	Interest Rate	Inflation	Age of Retirement	Life Expectancy	Present Value Today	Present Value at age 65
Assumptions	$100,000	5.5%	6.0%	65	90	$1,753,000	$1,911,000
Adjust:	$75,000	5.5%	6.0%	65	90	$1,047,000	$1,141,000
Adjust:	$100,000	7.0%	6.0%	65	90	$1,721,000	$1,876,000
Adjust:	$100,000	5.5%	8.0%	65	90	$3,148,000	$3,431,000
Adjust:	$100,000	5.5%	6.0%	70	90	$1,447,000	$1,577,000
Adjust:	$100,000	5.5%	6.0%	65	85	$1,437,000	$1,566,000

OPTIONS TO RETIREMENT NEED

Figure 9-5. Retirement needs change as assumptions change.

3. *Inflation.* If inflation is slightly higher or slightly lower than anticipated, it can also affect the amount of funds Anne and John have. Higher inflation requires more dollars to satisfy their standard of living. Conversely, low inflation ensures that money will be left over and goods and services can be purchased at a lower price than expected.

By structuring the transfer to include an inflation adjustment, and building hedges into their strategy, Anne and John can protect themselves against some of these variables.

4. *Age of retirement.* John and Anne may elect to work longer—say, to age 70. Delayed retirement provides additional income from the business for another three to five years. Although the inflation-adjusted dollars Anne and John will need at retirement may be slightly higher, there will be more years for those dollars to be accumulated.

5. *Life expectancy.* If, instead of assuming life expectancy to age 90, Anne and John assumed age 85, or age 95, the amount of dollars needed would be affected. Changing assumptions may affect calculations for how much money John and Anne will need to set aside, but it will not, of course, change reality. The less conservative the assumptions, the more risk they assume that they will outlive their nest egg.

Consider Retirement Needs When Selling to a Third Party

One client promised that if he ever sold his business he would offer it first to his key nonfamily employee. He had considered a range of values for the business. However, when the "financial independence" calculation was performed, the client learned that he and his wife would run out of money by the time they reached 80, based on the business value he had decided on.

He had intended to discount the sale price to this key employee in recognition for his valued service; however, he didn't want to run out of money during retirement either. My associates and I suggested having outside firms make an offer in order to establish a true fair market value. The client was surprised to learn that outside buyers would pay almost two times the price he originally considered for offering it to the key employee. The higher price would satisfy the client's need for financial security. The key employee was offered the business at 90 percent of what the outside firms would pay, but decided the pressure of becoming an entrepreneur would be too stressful. The decision was helped in part by the fact that the two outside buyers had both promised the key employee an attractive employment package, including financial incentives.

Ultimately, one of the outside firms bought the business. The client is more secure financially and the key employee is happy in his new role as senior manager.

References

1. Arlene Matthews, "This World," *Washington Post*, September 8, 1991.

10
Hurdle 7: Keeping Key Employees During a Transition

In the best of all possible worlds, the next generation is ready to take over the reins just as the older generation is letting go. But the world seldom works on cue. Often children are not yet seasoned enough to assume control. No problem, many owners think. Key nonfamily managers are often perfectly suited to fill the void until the next generation is ready. True, but there's a catch: To compensate for the increased responsibility, key employees frequently want a "piece of the action." Family business owners often reject this idea completely, seeing it as a potential threat to future family ownership.

When planning incentive packages for key people during a period of transition, an owner must:

- Be aware of their concerns about job safety, health of the business, and personal financial security
- Identify what role they can play to smooth the bumps during a transition
- Understand how they could obstruct or sabotage the owner's plans
- Assess whether or not the business would survive without them
- Consider the ramifications of the possibility that they might jump to a competitor
- Bring them "into the loop" regarding future plans for the business
- Create financial incentives ("golden handcuffs") geared to help the family and the owner achieve their goals

There are many creative ways to keep key employees happy without jeopardizing family control of the business. By tying additional rewards to long-term performance, the owner can create a "golden handcuff" that motivates valued managers to take a perspective that parallels the family's.

Incentive Stock Options

One client—I'll call him Paul Jordan—is owner of Jordan Supply, a $25-million wholesale plumbing business. As Paul was approaching retirement, he recognized that his two sons, both active sales managers for the company, still lacked the experience necessary to run the highly competitive business. Paul wanted ownership to remain in family hands. His general manager, Bill Galt, could bridge the gap until his sons were ready—if Paul could motivate this talented employee to groom his own successors. My associates and I discussed the situation at length with Paul and Bill. We looked at stock options—either an incentive plan or a nonqualified plan—and discussed phantom stock or cash bonuses.

Paul decided on an incentive stock option plan, giving Bill the right to acquire nonvoting shares. This plan would give Bill the financial benefits and motivation he sought, plus favorable tax treatment. Nonvoting common stock let Bill share in the company's growth. Coupling the plan with a stock redemption program would protect family control: Bill would have to sell his shares back to Jordan Supply when he reached retirement or if he terminated employment.

The incentive stock option (ISO) plan gave Bill an option to acquire shares in the company at a predetermined price, based on outside valuation of the stock's fair market value (in this case, book value). The granting or exercise of options is not a taxable event to Bill. Any subsequent increase in the company's book value also remains a tax-free benefit to Bill. Section 422A of the Internal Revenue Code permits Bill to exercise the options any time within 10 years. When he does, he can purchase his shares at the original grant price, regardless of current fair market value. Still, there is no tax consequence.

Once he buys the shares, Bill must hold them for at least two years to qualify for capital gains treatment on their sale. If he qualifies, Bill will pay capital gains taxes on the difference between the price for which he sells the stock back to Jordan Supply and the grant price. (The two-year holding period is waived for Bill's heirs in the event of his death.) If Bill sells before the two-year period, he pays ordinary income tax on the difference between his sale price and the grant price. The company gets a deduction equal to Bill's income, whenever Bill sells his shares.

The companion stock redemption agreement lets the company repurchase Bill's shares at market value when he retires, is terminated, becomes disabled, or dies. If Bill is terminated and has not yet exercised the options, he will have one year to do so. He can then hold the options for the two-year period to qualify for capital gains or sell them back to the company immediately, in which case he incurs ordinary income taxes on the gains and the company gets a deduction. (If Paul had been leery of letting a terminated employee hold even nonvoting shares, he could have insisted that Bill exercise the options, paying Bill a cash bonus at termination equal to the income taxes Bill paid in excess of the capital gains rates.)

The current book value of Jordan Supply is $3 million, or $3000 for each of its 1000 shares outstanding. Bill was granted options to acquire 30 shares, worth $90,000. He plans to exercise his option eight years from now, and then sell those shares back to the company two years later, just before his retirement. His cost will still be $90,000. Assume that the book value per share rises 7 percent a year, reaching $6000 by the time Bill retires. The $180,000 Bill would receive represents a $90,000 gain to be taxed at then-current capital gain rates. At some point, the company will have to be sure it has enough cash on hand to buy back Bill's shares.

The ISO plan gave Paul the missing link he needed for his own retirement. He already trusted Bill to run the company. Now, as an "owner," Bill had an additional incentive to protect Paul's interests as well as his own.

If a company extends its ISO plan to family members, additional restrictions are imposed on those participants. Options must be exercised at 110 percent (rather than 100 percent) of the stock's fair market value, and they must be exercised within five years rather than ten. These restrictions often make the plan less attractive to family members.

What about alternatives to the ISO plan? Incentive stock options are not the only way to share future growth with key nonfamily employees. Nonqualified stock options, phantom stock, or cash bonuses can be appropriate tools to motivate and hang on to nonfamily employees. Tax treatment, however, is more favorable to the company than to the recipient.

Nonqualified options result in ordinary income taxes when the options are *exercised* rather than when they are *sold*. The amount taxed is the difference between the grant price and the fair market value on the date the options are exercised. The corporation gets a deduction equal to the income reported by the participant. The various pros and cons of stock plans are summarized in Figure 10-1.

Phantom Stock

Phantom stock may be an attractive alternative. It is exactly what the name implies: no stock is transferred. Instead, a participant is granted "appreciation rights" to a specified number of shares. The appreciation may be defined by a change in book value or by another measure of growth. Annual valuations provide a method of reporting the phantom stock's performance to the participant. The participant in a phantom stock plan is a general creditor of the company; the value of the appreciation rights are analogous to an accrued bonus. The appreciation rights are paid on retirement, termination, disability,

	ISO Plan	Nonqualified Stock Options	Phantom Stock
THE PROS AND CONS OF STOCK PLANS			
Is employee taxed on purchase?	No	Yes	No
How is gain treated?	Capital gain	Ordinary income	Ordinary income
How are options and appreciation rights valued?	Fair market value	Any price set by board	Any price set by board
Are distributions to employee deductible to company?	No	Yes, equal to income reported by employee	Yes, equal to income reported by employee

Figure 10-1.

or death. They are taxed as ordinary income and are expensed by the company as paid.

A phantom stock plan may have higher administrative costs than an ISO plan because of the need to value and report appreciation rights annually. Here is an example of a performance-based valuation clause:

Shares of phantom stock shall be issued to the Participant by the Board of Directors of the corporation. In future years while the participant is still employed with the corporation, phantom stock will be credited in accord with the formula below:

Return-on-investment percentage	Annal shares
4.5	1.50
6.0	2.00
7.5	2.50
9.0	3.00
10.5	3.50
12.0	4.00
13.5	4.50
15.0	5.00
16.5	5.50
18.0	6.00
19.5	6.50
21.0	7.00

"Return on investment" of the corporation is defined as follows: net income divided by the company's adjusted value. Net income equals net after-tax income with adjustments for LIFO and expenses [associated with owner's buyout]. In determining adjusted value, long-term buyout debt on the books of the corporation shall be added to shareholders' equity. The return-on-investment percentage established from the formula shall be equated to the above schedule to arrive at the number of phantom stock shares granted in any one year.

In the above example, the phantom stock bonus to the executive could range from $6000 to $28,000 per year, based on a value of $4000 per share. This bonus can be in addition to existing cash bonuses already in place.

If performance-oriented managers want to build their net worth now rather than defer it, owners may consider cash bonuses based on current performance and paid out as earned. But cash bonuses do not handcuff that essential employee or provide any long-term incentives. Figure 10-2 illustrates how a phantom stock plan works.

Nonqualified Pension Plans

As alternatives to using stock, other financial incentives can stimulate key employees to remain with the company. The programs differ depending on what business owners are trying to provide and whom they wish to reward.

Family business owners are often insensitive to different perspectives that family members and key nonfamily executives have about the timing of business decisions. For instance, the family may take a long-term view in

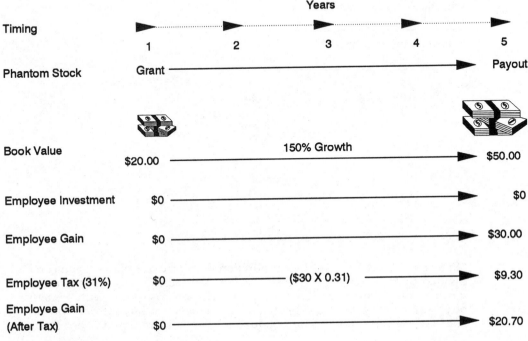

Figure 10-2. Phantom stock program.

managing the company's assets, but tie key executives' compensation to short-term performance measures.

One prominent family business that held a substantial amount of undeveloped real estate took a 40-year horizon regarding developing the real estate. The nonfamily executives, however, had financial incentives to maximize the company's return on assets. Their "view" was that the assets were underutilized in the form of raw land. Although the land value had been steadily appreciating, the executives wanted to develop the property, through a subsidiary, for industrial and commercial uses and then, through another subsidiary, provide ongoing property management services. The value of the company's asset would likely increase tenfold, resulting in higher year-end bonuses for the executive group.

The family refused to endorse the recommendation, which frustrated the management team.

What should be done here? Obviously, aligning the key executives' compensation with the family's long-term view would be ideal. Nonqualified pension plans, common in most large companies, could coordinate the two perspectives into a win-win solution. (See Figure 10-3.)

Other problems occur when the transition of ownership requires the key executives to "mentor" the next generation. Mentoring puts these executives in a lose-lose situation. Acting antagonistically to the new owners or to the transition could jeopardize their job; successful mentoring also could jeopardize their job when the person being trained takes over or leapfrogs the trainer's position.

Employment agreements, which usually protect an employee more than an

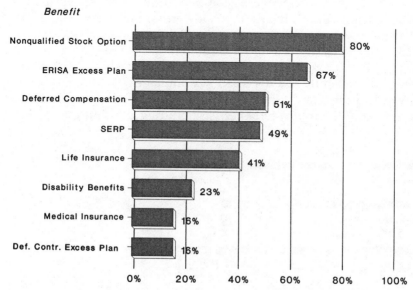

Figure 10-3. *Nonqualified plans.* The percentage of large companies offering nonqualified executive benefits. (*Source: Charles D. Spencer & Associates, 1989*)

Compensation	$30,000	$50,000	$70,000	$100,000	$150,000	$200,000
401(k) Plan Deposit (10% of Comp.) *	3,000	5,000	7,000	8,728	8,728	8,728
Benefit at Age 65 ** from 401(k) Plan	11,422	19,037	26,652	33,231	33,231	33,231
Social Security ***	11,952	14,832	15,552	15,552	15,552	15,552
Total	**$23,374**	**$33,869**	**$42,204**	**$48,783**	**$48,783**	**$48,783**
Percent of Compensation	**77.9%**	**67.7%**	**60.3%**	**48.8%**	**32.5%**	**24.4%**

*   The maximum amount that can be deposited into a 401(k) plan for 1992 is $8,728.

**   Benefits from the 401(k) plan assume deposits increase by 8 percent annually and that benefits are based on a life annuity.

***   Social Security benefits are determined based on the 1992 benefit scale. Currently, the maximum annual benefit is $15,552.

Figure 10-4. The need for an excess benefit plan grows as compensation increases.

employer, are often lacking in family businesses. The long-term employee may have 20 or 30 years of service, may lack formal education, and usually is making more money as a "number two" person in the family business than he or she could earn anywhere else. These are the folks whose loyalty is unquestioned and for whom selective nonqualified retirement-type benefits (as described below) can offer substantial rewards for their loyalty and years of service.

Another problem occurs when key executives analyze their qualified pension plan benefits and realize that the more they earn today, the lower their retirement benefits will be, as a percentage of compensation. In other words, the company's qualified plan may actually favor lower-paid employees and discriminate *against* the key executive group. Figure 10-4 illustrates this dilemma.

Nonqualified plans generally fall into a combination of three categories, as illustrated in Figure 10-5: retirement-type plans, growth-sharing plans, or survivor benefits for the family of a deceased key employee.

It is important to note the distinction between nonqualified plans and qualified plans. Qualified employee benefits, including pension and profit-

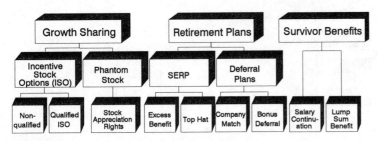

Figure 10-5. Overview of nonqualified benefit plans or "golden handcuff" programs.

sharing plans, must be offered to all employees, in accordance with various tax laws (ERISA in 1974, and later amendments in TEFRA in 1982, DEFRA and REA in 1984, and the Tax Reform Act of 1986). It is customary and advisable to seek advance approval of qualified plans from the IRS.

Nonqualified plans allow the employer to provide benefits to key employees who have exceeded the limits for qualified plans, or to provide selective benefits if qualified plans have been terminated or have never existed. The employer can provide these additional benefits on a discretionary basis to one key individual, or to many. The benefits are usually designed as either retirement-type plans or growth-sharing plans.

Nonqualified plans are further distinguished from qualified plans in that they do not need to be currently funded by the employer. Because unfunded plans are exempt from all ERISA requirements, the employer need not seek advance approval by the IRS. However, if the plan is funded, ERISA's reporting and disclosure requirements and fiduciary rules must be met and the funded plan is subject to ERISA enforcement provisions.

Unfunded, nonqualified deferred compensation benefits are not taxed until they are received, and the employer is not entitled to a tax deduction until the employee is taxed on the benefits. A comparison of the different features of qualified and nonqualified retirement plans is presented in Figure 10-6. The nonqualified plan is often referred to as a discriminatory benefit plan.

SERPs and Deferral Plans

Older, key employees may feel insecure or threatened by the next-generation successor's unproven skills, and not without cause. Often, successors respect the current owner's relationship with key employees, but don't want the financial burden of employees who may have become an unnecessary expense to the company. Nonetheless, during the transition period, the support of key employees is most needed. The most popular type of nonqualified retirement plan, the Supplemental Executive Retirement Plan (SERP), can provide financial and job security for key employees and ease some of the financial burden.

By providing a SERP to selected key people, the family business can send several messages. First, the company is sensitive to employees' personal retirement needs. Second, the company wants to relieve employees of any financial insecurity they may anticipate with the proposed changes. Third, the company wants to encourage key people to remain with the firm until normal retirement age. One indirect, but very real, benefit of a SERP is the additional financial security provided for older employees, allowing them to retire at the standard retirement age. Because ERISA requires no IRS filing and very few Department of Labor filings, SERPs are easy for an employer to install and administer.

There are generally two types of SERPs: excess-benefit plans and top-hat plans. Excess-benefit plans restore benefits to key people who may have lost

Qualified vs. Nonqualified Plans			
	Qualified Pension or Profit Sharing	Nonqualified Supplemental Pension	Nonqualified Deferred Compensation
Does the employer receive a current tax deduction?	Yes	No	No
Can the plan discriminate in favor of management or highly compensated employees?	No	Yes	Yes
Is Internal Revenue Service approval required?	Yes	No	No
Who establishes the ground rules?	The Government	Employer	Employer
Will the deposits be available to the company in the event of an emergency?	No	Yes	Yes
Will the benefits be forfeited by the participant if he/she terminates employment?	Limited	Yes	No
Are there likely to be annual administrative costs and fees?	Yes	Limited	Limited
Will annual Internal Revenue Service and Department of Labor filing and reporting forms be required?	Yes	No	No
Can the plan be terminated for any reason whatsoever without Internal Revenue Service approval or tax penalty?	No	Yes	Yes
Can the corporation recover its costs of funding benefits?	No	Yes	No
Is a bond required?	Yes	No	No
Is there fiduciary investment responsibility?	Yes	No	No

Figure 10-6.

some through curtailments in qualified plans. Such plans may also be used as recruiting tools. For example, assume a business owner wants to recruit a 50-year-old senior executive from another company. If the executive terminates employment at that company, he or she may lose significant benefits available under his or her current retirement plan. For that reason, the executive may be unwilling to change jobs. What can the business owner do? The excess-benefit SERP can fully replace all retirement benefits that individual lost at the former job.

A top-hat plan provides salary continuation to enhance postretirement income for key people. A top hat may provide a fixed annual benefit (a flat amount) or a percentage of the employee's annual or final pay. There are no limits to the benefits that can be provided. A properly designed SERP does not jeopardize or reduce Social Security or other benefits the employee may be eligible to receive.

A SERP can be provided *on a discriminatory basis* to key employees. Or the benefits can be different for each participant. Benefits in the top-hat SERP can "wrap around" any qualified pension, profit-sharing, or 401(k) plan benefits, and do not jeopardize any other benefits currently offered.

SERPs may be "informally" funded or remain an unfunded liability of the employer. Because the participant in SERP benefits becomes a general creditor of the company, the SERP is usually informally funded. Any contributions to an informally funded SERP remain an asset of the employer. If the employee terminates employment prior to normal retirement age, the employee could forfeit all benefits in the SERP. Vesting is at the discretion of the employer.

Deposits to the well-designed SERP grow tax-deferred until payout. Then the employer receives an income tax deduction as benefits are paid to the participant, and the employee recognizes income at the same time. During the years of participation in the SERP, the employee does not recognize any current income or pay any income tax.

One of the most important features of the informally funded SERP is cost recovery. *After* all benefits are paid to the participant, the employer can recover the entire corporate cost of funding the program from the SERP account—either after the benefits have been paid or at the time of the employee's death. Here's an example of how an informally funded SERP can work.

John is a 40-year-old manager making $50,000 per year. ABC Company is contributing $3500 per year to his profit-sharing account but wants to do more for John. By depositing an additional $3000 per year to a SERP account for John's benefit, ABC can provide John, at age 65, with approximately $25,000 *per year* for 10 years (based on current interest and mortality tables), *in addition* to any profit-sharing benefits John receives. At the end of the 10 years (John at age 75), ABC will recover the $75,000 it invested over the 25 years funded for John. Adjustments can be made to recover the entire cost plus interest. If John leaves ABC before age 65, he forfeits the entire SERP benefits package.

Deferred compensation plans also allow employees to defer the receipt of earnings to later years, but, unlike SERPs, some accrual is often added to the deferrals based on an interest rate or company performance. Deferral plans appeal to employees who do not need additional, current taxable income and are willing to defer the income—and the taxation—to a later time.

One caveat is that in order for the employee to avoid the constructive receipt of income and not be taxed currently, the employee becomes an unsecured, general creditor of the employer. The compensation deferred must be subject to a risk of forfeiture on the part of the employee; if it is not, it will become immediately taxable. Through the use of a grantor trust, this risk can generally be mitigated and taxation still avoided until benefits are received.

Deferred compensation plans provide a tax benefit through deferral; in order to turn this into a financial incentive to remain with the company, the company can provide a "matching" feature. Benefits provided by the company under the matching portion can be forfeited if the employee terminates before normal retirement age. With the company match, the difference between the nonqualified plan and the 401(k) is that the nonqualified plan can be discriminatory, while the 401(k) cannot.

Figure 10-7, a combination plan, shows a company-matching portion based on performance. The employer match can significantly enhance the employees' voluntary deferral; in this example, the deferral was projected for a 25-year period and 9.75 percent interest was credited to the deferred amount.

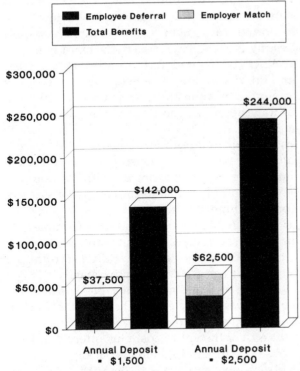

Figure 10-7. Deferred compensation plan—with and without employer match.

Securitizing the Benefits

The key employee in the family business may be comfortable with a general-creditor status regarding promised benefits as long as the current owner is around. However, if ownership succession is under way, that same key employee may feel insecure about his or her unsecured benefits with "the kids" running the company. The insecurity may be valid when those same kids are structuring the ownership succession plan along the lines of a leveraged buyout (LBO), adding debt to the company's balance sheet. Tying in key people as part of the LBO may reduce employees' insecurity about the succession process. Current management may need to be retained to maintain (and improve) the company's earnings during the LBO years.

There are two types of trusts which provide executives with some measure of security about promised benefits: rabbi trusts and secular trusts.

Rabbi trusts are irrevocable trusts established by the corporation. By irrevocably setting aside funds for the exclusive use of retiree benefits, rabbi trusts end uncertainties created by a change of control or a change of heart. The trust is called a rabbi trust because the first IRS letter ruling about this type of trust was issued to a rabbi whose congregation had contributed funds to an irrevocable trust for his benefit. The IRS said the rabbi would not be taxed on the funds until they were distributed to him or his beneficiary—that is, at retirement, death, disability, or termination of employment.

However, the company that establishes the trust is still deemed to control the funds; they are not beyond the reach of creditors in bankruptcy proceedings. Also important, funds deposited in a rabbi trust cannot be expensed by the company until they are actually paid out.

Secular trusts reverse that situation by giving the employee control of the funds. Creditors cannot claim the funds, and companies can immediately expense their contributions. Secular trusts are also irrevocable; the trust holds the executive's funds until retirement, death, disability, or termination occurs. Participants suffer because they must pay taxes on the amounts being set aside, although at retirement they can withdraw these previously taxed funds tax-free. Also, the plan no longer functions as a golden handcuff because the executives are fully vested; that is, they control the funding process at all times.

Whether establishing a golden handcuff is an objective or providing a secure deferred compensation plan is the goal, family business owners and successors may have to deal directly with the issues of plan security for participants.

Funding Variables

A basic question in providing a golden handcuff is whether to informally fund or not fund the plan. Virtually all funding vehicles have a cost. A fundamental question is which tool, or combination, is most likely to provide the greatest benefits per dollar spent and will be available as needed. Figure 10-8 shows

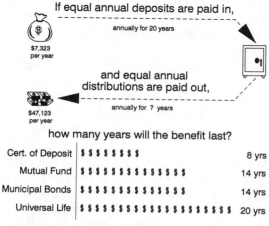

Figure 10-8. Which funding tool to use?

how four different funding alternatives might perform to offset the future liability of a plan. The funding assumptions illustrated are:

Vehicle	Interest rate assumed
Certificate of deposit	7.0%
Mutual funds	10.0%
Municipal bonds	6.5%
Universal life insurance	8.5%

As can be seen, universal life insurance provides the annual benefit for 20 years, longer than municipal bonds, mutual funds, or certificates of deposit.

Since the distribution is tax deductible to the company, the company needs to withdraw only the "net" amount from the funding account. In other words, the company's tax savings is factored into the payout. If a company in a 34 percent tax bracket owes $47,123 in annual benefits, it will get a tax refund of $16,000 from Uncle Sam. The company will therefore need to withdraw only $31,123 from the account.

The advantage of the insurance product is its tax-free compounding both during the accumulation period and during the distribution phase. In addition, the insurance product has a death benefit feature. If death occurs any time during the 20-year accumulation period, the participant's survivor would receive the deceased spouse's full benefit. The deposits and distributions are illustrated in Figures 10-9 and 10-10.

Summary

To a large extent, a successful transition depends on the support of key employees. Because the key group often has labored many more years in the business than the successor(s), some extra benefits or financial incentives may facilitate the employees' support of the next generation. As existing employees retire or quit, it is important for the next generation to have incentives that can help them recruit their own key people.

Nonqualified plans can enable family businesses to recruit new managers and reward existing key individuals for their loyalty, commitment, or performance. Nonqualified plans are extremely flexible and can be individually tailored to each situation. The provision of golden handcuffs through forfeiture conditions can deter key individuals from leaving the family firm.

No matter which program, or combination of programs, a family firm provides its employees, it is important to remember to communicate with them, respect them, empower them, and to reiterate the advantages of working for a family firm. The interpersonal strategies may be as important as the financial incentives. The retention of key personnel, along with their support of and commitment to the successors, can help smooth a bumpy transition and significantly enhance the success of the next generation.

FUNDING VARIABLES

Accumulation Phase

Male Age 45
Retirement Age 65

	CD	Mutual Fund	Municipal Bonds	Universal Life
Annual Deposit	$7,323	$7,323	$7,323	$7,323
Corporate Tax Cost at 34%	3,772	3,772	3,772	3,772
Interest Rate	7.0%	10.0%	6.5%	8.5%
After Tax Interest Rate	4.6%	6.6%	6.5%	8.5%

Account Balance at End of Year

Age				
45	$ 7,661	$ 7,806	$ 7,799	$ 4,664
46	15,677	16,128	16,105	9,584
47	24,062	24,999	24,951	15,105
48	32,835	34,455	34,372	21,130
49	42,013	44,535	44,405	27,706
50	51,616	55,281	55,090	36,271
51	61,662	66,736	66,470	45,593
52	72,172	78,947	78,589	55,751
53	83,168	91,963	91,497	66,815
54	94,671	105,839	105,243	81,270
55	106,706	120,631	119,883	95,179
56	119,298	136,399	135,474	110,360
57	132,470	153,208	152,079	126,914
58	146,252	171,126	169,763	144,923
59	160,670	190,226	188,597	164,554
60	175,754	210,587	208,654	185,900
61	191,535	232,292	230,016	209,262
62	208,046	255,430	252,766	234,879
63	225,319	280,095	276,995	263,032
64	243,390	306,387	302,798	313,772

Survivor's Benefit if Executive Dies Before Reaching Retirement	Account Balance Only	Account Balance Only	Account Balance Only	Full Benefit of $47,123 for 20 years

Figure 10-9.

FUNDING VARIABLES

Distribution Phase

Male Age 45
Retirement Age 65

	CD	Mutual Fund	Municipal Bonds	Universal Life
Annual Benefit Paid	$47,123	$47,123	$47,123	$47,123
Annual Withdrawal From Account	31,101	31,101	31,101	31,101

Account Balances at End of Year

Predistribution Balances	$243,390	$306,387	$302,798	$313,772

Age				
65	$222,096	$293,455	$289,358	$309,473
66	190,995	279,669	275,043	304,718
67	159,894	264,974	259,798	299,466
68	128,793	249,308	243,562	293,660
69	97,692	232,608	226,271	287,205
70	66,590	214,807	207,856	279,950
71	35,489	195,830	188,244	271,878
72	4,388	175,601	167,357	262,943
73	0	154,037	145,112	253,120
74	0	131,049	121,422	242,382
75	0	106,545	96,191	230,717
76	0	80,423	69,321	217,693
77	0	52,577	40,704	203,147
78	0	22,893	10,227	186,902
79	0	0	0	168,758
80	0	0	0	148,493
81	0	0	0	125,865
82	0	0	0	100,608
83	0	0	0	72,423
84	0	0	0	40,974

Benefit Payout Period (Years)	8	14	14	20

Figure 10-10.

PART 2

Business Valuation

11

What's the Family Business Worth?

The Internal Revenue Code mandates that whenever property is transferred—during a lifetime or at death—the fair market value of the property transferred must be determined in order to tally the income, gift, or estate tax bill.[1] In 1990, Congress enacted a new tax act that included special valuation rules for corporations, partnerships, and trusts. These new rules also apply to buy-sell agreements and valuing voting rights. The new rules reaffirm that fair market value is the standard by which transactions with family members will be measured for tax purposes.

The courts and the IRS have long held that the definition of the fair market value of a business is "the price at which a property would change hands between a willing buyer and a willing seller, neither being under any compulsion to buy or to sell and both having reasonable knowledge of the relevant facts."[2]

When a family business tries to determine fair market value, the intended transaction often lacks both a willing buyer and a willing seller, such as when the transaction is the gifting or transfer of stock at death through wills and trusts. Another impediment to figuring fair market value is that closely held family business stock is not traded on the open market; comparable valuations cannot be easily determined. Many times only a fractional part of all the outstanding shares is being valued, making the valuation assignment even more complex.

Estate-planning attorneys for many years have attempted to "freeze" value for tax purposes by creating different classes of stock and/or ascribing different rights to different classes, all of which affect the determination of fair market value.

Since 1952 both the courts and the IRS have recognized how tough it is to calculate the fair market value of closely held stock. An opinion from the Eighth Circuit Court stated: "No single formula is universally applicable and the ultimate fair market value determination is basically a question of judgment rather than mathematics."[3] In 1967 the Tax Court went a step further: "A publicly traded stock and a privately traded stock are *not* the same animal distinguished only by the size, frequency or color of its spots. The essential nature of the beast is different."[4]

Over the years, general IRS guidelines on valuing closely held or family-owned businesses have been subject to substantial differences in interpretation. With the passage of the 1990 Tax Act, the IRS is likely to scrutinize more closely the business valuation methodology applied to ownership succession planning or estate planning for the family business owner. Business valuations will be increasingly important in order to determine whether gift taxes are due on lifetime transfers. Shareholder agreements that used book value or formula-derived pricing mechanisms in the past will need to be revised; they will be acceptable to the IRS only if they resemble a fair market value determination.

Family business spin-offs and split-offs undertaken for cashflow, regulatory, or operational reasons—as well as tax-free reorganizations, recapitalizations, stock buybacks, and tax-deductible charitable contributions of family business stock—all require independent, third-party documentation of the business's value.

Although value is always in the eye of the beholder, "beholders" are becoming more sophisticated, as substantial merger and acquisition activity in many industries provides a track record of valuations. Further, an increasing divorce rate means that businesses must be valued for determining property settlements. Another factor is the level tax rate for capital gains, which makes the value of the deal relatively more important and the terms of the deal less so.

The IRS is always interested in the value assigned to the transfer of a business interest; it typically hopes it can show that the value was higher than reported, in order to increase the tax bill on the transaction—whether income tax, gift tax, or estate tax.

Where Do You Start?

What is the fair market value of the family business? Look around at tangible assets: the real estate, buildings, machinery and equipment, rolling stock, and inventory. Include also the intangibles: the loyalty and dedication of employees, the manufacturing processes, the quality of services provided, the customer base, the business's reputation and standing in the community, patents on products, and new technologies. Although it is difficult to quantify these "intangibles," they are an important part of what makes up the family business.

How do intangible assets affect business value? Consider the following from a client's employee handbook:

> The corporate mission of Family Industries, Inc., is to provide plastic products and services that fully satisfy our customers' needs. Our performance will enhance our customers' product, profitability, and

efficiency. We will design, produce, and deliver our products in an environmentally responsible manner.

Living up to our mission requires *total quality performance* in all areas of our business. It means satisfying our customers' requirements with products and services; this is the ongoing responsibility of every Family Industries employee. *Total quality performance* means that each of us is working in a way that can't be matched by our competitors. It means being the best in our industry.

The commitment by the 400 employees of this family business to total quality performance has a definite impact on the company's earnings and therefore on its value, as we'll see below.

There are many additional questions to address. Is the company worth more than its assets? Is it worth more than its retained earnings? Are there future opportunities waiting to be realized by the successors as new owners? Are the earnings or cashflow from the business predictable and steady? Will these stable earnings continue in the future? Although the owner may know everything there is to know about the business, he or she may have no idea of its true fair market value. Putting the company up for sale just to determine its value to an outsider is rarely an option.

The question of value becomes more complicated when family members attempt to put a price tag on it for succession planning. The price can vary depending on the circumstances: The "price" for the children may be less than the price asked from a large company that is attempting to buy the business. The determination of value can be motivated by other factors as well. Personal financial security is one. Another relates to potential estate taxes: The family would want its attorney to argue to the IRS that the company has minimal value. If there are currently stock purchase or buy-sell agreements, which establish a selling price for the shares, the agreements may not reflect the fair market value the owners believe the business is worth.

Although value can be subjective, objective resources are available to help determine worth. When seeking the value of a car, consulting the *Kelly Blue Book* is a solution for prices on all makes, models, years, and options of cars and trucks. The *Blue Book* tells what the seller can expect from a sale of the car, or what a buyer must pay for a car he or she is considering purchasing.

The assets of the business can be appraised by an outside third party. A value will be established for the machinery, real estate, inventory, furniture, and fixtures. An appraisal of the business assets, however, does not take into account the "intangibles" discussed earlier.

Valuation Methods

A business valuation is essentially an attempt to predict future events: an anticipated growth or contraction of the business, a guesstimate of the rate of inflation, projected appreciation of real estate and other asset values, and projected costs and expenses of running the business. These predictions are based on historical and financial records of the business, the judgment of the owner, the expertise of the valuation firm, and other knowledgeable resources.

The Tax Court has regularly confirmed this view. In 1961 the court noted that "financial data is important only to the extent it furnishes a basis for an informed judgment of the future performance of a particular company."[5]

The IRS provided guidelines for the valuation of stock in a closely held business for estate or gift tax purposes in Revenue Ruling 59-60. These factors are appropriately considered in valuing any company—whether a corporation or an unincorporated entity—or in valuing a partial ownership interest in a company. Under "Factors to Consider," the ruling states that the following are fundamental and require careful analysis in each case:

    (a) The nature of the business and the history of the enterprise from its inception;

    (b) The economic outlook in general and the condition and outlook of the specific industry in particular;

    (c) The book value of the stock and the financial condition of the business;

    (d) The earning capacity of the company;

    (e) The dividend-paying capacity;

    (f) Whether or not the enterprise has goodwill or other intangible value;

    (g) Sales of the stock and the size of the block of stock to be valued; and

    (h) The market price of stocks of corporations engaged in the same or a similar line of business having their stocks actively traded in a free and open market, either on an exchange or over-the-counter.

These factors are critical elements of a business appraisal; they should be combined with common sense, informed judgment, and reason in arriving at a value. As shown in Figure 11-1, the methods for calculating value fall into four broad categories: income approaches, market approaches, asset approaches, and hybrid approaches.

Income Approaches

Value to a buyer lies not in what the business has produced in the past but in expected future benefits. Income-based valuation approaches calculate expected future benefits. Examples of income approaches are capitalized earnings, discounted future cashflows, and discounted future earnings.

The *capitalized earnings method* requires first an estimation of the future earnings of the company, and then a determination of the rate of return that an investor would require from an investment of this type. The earnings estimate is then divided by the rate of return required, to arrive at a value figure. For example, if the annual earnings of a business are $100,000, and a typical rate of return for a closely held business in the particular industry is 25 percent, then the value of the business according to the capitalized earnings method is $100,000 ÷ .25 = $400,000.

The *discounted future cashflows method* involves a projection of the future cash

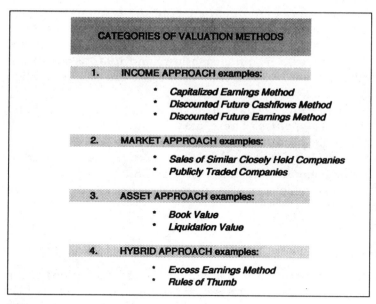

Figure 11-1.

receipts and disbursements of the company, based on historical performance and the judgment of the owners and others regarding future events. The present value (or value in "today's dollars") of the projected cashflows is then calculated using a discount rate, which represents the rate a prudent investor would expect on an investment in the business. For example, if the prospective buyer expects the business to generate $150,000 annually in cashflows for the next 10 years, and requires a 25 percent return on investment, the value of the business under the discounted future cashflows method (based on the present value of the projected cashflows) would be $536,000.

The *discounted future earnings method* follows the same pattern as the discounted cashflow, but uses projected earnings rather than cashflow.

Market Approaches

A market approach uses values assigned to similar businesses that are bought and sold in an active market, and adjusts that figure for differences in the family business to determine value.

In using a *comparable sales approach* to find the value of a machine shop, the appraiser would search for other machine shops that were sold recently, determine the price of the sale, and use that price as the value of the machine shop. An obvious weakness in this theory is that no two businesses are identical, even though they may be in the same industry, in the same town, and have the same number of employees. Timing can make a huge difference in value. (A machine shop sold a year ago under a favorable economy might fetch a great deal less in a recessionary period.) And even if an identical business is sold in the same week, information about the price and terms of the sale would not be available to the public. When information is available about recent sales of similar closely held businesses, the appraiser makes comparisons of the sale price to income, cashflow, and total assets of the business sold. The ratios derived from the comparable sale can then be applied to the business being valued.

Another method of using market data to value a closely held company involves *publicly traded companies*. There may be similar businesses—companies with comparable product lines, customer bases, or other critical business factors—whose stock is traded in the stock market. Published information about public companies includes financial ratios such as *price to earnings* and *price to revenues*, which can be evaluated and applied to the family business to estimate its value.

Asset Approaches

Asset approaches tally a company's assets less its liabilities. Valuations of the company's receivables, inventory, fixed assets, investments, and intangibles (such as goodwill, patents, and customers lists) are combined. Accounts payable and accrued expenses, notes and loans payable, and other debts are subtracted. The resulting amount is one measure of value for the business.

A common asset-based method is *book value*, which is the historical value of the assets of the business, less the company's liabilities, as recorded on the company's books and reflected in its financial statements. Book value is not usually considered an accurate reflection of current value.

The *liquidation value* usually is a worst-case scenario. The book value of assets may be discounted and sold piecemeal in order to raise cash. No one wants to liquidate their company; it's usually caused by a lack of planning. Unfortunately sometimes shareholders can earn a higher rate of return if the company's assets are sold and the proceeds placed in a savings account rather than continuing to leave their stake in a poorly managed company that has marginal earnings.

Hybrid Approaches

Hybrid approaches combine two or more elements of the other categories. The excess earnings method and industry rules of thumb are two examples of hybrid approaches.

The *excess earnings method* (often referred to as the IRS method or the ARM 34 method) attempts to quantify the goodwill of a business as being equal to the intangible value in earnings power, over and above the intrinsic value of operating assets. The earnings of the business are compared with the average return earned by other companies in the industry. The excess of the company's earnings over the average industry return is then multiplied by a factor to arrive at the calculated goodwill value. The goodwill is then added to the value of tangible assets, and liabilities are subtracted to arrive at a total value for the company.

Many industries use *rules of thumb* to approximate value. In particular, business brokers and acquisition companies use the rule of thumb to determine whether a businesss is a candidate for further investigation. Rules of thumb (sometimes referred to as industry standards) may fall into any of the three groups of valuation approaches:

- Multiple of gross revenues ("one times gross")

- Revenue unit multiplier ("X dollars times the number of square feet of selling space")

- Asset value ("you won't get more than book value for a building material distributor in the current market")

Rules of thumb can be very misleading and should be used only as a rough estimate of value, since they ignore the peculiarities that make one company strong and profitable while its crosstown counterpart in the same business limps along at breakeven level.

Case Study

Smith Enterprises, Inc., is a second-generation, family-owned plastics manufacturing company. The company's stock is owned by Bob Smith, his son David, and his son-in-law Brett:

Stockholder	Number of shares	Percent of total
Bob Smith	3,500	87.50
David Smith	350	8.75
Brett Adams	150	3.75
	4,000	100.00

The company has hired an appraiser to determine its value under several different valuation approaches.

Book Value

The company's balance sheet (see Figure 11-2) shows total assets of $11,193,000 and total liabilities of $4,431,000. The book value of the company is $6,762,000.

Excess Earnings Method

The appraiser first analyzed the balance sheet of Smith Enterprises to determine the fair market value of the individual tangible assets and liabilities; the result is a market value of the net tangible assets of the company of $6,000,000.

SMITH ENTERPRISES, INC. BALANCE SHEET DECEMBER 31, 19XX		
ASSETS		
Cash		$1,167,000
Accounts Receivable		3,430,000
Inventory		2,519,000
Other		220,000
Total Current Assets		7,336,000
Property and Equipment	$10,490,000	
Less Accumulated Depreciation	(6,840,000)	
		3,650,000
Other Assets		207,000
TOTAL ASSETS		$11,193,000
LIABILITIES		
Accounts Payable		$1,977,000
Accrued Expenses		1,376,000
Current Debt Payments		125,000
Total Current Liabilities		3,478,000
Long–Term Debt		953,000
Total Liabilities		4,431,000
STOCKHOLDERS' EQUITY		
Common Stock		18,000
Retained Earnings		6,744,000
Total Stockholders' Equity		6,762,000
TOTAL LIABILITIES AND STOCKHOLDERS' EQUITY		$11,193,000

Figure 11-2.

A normal rate of return on assets in the plastics manufacturing business was determined to be 14 percent, which results in expected earnings of $840,000 (net assets of $6,000,000 times 14 percent). The earnings of Smith Enterprises were $855,000, as shown in Figure 11-3, so its "excess" earnings were $15,000.

The excess earnings were capitalized using a capitalization rate of 20 percent: $15,000 earnings divided by 20 percent yields a value for goodwill of Smith Enterprises of $75,000. Adding the calculated goodwill value to the fair market value of the net tangible assets results in an excess earnings method value of $6,075,000.

Capitalized Earnings

Dividing expected earnings of $855,000 by the 20 percent capitalization rate determined above yields a capitalized earnings method value of $4,275,000.

Discounted Future Cashflows Method

Management has projected its cashflow expectations for the next five years. Applying an appropriate discount rate, determined by the appraiser to be 24

```
┌──────────────────────────────────────────────────────────┐
│                   SMITH ENTERPRISES, INC.                │
│                    INCOME STATEMENT                      │
│           FOR THE YEAR ENDED DECEMBER 31, 19XX          │
│                                                          │
│                                                          │
│   Sales Revenue                            $33,420,000   │
│   Cost of Goods Sold                       (28,245,000)  │
│        Gross Profit                          5,175,000   │
│                                                          │
│   Expenses                                  (3,750,000)  │
│        Operating Income                      1,425,000   │
│                                                          │
│   Income Taxes                                (570,000)  │
│        NET INCOME                             $855,000   │
└──────────────────────────────────────────────────────────┘
```

Figure 11-3.

percent, the resulting value is $3,890,000. The appraiser then added estimated residual value of the net assets of the business after the five-year period, estimated to be $7 million. Adding the two amounts yields a discounted future cashflows value of $10,890,000.

Sales of Similar Companies

The appraiser analyzed recent sales of comparative companies and found that several companies were sold at approximately six times pretax earnings. Applying the multiple of 6 to Smith's operating income of $1,425,000 (from Figure 11-3) results in a comparative sales method value of $8,550,000.

These results are summarized in Figure 11-4. Figure 11-5 displays the price per share range.

Summary

There are many ways to value a family business. Any of the above approaches might be used. As we'll see in the next chapter, the value of the stock can also be engineered through the use of valuation discounts and other techniques. Underlying all valuation methods are the following assumptions:

1. "Profitable" businesses are worth more.
2. Profitability is determined *after* adjusting for owners' salaries, benefits, and perks.
3. Earnings power is as important as earnings trends for future projections.
4. Future earnings are viewed in terms of present value.
5. Industry standards and ratios change constantly.
6. Financial statements do *not* accurately reflect value.

SMITH ENTERPRISES, INC.

VALUATION SUMMARY

As of December 31, 19XX

Stockholder	# of Shares	% of Owner-ship	Buy–Sell Agmt at Book Value	Excess Earnings Method	Capitalized Earnings Method	Discounted Future Cashflows	Comparative Companies 6 X Pretax Earnings
Bob Smith	3,500	87.5%	$5,916,750	$5,315,625	$3,740,625	$9,528,750	$7,481,250
David Smith	350	8.8%	591,675	531,563	374,063	952,875	748,125
Brett Adams	150	3.8%	253,575	227,813	160,313	408,375	320,625
Total	4,000	100.0%	$6,762,000	$6,075,000	$4,275,000	$10,890,000	$8,550,000
Per Share Value			$1,690.50	$1,518.75	$1,068.75	$2,722.50	$2,137.50

Figure 11-4.

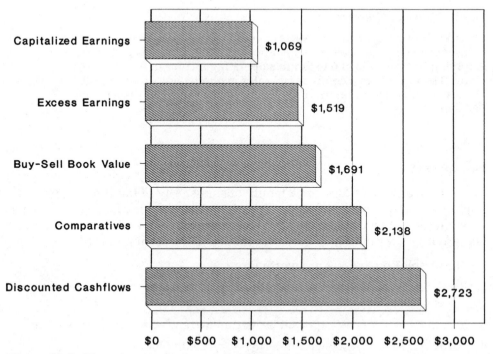

Figure 11-5. The price per share range for Smith Enterprises, Inc.

References

1. Estate Tax Regs 20.2031-1(b).
2. *U.S. v. Cartwright,* 411 U.S. 546, 551 (1973).
3. *O'Malley v. Ames,* 197 F.2d 256, 258 (8th Cir. 1952); *Hamm v. Commissioner,* 325 F.2d 934, 940 (8th Cir. 1963).
4. *Morris Messing,* 48 T.C. 502 (1967).
5. *Snyder's Estate v. U.S.,* 285 F.2d 857, 861 (4th Cir. 1961).

12

Valuation Discounts: Managing the Value of Your Business

Two difficult but critical factors affecting the value of an ownership interest in a closely held company are *lack of marketability* and *lack of control*. In 1925 the U.S. Supreme Court ruled, "The capital stock of a corporation, its net assets, and its shares of stock are entirely different things...the value of one bears no fixed or necessary relation to the value of the other."[1]

Shannon Pratt, a noted valuation expert, has written, "All other things being equal, an interest in a business is worth more if it is readily marketable or, conversely, worth less if it is not." Pratt adds that "in many valuations of closely held businesses or business interests, the discount for lack of marketability turns out to be the largest single issue to resolve."[2]

Similarly, determining the value of a minority interest in a business—as opposed to a majority interest, which controls the voting power and therefore the management of the company—is a challenging assignment. But it is not hard to understand that a minority ownership interest—which cannot control the election of the board of directors, direct the payment of compensation or dividends, force the business to be sold, or prevent the selling of the other ownership interests—would be worth less than a pro rata share of the total value of the company.

In transferring a family business to children or key employees, the owner's dilemma is often to balance the position of entrepreneur with the position of parent. As an entrepreneur and founder of a company, the business owner wants to realize the highest value possible when selling or disposing of the company. The sale price establishes the measure of the business's success. The founder's years of effort can all be condensed into negotiations over the sale of the business. During the negotiations, the owner's representatives attempt to secure the highest price possible from the third-party buyer.

The parent-owner knows that the children, or the key employees, cannot compete with large acquisition firms and emotionally recognizes that it will be difficult to get "top dollar" from an internal sale. The parent-owner also recognizes that the children or the employees have contributed greatly to the value of the company—through their efforts, their years of service, their loyalty, and their personal sacrifices.

When transferring the business to offspring or key employees, the owner should begin by determining the fair market value of the business as a whole. (I recommend hiring an experienced business appraiser to do a preliminary valuation.) This method of pricing should satisfy the entrepreneurial desire to establish the highest possible value for a life's work.

However, the owner is not locked into that premium price when considering a sale to internal buyers. By selling to the kids or to key employees at an appropriately discounted price, the owner recognizes their contributions to the business and can provide them with a more affordable opportunity.

Discounting the price also makes the gifting or sale of fractional interests over time more efficient. Small blocks of ownership are discounted. Once owners know the discounted value of a single share of stock, they can calculate the number of shares their offspring can afford to buy, and can transfer ownership with less impact on an offspring's personal cashflow. In addition, the owner can transfer more stock at a discounted value and stay within the annual gift tax exclusion, making gifting less costly from a tax standpoint. More stock can be transferred without a gift tax once appropriate discounts have been applied to the value of the stock.

Discounts and Premiums

The previous chapter suggests that the value of an ownership interest in a business could be calculated simply by multiplying the number of shares by the per share value. In other words, if Mom owns 900 shares of the company, and Son owns 100 shares, then the mother's interest would be worth 90 percent of the total value, and the son's interest would be worth 10 percent. In this case Son has a "minority interest" and Mom is said to have "control."

As a 10 percent owner, Son has only 10 percent of the vote on business issues, and can be outvoted by Mom every time. Although he owns 10 percent of the equity of the company, and is entitled to 10 percent of all dividends paid, he effectively has no say in the running of the company. Son can voice his opinion, and he may be able to influence his mother's decisions by means other than a formal vote, but Mom has the legal right to disregard his wishes in the management of the family business. In the extreme, Mom could fire Son or sell the business out from under him.

Because 10 percent represents a minority interest, an outsider would be unlikely to pay the full 10 percent the son's stock was worth, based on a simple per share computation. The outsider would probably say, "I'm interested in owning a piece of this successful venture, but I won't pay 10 percent of the total value of the company, when my 10 percent vote is actually ineffective. Instead, I'll pay you 75 percent of what you think it's worth."

The outsider has applied a *discount* to the minority interest being sought. Minority discounts upheld in estate and gift tax court cases vary widely. One study indicates that average minority interest discounts in the public marketplace ranged from 27 percent to 29 percent for 1980 through 1989, based on a comparison of controlling interest and minority interest transactions on the stock exchanges.[3]

Data from the closely held company marketplace show even higher discounts: Studies have shown discounts averaging 40 percent, and ranging as high as 78 percent![4] Note that these discounts are from book value, not from the value of the enterprise as a whole. Assuming the value of the business is in excess of book value, then the surveys would indicate a greater disparity when the minority interest discount is applied to the fair market value of the business instead of its book value.

H. Calvin Coolidge, a former bank trust officer experienced in selling minority interests in closely held companies, presents the following analysis:

> A willing buyer contemplating a purchase from a willing seller of a minority interest, being under no compulsion to buy...would suffer the same disadvantages of lack of control. The buyer is asked to make an investment with no insurance as to certainty of current yield or as to when, or the amount at which, he may be able to liquidate his investment. Regardless, therefore, of the value of 100 percent of the corporation, the buyer will not purchase a minority interest except at a discount for a proportionate share of the value of 100 percent of the corporation.[5]

Marketability Discount

Continuing with the preceding hypothetical conversation, suppose Outsider offers Son 75 percent of what Son feels his 10 percent is worth. While Son contemplates this offer, Outsider explains that the business is not readily marketable. "In fact," says Outsider, "compared with other investments, it is illiquid. I can't call my broker and just sell the stock. I may not be able to find a buyer when I am ready to sell." Therefore, Outsider believes the offer for Son's stock should be further discounted for its lack of marketability.

In a well-documented study, J. Michael Maher found that discounts for closely held business interests averaged approximately 35 percent for lack of marketability. Maher's report concludes:

> The result is that most appraisers underestimate the proper discount for lack of marketability. The results seem to indicate that this discount should be about 35 percent. Perhaps this makes sense, because by committing funds to restricted common stock, the willing buyer (a) would be denied the opportunity to take advantage of other investments, and (b) would continue to have his investment at the risk of the business until the shares could be offered to the public or another buyer is found.

The 35 percent discount would *not* contain elements of a discount for a minority interest, because it is measured against the current fair market value of securities actively traded (other minority interests). Consequently, appraisers should also consider a discount for a minority interest in those closely held corporations where a discount is applicable.[6]

More recent studies continue to indicate an average discount of 35 percent for lack of marketability.

In 1977, the IRS specifically recognized the importance of valuation discounts when it published Revenue Ruling 77-287. The purpose of this ruling was "to provide information and guidance to taxpayers, Internal Revenue Service personnel, and others concerned with the valuation, for federal tax purposes, of securities that cannot be immediately sold because they are restricted from resale pursuant to federal security laws."[7]

Referenced in Revenue Ruling 77-287 is a 1977 accounting release by the Securities and Exchange Commission (SEC) which specifically notes that the discount for lack of marketability can be substantial: "This reflects the fact that securities which cannot be readily sold in the public marketplace are less valuable than the securities which can be sold...."[8]

When a minority interest discount is combined with a marketability discount, the total discount can exceed 50 percent of full fair market value for stock transferred to family members. By carving up the ownership of the family business into separate interests—minority interests—Mom and Dad can use minority and lack of marketability discounts to their advantage. Pieces of the business ownership can be gifted or sold to family members or key employees with no gift tax on the transfer. And a partial interest remaining in the parents' estate can be worth significantly less for estate tax purposes than full ownership. Figure 12-1 shows how discounts reduce gift taxes.

Premiums for Control

In the preceding example, Outsider discounted Son's interest both for a minority position and for lack of marketability. If Outsider now decides to talk with Mom about her 90 percent interest, he might also suggest discounting the price for lack of marketability. However, Mom may counter that her 90 percent should be entitled to a control *premium*. The 90 percent stock ownership carries the entire effective voting power of the corporation, so the value of the 90 percent majority interest could actually be *more* than the per share value. Frequently, control premiums range from 10 percent to 50 percent of the value of the company, with various studies showing an average premium of about 40 percent.

Thus the value for part of a company does not necessarily equal the pro rata share based on ownership percentage. A minority interest may have only nominal value relative to the total business, while a controlling interest of 75 percent may be worth 90 percent of the total value of the business. Figure 12-2 applies discounts to Smith Enterprises, Inc., and revises the values discussed

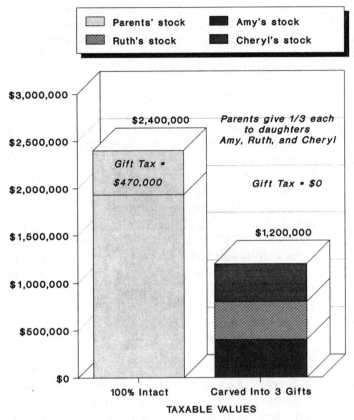

Figure 12-1. Discounts reduce gift taxes. Substantial value can be gifted tax-free if partial interests are created.

in the preceding chapter. Smith Enterprises was appraised as a whole company as opposed to an appraisal of an ownership interest. The control premium was built into the appraisal method. The control block of shares (87.5 percent) was discounted 10 percent because they were not readily marketable.

Other Techniques to Manage Value

In addition to the application of minority interest and marketability discounts, or premiums for control, on the value of the business today, techniques can be utilized to manage value *prior to* the valuation being conducted. In this case, the value can be manipulated by entering into contracts or accruing liabilities that would have a direct impact on the financial statement and strength of the company. For example:

Dad wants to transfer shares to Son, and is concerned about using book value because of gift tax implications. A preliminary valuation, even after the application of discounts, results in a per share price which is currently

SMITH ENTERPRISES, INC.

	Smith Enterprises 100%	Bob's 87.5%	David's 8.8%	Brett's 3.8%
Appraised value of the company as a whole and pro rata interests	$8,000,000	PRO RATA VALUES		
		$7,000,000	$700,000	$300,000
Less 35% discount for lack of marketability of minority shares	(350,000)		(245,000)	(105,000)
Less 10% discount for lack of marketability of control shares	(700,000)	(700,000)		
	6,950,000	6,300,000	455,000	195,000
Less 25% discount for minority interest	(162,500)		(113,750)	(48,750)
		VALUE OF INDIVIDUAL OWNERSHIP INTERESTS		
	$6,787,500	$6,300,000	$341,250	$146,250

Figure 12-2. The value of individual ownership interests after valuation discounts.

unaffordable to Son. In addition, Dad does not need the income to support his personal lifestyle and is willing to defer receipt of part of the purchase price. The price can be reduced further through some additional restructuring. The corporation can recognize Dad's many years of service (for which he was never fully compensated) and can provide, on a discretionary basis for Dad alone, a supplemental pension agreement in addition to any other retirement benefits to which he might be entitled from the company. The company's board decides at its annual meeting to adopt a resolution providing for a supplemental pension to Dad.

Let's assume that Dad is 65 years old, and beginning at the normal retirement age of 65, the pension benefit provided by the company is $50,000 per year for 20 years. Although the total payments equal $1,000,000, the present value is considerably less. The company's accountants determine that the present value of the pension payments is $567,000: the amount the corporation would need to set aside today, assuming 7 percent interest, in order to provide twenty $50,000 payments. At the end of twenty years, the $567,000 plus interest earned would have been fully paid out to Dad. The present value of the retirement payments is a new corporate liability, which will be reflected as a liability on the company's financial statements, and would reduce the value of the corporation.

After the supplemental pension plan is adopted and the liability has been booked, Dad begins his stock transfer plans. The valuation discounts discussed previously still apply. The effect here is to reduce the value of the company by $567,000 *before* any discounted stock transfers take place.

In Figure 12-3, a progression of adjustments was applied beginning with the supplemental pension and proceeding with marketability and minority discounts. Ultimately the value is reduced by almost 55 percent.

Now let's look at an opposing scenario: Dad has come to accept that none of his children is interested in perpetuating the family business. He realizes that selling to a third party is his only viable option, but he wants to be sure he gets the best possible price. Dad can take a number of steps to *increase* the value of the company and maximize his price: Grooming a management team (whether already on board or hired from outside) to carry on in his absence will enhance the value of the company. Taking a hard look at historical expenses and controlling expenses in the future will enhance cashflow and improve value. Developing or strengthening supplier or distributor relationships can also increase the price an outsider would pay for the business.

Summary

There are a number of approaches to valuing the closely held company. Beyond valuing the assets with their earning power, an owner needs to ask, "What do I need from the business in order to provide a comfortable and secure retirement for myself so that I won't *have* to sell the business?"

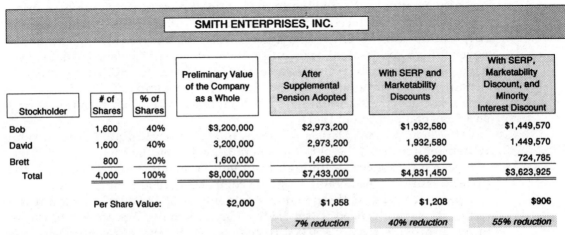

Stockholder	# of Shares	% of Shares	Preliminary Value of the Company as a Whole	After Supplemental Pension Adopted	With SERP and Marketability Discounts	With SERP, Marketability Discount, and Minority Interest Discount
Bob	1,600	40%	$3,200,000	$2,973,200	$1,932,580	$1,449,570
David	1,600	40%	3,200,000	2,973,200	1,932,580	1,449,570
Brett	800	20%	1,600,000	1,486,600	966,290	724,785
Total	4,000	100%	$8,000,000	$7,433,000	$4,831,450	$3,623,925
Per Share Value:			$2,000	$1,858	$1,208	$906
				7% reduction	40% reduction	55% reduction

Figure 12-3. *Valuation management.* The company has adopted a SERP for Bob, and Bob has gifted additional shares to David and Brett.

References

1. *Ray Consolidated Copper Company v. United States,* 45 S.Ct. 526 (1925).

2. Shannon Pratt, *Valuing a Business: The Analysis and Appraisal of Closely Held Companies,* 2d ed. (Homewood, IL: Dow Jones–Irwin, 1989), p. 239.

3. *Mergerstat Review 1989* (Schaumburg, IL: Merrill Lynch, 1990).

4. H. Calvin Coolidge, *Estate Planning,* Spring 1975, p. 141, and *Estate Planning,* September 1983, p. 282.

5. H. Calvin Coolidge, "Discount for Minority Interest: Rev. Rul. 79-7's Denial of Discount Is Erroneous," *Illinois Bar Journal,* vol. 68 (July 1980), p. 744.

6. J. Michael Maher, "Discounts for Lack of Marketability for Closely Held Business Interests," *Taxes,* September 1976, pp. 562–571.

7. IRS Revenue Ruling 77-287 (1977-2 C.B. 319), Sect. 1.

8. Securities and Exchange Commission, Acct. Series Release 113: *Statement Regarding Restricted Securities* (Chicago: Commerce Clearing House, Federal Securities Law Reports, 1977), pp. 62 and 285.

PART 3

Ownership Transfer: Four Options to Choose From

13
Option 1: Gifting

Gifting the business to "the kids" may create more problems than it solves. Before we look at the problems, let's cover basic facts.

Each year a parent or donor can give $10,000 to a child without any tax consequences. That means no gift taxes have to be paid, no gift tax return has to be filed. The recipient doesn't pay any taxes on the gift either. If the donor's spouse joins in, the donee can receive two $10,000 gifts: a total of $20,000 each year. And if the donee's spouse is a recipient, the maximum annual tax-free gift can jump to $40,000 each year. The tax-free gift limit increases by $10,000 for each grandchild, per donor.

What happens if the donor wants to give *more than* $10,000? There are two possibilities. The first is to pay gift tax on any amount over $10,000. (A gift tax schedule is illustrated in Figure 13-1.) The second is to use some of the donor's $600,000 unified credit.

Beating the IRS Clock

In addition to gifting $10,000 *each year,* each donor has a credit of $600,000 (called the unified credit amount) that can be used during his or her lifetime or at death. If the donor saves the credit until death, the first $600,000 in assets will go to the beneficiary of the estate, tax-free. After that, there's a tax (unless the donor was married at the time of death, in which case the tax is deferred until the spouse's death).

Therefore, a married couple can give away up to $1,200,000 (both using their unified credits) during their lifetime. Anything not used during the lifetime is "saved" and used at death. Additional amounts can be transferred tax-free using generation-skipping devices, which are covered in Chapter 26. Our focus here is on immediate, rather than deferred, gifts.

Most attorneys who recommend using the $10,000 annual exclusion suggest not giving more than $10,000 each year so that the donor won't have to file a

GIFT AND ESTATE TAXES (Unified Transfer Tax)			
Amount Subject to Tax		Tax on Amount in Column A	Tax Rate (%) on Excess Over Amount in Column A
(A) Exceeding	But not Exceeding		
$ 0	$ 10,000	$ 0	18
10,000	20,000	1,800	20
20,000	40,000	3,800	22
40,000	60,000	8,200	24
60,000	80,000	13,000	26
80,000	100,000	18,200	28
100,000	150,000	23,800	30
150,000	250,000	38,800	32
250,000	500,000	70,800	34
500,000	750,000	155,800	37
750,000	1,000,000	248,300	39
1,000,000	1,250,000	345,800	41
1,250,000	1,500,000	448,300	43
1,500,000	2,000,000	555,800	45
2,000,000	2,500,000	780,800	49
2,500,000	3,000,000	1,025,800	53
3,000,000	10,000,000	1,290,800	55
10,000,000	21,040,000	5,140,800	60
21,040,000		11,764,800	55

Figure 13-1.

gift tax return. Attorneys also usually recommend that clients save the $600,000 unified credit until death.

Another school of thought goes as follows: "Give *more than* $10,000—in fact, give an amount in excess of $10,000 so the donor will need to file a gift tax return and pay at least $1 in gift tax on each transaction." The gift tax on amounts between $10,000 and $20,000 is only 18 percent of the value of the gift in excess of $10,000.

The reason behind filing a gift tax return is to build a valuation history. When the time comes to calculate estate tax, the IRS is not bound by the value it accepted for gift tax purposes. By filing gift tax returns and paying modest gift taxes, the donor establishes a record of appraised values, the various factors that influenced the value, and the valuation methods that the IRS found appropriate at the time of the gifts. This can be especially important when gifts of stock in the family business are transferred.

For example, the business owner might give one share of her company's stock, valued at $12,000, to her daughter each year for three years, using the $10,000 annual exclusion each year. At 18 percent, the gift tax each year would be $360. Let's assume that the IRS audits two of the gifts, and agrees on a value for those gifts of $13,500 each. That adjustment will cost an additional $540 in gift tax. For a gift tax cost of under $2000, the mother has established that her company's stock was worth $13,500 per share, and she has a record of the methods and factors that determined that value. At her death a few years later, the IRS will find it difficult to argue that the stock was worth substantially more. If gifts of hard-to-value assets, such as family business stock, are to occur, a thoroughly documented appraisal is in order. More than one appraisal would be recommended.

One of the provisions of the 1990 Tax Act starts the statute of limitations running even when gifts are deemed to be nontaxable (i.e., less than $10,000 per donee). The donor should disclose the transaction to the IRS in a statement attached to a gift tax return, which will then begin a three-year period that the IRS has to challenge the value of the gift.

That same school of thought also argues that it's better to use the $600,000 unified credit during a lifetime than save it until death. There are three reasons for listening to this thinking.

1. Tax laws are changing rapidly; the U.S. government still has a large deficit that is not being offset by tax collections. There is no guarantee that the $600,000 unified credit will still be available at death. The tax laws may eliminate that credit entirely (resulting in more tax revenue for the government). The thinking here: "Use it or possibly lose it."

2. The present value of the $600,000 credit is higher *today* than it will be in the future. The longer a donor waits to use it, the less valuable it becomes. A brief example of how inflation erodes the credit may be helpful. Keep in mind that the credit amount, $600,000, is fixed and does not change from year to year. The variables are (a) time until the credit is used and (b) inflation rates. (See Figure 13-2.) Assuming a conservative 4 percent inflation rate, if the credit isn't used for 20 years (very likely for a 60-year-old today), it will then be worth less than half its current value!

3. Removing a $600,000 asset (let's say, stock in the company) from the estate today provides a double benefit. The donor removes $600,000 of stock; all the future growth on those shares is also removed from the estate. Assuming the stock will appreciate at 6 percent a year, in 20 years a $600,000 stake will be worth about $2 million. The estate might have had to pay $1 million of estate taxes if those shares remained in the estate. Using up the $600,000 gift today prevents $1.4 million of future value from being subject to estate tax.

Gifts of Present versus Future Interest

The annual exclusion was introduced into the federal gift tax law with the Revenue Act of 1932. Congress has continually been aware of the problem of keeping track of small gifts. The annual exclusion ranged between $3,000 and $5,000 from 1932 until 1982, when it was increased to $10,000 and computed on an annual basis.

It is important to note that these exclusions relate to gifts of a present interest. The exclusions are denied for gifts of a future interest. Congress defines a future interest in property as "any interest, whether vested or contingent, including reversions, remainders and other interests,...which are limited to commence in use enjoyment or possession at some future date or time."[1]

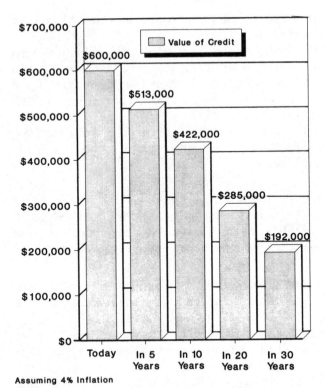

Figure 13-2. When should the $600,000 unified credit be used?

In regard to gifts made in trust, the gift will be of a present interest if the trust provides the beneficiary with the power to demand immediate possession of the transferred property. The right of demand can lapse after 45 days. This is commonly referred to as a "Crummey power of withdrawal," named after the Crummey family, who took the IRS to court in 1968 (and won). This provision, often used in conjunction with an irrevocable life insurance trust, is explained in Chapter 26. An example paves the way.

Dad and Mom are concerned about the lack of liquidity in their estate, which is made up primarily of stock in the family business. They plan to acquire survivor life insurance in an irrevocable trust so that funds will be available to pay estate taxes on the second death. The insurance policy, owned by the trust, if properly structured, should not be included in their estate. The trust is beneficiary of the insurance policy, and the two children are beneficiaries of the trust. The insurance premium will be gifted by the parents to the trust, and the trustee will then pay insurance premiums as they come due.

The parents plan to gift sufficient funds each year to the trust 45 days before the insurance premium is due, so there is adequate money for the trustee to pay the premium. Each year the trustee will notify the children, as trust beneficiaries, that they have 45 days to withdraw the funds from the trust. Assuming the 45 days pass and no withdrawal is made, the trustee then would pay the insurance premium. The parents' gift to the trust would be treated as a present-interest gift, of which up to $40,000 can qualify for the annual exclusion ($10,000 per donor with two donees).

Gift Taxes and Estate Taxes Are Different

Most people believe that because the top gift and estate tax rate is 55 percent, they are timing differences of the same animal. But, that's not true. Although they both use the same rate schedule and they both use the unified credit, they are different. Estate taxes impose a greater tax burden on the transfer of assets. Although the top tax rate is 55 percent, the question is 55 percent of what?

Hillery James Gallagher explains that the meaning of "transfer" is the key to understanding this important difference.

> A transfer is not what is given, but what is received by the donee....Using a 55 percent gift tax rate, a gift of $100 requires a tax of $55, both of which come from the donor. The donee receives $100; the tax of $55 is exactly 55 percent of the amount transferred. To produce the same result from a decedent's estate in the 55 percent bracket—that is, a transfer of $100—requires a tax payment of $122...in the estate tax process, tax rates are applied to what a decedent possesses. When the tax is 55 percent, 45 percent is left to be transferred. The heir will receive $100 (the transfer) out of $222 of estate assets. The tax is 122 percent of the amount transferred.[2]

Valuation of the Gift

The 1990 Tax Act repealed a section of the Internal Revenue Code called 2036(c) but added some new sections. One of the new sections is of particular importance to family businesses. In the past, a donor's accountant might have used the book value of the company (when stock in the family business was transferred) to determine the value for gift tax purposes. Today, under the new code, the accountant would need a certified valuation opinion which might still use book value, but *only* if book value represents the fair market value of the shares, based on comparable transactions.

As we saw in Chapters 11 and 12, the value of stock in a family business is not a fixed price and depends on many factors. If the business is not incorporated, this may be a good time to consider doing so. Alternatively, consider a family limited partnership, as described in Chapter 23.

A corporate entity allows an owner to transfer the business in pieces—namely, in shares of stock. A family partnership creates limited partner units that can also be transferred in increments. Each piece—stock of a corporation or limited partner units in a partnership—can have its own value determined, thereby making a transition more easily accomplished over time. An owner can transfer a number of shares each year to successors until the objective is accomplished.

Using minority and marketability discounts established by an independent valuation, a greater number of shares can be transferred each year. For example, assume the stock has a value of $2000 per share, and the current owner owns all 1000 outstanding shares. Total value of the business is $2 million ($2000 × 1000). Two children, a son and daughter, are active in the business.

Using the annual exclusion of $10,000—and assuming the spouse enters into the gift—the parents can give $40,000 to their son and daughter. (They may also gift $40,000 to the son-in-law and daughter-in-law, if they don't object to in-laws owning shares.)

Giving $40,000 per year, and assuming the shares remain level at $2000 per share (which they probably won't), the parents can give away only 20 shares each year. It will take 50 years to complete the gifting—and that's assuming, for the sake of simplicity, no increase in value. Applying a marketability discount in the transaction provides a method to accelerate the timing of the gifts.

What about using a minority discount along with a marketability discount? The IRS might argue that a minority discount should not be allowed, since the stock owned by the children is really attributed to the family and does not represent a true minority position. Most valuation consultants would claim that if the son and daughter are over 21, they can be treated as independent owners. For valuation purposes, this reasoning goes, they are not required to vote their stock along with other family members, so a minority discount *along with* a marketability discount could be used.

The following illustration adopts a conservative line and assumes only one discount: a 35 percent lack of marketability discount. With the gifted shares now valued at $1300 per share, 30 shares can be gifted annually. Because it will still take over 33 years to complete the gifting, the parents should consider using part of their $1.2 million unified credit to accelerate the process. Figure 13-3 examines the results.

However, the shares are usually going up in value because the company is retaining some of its profits for growth and expansion. Consider this very real "Catch-22": The owners are gifting shares to a son and daughter active in the business. The business is becoming more profitable than it has been because the gift of stock motivates the kids to work harder. Next year another gift is made; the valuation report indicates the shares have increased from $2000 per share to $2200.

Even applying the 35 percent discount, the stock value has increased from $1300 to $1430 per share. Everyone is faced with a new problem: Fewer shares can be gifted. Next year could bring the same problem. What to do?

Let's assume the $1.2 million exclusion was used. What other options are there? The real question here is how to "freeze" the value so that future growth in the value of the shares retained by the parents would not be included in their estate for estate tax purposes. Later we'll look at other ways to freeze value: Subchapter S elections (Chapter 17) and preferred stock recapitalizations (Chapter 25).

GIFTING CALENDAR				
Value of the Company as a Whole				$2,000,000
Per Share Value of the Company as a Whole				$2,000
Per Share Value of Fractional Interests *discounted for minority interest*				$1,300
	Dad and Mom		**Son and Daughter**	
	Number of Shares	Value	Number of Shares	Value
BEFORE GIFTING	1,000	$2,000,000	0	$0
		100%		
Year 1 Gifts Using Unified Credit	(340)	($442,000)	340	$442,000
Year 1 Gifts Using Annual Exclusion	(30)	($39,000)	30	$39,000
Ownership at End of Year 1	630		370	
Year 2 Gifts Using Annual Exclusion	(30)	($39,000)	30	$39,000
Ownership at End of Year 2	600		400	
Year 3 Gifts Using Annual Exclusion	(30)	($39,000)	30	$39,000
Ownership at End of Year 3	570		430	
Year 4 Gifts Using Annual Exclusion	(30)	($39,000)	30	$39,000
Ownership at End of Year 4	540		460	
Year 5 Gifts Using Annual Exclusion	(30)	($39,000)	30	$39,000
AFTER GIFTING	510	$1,020,000	490	$637,000
		51%		49%
VALUE TRANSFERRED USING DISCOUNTS				$343,000

Figure 13-3.

Voting and Nonvoting Shares

Often business owners face a dilemma when some children are active in the business and others are not active. Gifting shares of stock to active kids poses a problem. What should be given to the inactive kids? And when? The first question owners should resolve is whether gifting to active kids needs to be equalized or offset with the inactive children.

The answer may be no if the following reasoning is applied: Each year the parents are gifting a few shares (truly a minority interest!) to the kids who are working hard in the company. The kids may receive the stock subject to restrictions, such as a shareholder's agreement. It may not have any current value to them. If no dividends are paid, the stock doesn't increase their standard of living or income. Basically it's a tax-motivated transaction to get assets out of the parents' estate. In fact, the fair market value of the stock will be established and can be used to offset future bequests in the estate plan through an equalization clause. (More on this line of reasoning in Chapters 20 and 23.)

As logical as this approach may be, there is still a potential emotional dilemma: "It doesn't feel right," Mom or Dad may say, "to give something to active kids without also doing something for the inactive kids." Reorganizing the capital structure of the business into voting and nonvoting (common) stock may be the answer here. In essence, the *value* of the shares is the same for all parties. What changes is that some shares have voting rights, others do not. The nonvoting shares, however, have the same value as the voting shares.

For example, in the prior illustration, Mom and Dad have 1000 shares and two children in the business. What if they also have an inactive third child? They can exchange their 1000 shares of common stock, through a corporate reorganization, into 666.6 shares of voting common and 333.3 shares of nonvoting common. Voting stock would be gifted to the active children, nonvoting would be gifted to the inactive child.

A comprehensive shareholder's agreement with "puts" and "calls" could provide a method for the inactive child to sell his or her stock back to the company at some future date (e.g., death of the parents), based on a fair market value determination of the nonvoting shares.

Don't Gift Until You Read This

The previous discussion outlines some of the tax-oriented approaches to gifting stock in the business. But there are five important psychological issues to consider carefully *before* any gifts are made. A client situation sets the stage.

Steve owned three successful retail gardening centers. As he approached 65, he wanted to spend less time in the business and more time pursuing other interests. At the same time, Steve kept resisting his advisers' recommendations to gift stock to his three sons, all active in management.

Whenever Steve's advisers suggested gifting stock, Steve's answer was always the same: "They're not ready." Steve was concerned about the boys' inability to get along. Granted, Joe and Mike had been in the business with him for seven years each, but Pat, the youngest son, had joined his two brothers only six months ago. Steve also believed that the boys weren't committed the way he and Susan, his wife, were when they started the company.

Frustrated, the three boys, with the help of outside consultants, approached Steve with a buyout plan. The proposal reflected the value of the business on the open market and included a structure allowing Steve to protect his personal cashflow and minimize his income tax liability from the transfer. No gifting was involved. The sons' cashflow projections for the business indicated that the deal was affordable and provided them with an opportunity to increase their personal income and net worth.

Everyone was surprised at how readily Steve was willing to discuss a buyout. All documentation was completed and signed within three months. The three boys purchased the business for $3.5 million, including a modest cash down payment and notes with terms that avoided any adverse estate tax issues. Steve has let go of the business and the boys are learning to work as a team.

The buyout solved several problems that gifting could not address. Steve was impressed that the boys were willing to make a buyout offer and saw this as evidence of increased cooperation among them. Their businesslike approach and willingness to shoulder payment obligations indicated they really were committed. For Steve, who had built his business from zero to $3.5 million, gifting wouldn't have realized the value of what he had created. For him, his kids, and his company, a buyout proved more beneficial than gifting would have.

There are other compelling reasons to question gifting as an appropriate transfer strategy:

1. Gifts often have strings attached. Offspring can't challenge parents without appearing self-serving or jeopardizing "the next gift." What's more, although the kids own some stock, they know it's still Mom and Dad's company. Gifts are usually made with the understanding that "nothing really changes."

2. Gifting doesn't create family heroes. Often the family culture is built around the parents' struggles to build the business and overcome substantial obstacles. Mom and Dad's early poverty creates family stories that bind family members to a heroic ideal. When the parents gift ownership, they eliminate any struggle that might make their children heroes in their own eyes.

3. Gifting makes estate planning and estate equalization planning very complex when there are active as well as inactive children in the family business. If the owner gifts stock to all children, later family problems are almost guaranteed—when the current owner is no longer around to referee. If only active children are gifted, what is done for the inactive children? And when? If other assets are gifted, are they assets the owner will need for financial security in retirement? The owner may even fail to complete the gifting program because of concern about fairness to different children—at just the time that the reins should be handed over to the next generation.

4. If a company is healthy and growing, gifting may not even cover the growth. In Steve's case, if he and his wife made maximum use of the gift tax exclusion, they could give up to $60,000 in stock annually, tax-free, to their three sons. If the $3.5 million business were growing at a modest 5 percent a year, that $175,000 increase in value would dwarf their gift. The fewer shares of stock retained by Steve would be worth more in his estate than the majority stake he gifted in prior years. As Alice observed in Wonderland, "You have to run harder just to stay in the same place."

5. When gifting enters the transfer equation, what *should* be a business decision—continuity and management of the business—gets confused with family issues. The demands of a family system (equal treatment for all) conflict with business system requirements (rewards on the basis of performance). These conflicting issues cause confusion, procrastination, and indecision for the owner who wants to "do right" and simultaneously "be fair."

The action taken by Steve's family—the children buying out the owner—is an alternative. The leveraged buyout, so prevalent in large corporate takeovers, works especially well in the family business. The current owner is able to realize full, fair market value. Psychologically, a sale cuts the strings associated with gifting. In addition, the children's commitment is evidenced by their willingness to assume personal guarantees on the debt associated with the transaction. For tax purposes, there are many ways to structure the transaction to help the buyer group make the payments.

Most important, the buyout simplifies some of the emotional dilemma associated with estate planning. If the owner sells the company to active children for fair market value, then he or she has the satisfaction of giving equal treatment to both the active and inactive ones. The value received (cash, notes, and so on) by the owner's estate can be worked into an estate plan that is equal for all children. The estate plan can thus be untangled from issues of business continuity.

More Cautions

Any gift of shares should always be accompanied with a stock purchase or buy-sell agreement signed at the time the gift is made. (Chapter 20 covers the provisions in detail.) The agreement can include future gifts, by reference, so the agreement does not have to be reexecuted each time. Consider the possibility that the recipient (son or daughter) divorces a current spouse. Without a preexisting agreement, the shares may wind up in the divorce settlement, or the current owner may end up with a new minority shareholder!

Include in a stock purchase agreement an option for the corporation to reacquire shares if a divorce petition is filed. By doing so at the time of the petition, the company (or other shareholders) should be able to repurchase the shares on the basis of the valuation method established in the agreement. The buyback clause probably won't prevent the value from being included in the divorce, but it should prevent the shares themselves from being split between the divorcing parties.

Even if a spouse is party to a shareholder's agreement, the agreement is usually *not* binding (subject to state statutes) unless the spouse actually sought and obtained *separate and independent* counsel for advice on his or her rights. In some community property states, although the gift may be "sole and separate" at the time it is made, the *increase* in the value of the gift may be a community property interest. For example, if stock is worth $10,000 when the gift occurs, but $100,000 at the time of the divorce, $90,000 may wind up as a community property interest.

If the possibility of children's divorce prevents the parents from taking action regarding their own estate planning and the stock of the business, an irrevocable trust can be used to hold stock for children during the parents' lifetime (see Chapter 26). A properly drafted irrevocable trust should remove the current value of the stock from the parents' estate, and also prevent both the current *and* future value of the stock from being in the child's estate until such time as the trust terminates or distributes the shares to the child.

One last option to consider is a completion clause. What happens if midway through the gifting program one or both parents die? The remaining, ungifted shares would pass through the estate and possibly be divided equally among all family members, inactive and active. The active children may have to report to their inactive brothers and sisters on how to run the business. A completion clause protects the current owner and the business by specifying that if death or disability occurs before the completion of the gifting program, the ungifted shares are valued and then distributed to the designated heirs. Other assets, of equal value, could be directed to children inactive in the business.

Spoiled Gift

Consider the following true situation: Mom and Dad worked 40 years to build a successful chain of clothing stores, located in several states. The business had more than 200 employees and $20 million in annual revenue. Two of Mom and Dad's four children had gained experience in retailing and had entered the family business. When he turned 65, Dad agreed to gift a controlling interest in the business to the two active children over seven years.

Mom and Dad were prudent. They didn't enjoy a lavish lifestyle and paid themselves only enough to maintain a moderate standard of living. The business accumulated more than $4 million in cash.

Two years into the seven-year program, the two active sons became increasingly frustrated with Mom and Dad because they were not ready to "let go." Mom and Dad recognized that their sons had worked hard for the business, and after some emotional confrontations they agreed to step aside. Mom and Dad proposed that the company buy in the ungifted shares through a stock redemption plan. Since they had lived so modestly, Mom and Dad needed the funds from the proposed stock redemption to support them in a comfortable lifestyle during retirement.

The sons, however, refused to agree that the company pay the price established by an outside valuation firm. The family was polarized. The two active children sided against the other two, who supported Mom and Dad.

The two active sons threatened a minority shareholder's suit, and attorneys were employed by both sides. Finally, Mom and Dad voted their controlling interest in the stock to oust the two sons. A previously signed shareholder's agreement required the sons, on termination of employment, to sell their stock back to the company, and that is what happened. The sons, now in another business, no longer communicate with their parents. What began as Mom and Dad's legitimate attempt to create and share the wealth of the business resulted in a divided family and great legal and emotional expenses.

Gifting stock of a family business can be a blessing for some and a curse for others. Before making a decision, understand motives and protect everyone with contractual agreements in the event that things go wrong, because they often do.

References

1. Treasury Regulations Sec. 25.2503-3(a).
2. Hillery James Gallagher, "Life Insurance for the Liquid Estate," *Journal of the American Society of CLU,* March 1992, vol. XLVI, no. 2, p. 38.

14

Option 2: Transferring the Business Through the Estate Plan

Many business owners, when asked how they are "passing the torch" answer, "It's all taken care of—in my will." They are not aware, or are not willing to admit, how many problems this approach can cause for the family and the business.

Obstacles to Address

Retaining the business in the estate creates countless obstacles. If, after their death, Mom and Dad could observe some of the tragic consequences, they would never consider this strategy. The potential problems include active heirs with fractional ownership in the family business quarreling with inactive siblings who also own part of the business—all because Mom or Dad thought that being "fair" meant treating all children equally.

Imagine the plight of the loyal successor. He or she works faithfully for many years in the shadow of the owner, and is the epitome of the "key employee." The successor handles the day-to-day operations and is the "number 2" person in the company.

Meanwhile, the successor gets old waiting for Dad or Mom to let go. Aging successors move through their own stages of life, often frustrated at not having an ownership opportunity and the chance to "strut their stuff." Alcoholism and divorce are often symptoms of this frustration. By the time Dad or Mom passes away, the kids are approaching retirement age. With Dad and Mom now gone, the kids often sell the business and begin to enjoy life for the first time.

One client, in his early fifties, confided that he would "sell the business in a heartbeat"—that is, as soon as Mom's heart stopped beating. Daily, his mother's death symbolized his freedom! How would Mom feel if she knew what her son was really thinking?

The business owner rarely grasps how much in estate taxes will be due when the full value of the business is retained in the estate. Owners who do not project estate taxes also tend to neglect to plan *how* the family will pay estate taxes. Often the only option is assuming heavy debt. If the business is the primary asset in the estate, it may not have much cash, but it may have assets such as plant and equipment that can be pledged as collateral for a bank loan. The business's cashflow then gets diverted for 5 to 10 years to pay the bank note.

Cash for business expansion or growth, or refurbishing plant and equipment, is not available. In a competitive industry, this business will not survive; sales and profits will decline as expenses increase—the aging equipment will break down more often, requiring more and more repair. New, more efficient equipment is unaffordable. Shrinking profit margins will likely ignite shareholder disputes among the heirs over the "right way" to run the company. More time spent on shareholder disputes means less productive time (and lower morale) in the company. The spiral continues until selling the business—or what's left of it—becomes the only viable option. And it all could have been avoided.

Here's another bleak scenario: Dad dies, leaving his stock in the business to an inactive spouse. Mom, who was discouraged from being involved in the business during Dad's lifetime, may choose one of these paths: (1) she becomes active in the business but knows very little about it; (2) she is concerned about personal financial security and stops expansion or growth plans that were in the works; or (3) she recognizes her personal limitations and hires an adviser to run the company by proxy, yet retains veto power over all decisions, thereby creating confusion over who's really in charge.

Owners who still insist on using the estate plan as the ownership succession plan can avoid the above scenarios with some advance planning.

Project Future Estate Taxes

Estate taxes can be as high as 55 percent of the estate's assets. If the primary estate asset is a family business, the IRS will value it at death at its fair market value.

If an owner does nothing, a small estate can become a large estate for tax purposes. A future tax bill can actually increase faster than the estate's growth. Figure 14-1 shows how an estate worth $3 million today, growing an average of 7 percent a year, can be worth $8.5 million in 15 years.

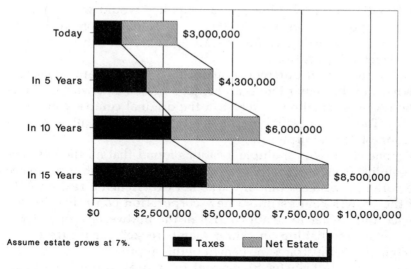

Figure 14-1. *Do Nothing.* The tax bill grows faster than the net estate.

A 60-year-old owner today, with a 60-year-old spouse, is likely to live for an additional 15 years. Consider what happens to the estate when that occurs:

Assets	Today's value	Annual growth rate	Value in 15 years (rounded)
Family business	$1,500,000	9%	$5,500,000
Business real estate (owned separately and leased to company)	650,000	5	1,350,000
Profit-sharing plan (assume some distributions are taken)	500,000	5	1,000,000
Residence	250,000	3	375,000
Other assets	100,000	7	275,000
	$3,000,000	7% avg.	$8,500,000

As the estate grows in size, so do the estate taxes due. Where will the family get $4 million for estate taxes?

- If the family borrows the money from a bank on a 10-year note, the payments (principal and interest at 10 percent) would be $650,000 a year!

- If the family borrows part of the money from the government under a 6166 election (see Chapter 27) and the balance from a bank, the payments would range from $410,000 to $738,000 over a 10-year period.

Freeze Growth in the Taxable Estate

The money in the profit-sharing plan could be used for taxes, but that would trigger an *income tax* of 35 percent to 40 percent on the distributions. A $4 million second-to-die or survivor life insurance policy would work, but the premium on such a policy could run $50,000 a year for 10 or more years. The least costly solution is freezing value or shifting some growth to the next generation, while retaining control.

One approach is to spin off different components of the operating business to different heirs, and then enter into shareholder's agreements with the heirs to buy out the owner's remaining interest in the original company at death (see Chapter 18). The core operating business after the spin-off might have a reduced value for estate tax purposes.

For example, one client with multiple locations found that all the business growth was coming from the East Coast offices, which his children were running. The core midwestern company was not experiencing real growth. Spinning off the growth centers into a new corporation controlled by the children allowed this owner to retain control of the midwestern operations (his baby) while accomplishing an estate "semi-freeze" for future taxes. Strategy 1 in Figure 14-2, illustrates the benefit of this approach.

Another approach is to transfer 51 percent (or more) to the heirs now, through gifting or installment sales, with the owner retaining 49 percent (or less). To avoid giving up full control, current owners could change the corporation's bylaws to require a supermajority vote for major decisions (see Chapter 21). The reduced ownership interest retained might be valued at a discount at death for lack of marketability and for being a minority block. The real estate could be put into a family limited partnership or into a GRAT (grantor-retained annuity trust), explained fully in Chapter 26. The result is shown as strategy 2 in Figure 14-2.

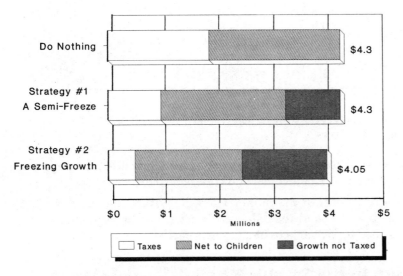

Figure 14-2. Why focus on estate planning now? Compare the 20-year results from two estate-planning strategies with a decision to "do nothing."

A third approach is to recapitalize the corporation into common and preferred stock, with the preferred stock representing all the current value and the common stock representing all future value. Gifting the low-current-value common to the heirs, or a portion of it, would remove from the estate's future growth of those shares. To satisfy IRS requirements, the company would have to pay a dividend on the preferred stock. Therefore, the preferred could conveniently be used as an income-producing device during the parents' lifetime and then could be redeemed by the corporation at death. Properly structured, the preferred stock should not appreciate in value; appreciation would be in the common.

Sometimes a recapitalization occurs *after* the parents' death. This can provide preferred stock to inactive children and common stock to the children who will run the company. The parents provide in their will or trust that the fiduciary of the estate will recapitalize the company in order to make the appropriate distributions of stock.

For the family business owner who cannot decide between being "fair" or being "equal," the recap at death allows equal distributions to all children, whether active or inactive. At the same time, the recap provides a mechanism to allow the active children exclusive enjoyment of the fruits of their future labor, while freezing the inactives' shares at the date-of-death value. Additional techniques for freezing value are discussed in Chapter 25.

Provide Liquid Assets for Estate Taxes

Another important consideration for the owner who doesn't want to "let go" is how the estate will fund estate taxes. Many companies have had to sell out or go public in order to raise funds to pay estate taxes. Cash and securities set aside during the parents' lifetime may be needed as nonbusiness assets to provide equal value for inactive children. The family business arena is full of stories about how the estate's liquid assets (cash), earmarked for inactive children, were used instead for taxes, leaving the active children with the family business and the inactive children with empty promises and hard feelings.

Funded shareholder agreements, qualifying Subchapter S trusts, or Subchapter S elections with voting and nonvoting shareholders can create liquid assets—if planned in advance (see Chapters 17 and 27).

Make Written Contractual Agreements

What happens if, because of the owner's uncertainty about successors, plans for the transfer of ownership are not in place and the owner dies? Who will run the company? Who will own it? Would the family want it to be sold? What if the business has been transferred, but other business assets, such as real estate, are owned by inactive family members?

Many issues need to be resolved as stopgap measures or when there's just plain confusion on the part of the owner as to what he or she really wants to do. Having contractual agreements may be the key so that an intended transfer to family members can be completed in the event of an untimely death. If the current owner is waiting for a family member to mature, or to become more responsible, he or she may postpone the transfer of ownership. If an untimely death occurs, and no contracts exist, the children who are working in the business may be deprived of any ownership. The business could be sold to outside parties, eliminating the family's future employment as well.

Consider this example of verbal agreements. A grandson had been working in the family business for a number of years and had reached a verbal agreement with his grandfather on ownership of the company. It was common knowledge in the company that Grandfather intended to transfer the business to Grandson when Grandfather died. Before Grandfather got around to committing his intentions in writing, he died of a heart attack. Although the aunts and uncles sympathized with the grandson, they pointed out that he didn't have a formal contract with his grandfather. The aunts and uncles overruled Grandson (and his dad) and insisted that the company be sold to the highest bidder in order to realize value for the other members of the family. Grandson was outbid by a large conglomerate, and ultimately left the family business.

Often business owners with only one child feel that a testamentary bequest (via the will) to the son or daughter is an effective way of transferring the business. How wrong they are! If the will requires that the business be transferred at the first death to the active child, the owner may be creating an unnecessary estate tax liability. If the value of the stock being transferred exceeds $600,000, the excess portion will be taxed in the estate. If there is insufficient liquidity in the estate to pay the tax, an unnecessary burden may be placed on the family. Intentions, of course, may be quite the contrary.

Another common response on the part of the owner is to leave the stock in trust for the life of the surviving spouse; after the spouse's death, the stock is distributed to the active child. Although this arrangement may eliminate estate taxes at the first death, it can create additional problems at the second death. If the child enhances the business's value, the value of the stock in the spouse's estate will be that much greater than the value was at the first death. Because the second estate may not be eligible for the unlimited marital deduction, the estate taxes may be greater at the second death, provided the spouse doesn't remarry. Inadvertently created, then, is an incentive for the son or daughter to be a mere caretaker—maintain the company, not build it— rather than adopt an entrepreneurial role. Any value created by the active child for the duration of the spouse's life will be partially lost (up to 55 percent) by the higher estate taxes the successor has to pay.

If a stock transfer plan has begun—whether via gift or sale—to other family members, and the owner is unsure of their maturity or ability, the owner should be sure to include a clause in the stock purchase or buy-sell agreement that gives them an option to buy the remaining interest at fair market value, or to have a first right of refusal if, in the event of the owner's death, the spouse decides to sell the company. In this way, the other family members have the option to match an offer from an outside party. If they are willing and able to retain the business, they will eliminate potential disappointments in later years from children who "never had a chance to keep the business in the family."

Solve Succession Issues with a Contingency Plan

The unresolved issues that should be addressed in a contingency plan are the same issues that should be resolved in the "incomplete" estate plan. That is, what were the deceased owner's desires, wishes, concerns, and fears that were never communicated? A recent client situation illustrates the importance of the contingency plan.

Joe was an extremely successful entrepreneur. He had taken over the family funeral home business at age 25, when his dad died in a sudden accident. Joe matured as his dad's peers coached him. He took calculated business risks and, over time, successfully expanded his business into several states. He built a dedicated staff and, at age 55, still wasn't ready to think about a succession plan. Joe was enjoying his business; he had just completed a new acquisition. His 30-year-old son, Joe Jr., "wasn't ready," but "there's plenty of time" Joe would say.

"What if something happens?" my associates and I asked Joe as we reviewed his incomplete estate plan. "We'll work on that at our next meeting," Joe responded. Tragically, Joe, an accomplished pilot, was killed a few weeks later when his small single-engine plane crashed. At the funeral, everyone wondered if Joe Jr. could handle the business.

Joe hadn't established a contingency plan. There were a lot of assumptions as to what Joe would have wanted, but no one knew for sure. The family and the staff were understandably angry as they dealt with their grief.

The contingency plan is different from the succession plan. It can be as simple as a brief letter or as complex as a long document. At the least, it should leave instructions, names, and phone numbers for the survivors. If the current business owner died, what would the survivors need to know? What should they do first? Who should they consult regarding business decisions?

One business owner commented after Joe's funeral that his own family tradition was to exclude spouses. They weren't supposed to know anything about the business. Maybe this type of thinking should be revisited in light of an incomplete contingency plan. Are there peers or study group members who could offer a spouse unbiased business advice? Lawyers and accountants can provide legal and tax counseling; but what is most needed—and most often lacking—in the contingency plan is a trusted person to provide sound business advice.

In laying out a contingency plan, the current owner should write a personal letter to the survivors stating the challenges and opportunities the family business will likely face in coming years. The letter should analyze the strengths and weaknesses of potential heirs to the business and suggest courses of action (e.g., finishing school, completing a graduate program, getting industry training).

The letter should also describe the owner's vision had he or she lived to develop a succession plan, and express specific ideas for conflict resolution in the family. This can rally the family behind a common goal and direct survivors toward meaningful future activities.

Finally, the letter should describe the owner's vision for the family—outside of the business. What are the values cherished by family members? What ideals have they adopted?

Communicating these thoughts to the family, business partners, children, and spouse may not ease the pain or reduce the grief. However, it can go a long way toward reducing anger, eliminating confusion, and binding the family to a common purpose.

Interim management needs to be established if children are not yet ready psychologically and experientially to carry on as managers and owners. One of the tasks of interim management is to mentor family members until they are ready. Tying in key employees during a transition of this type may require the family to adopt incentives, such as those outlined in Chapter 10. "Bridge managers," who specialize in running companies on a temporary basis, may be useful. Bridge managers are often former family business owners who have successfully "let go" of their own company and are available on a consulting basis to other companies in their industry or trade group. Strategic alliances are another alternative for finding a transition manager (see Chapter 22).

Transferring business ownership through the estate plan is fraught with obstacles and potential problems. Many owners—through procrastination or indecision—decide to go this route. But with a little planning they can still ensure that the business and family will live on.

15
Option 3: Selling the Family Business to a Third Party

Sometimes the best way to "pass the torch" is to transfer the business to a third party instead of a family member or key employee.

There are a number of reasons why selling to outsiders can be the best solution for the family and the business. In 1990, *Inc.* magazine conducted a survey on the reasons family businesses have been sold.[1] Respondents reported the following motivations:

Reason	Percent responding
Boredom or burnout	54%
Lack of capital	11
Children have no interest in the business	10
Desire for liquidity	10
Age and health	8
Other interests	7

Many business owners, after deciding to sell the business, don't know what to do next. The value of the family business often represents retirement security for the prospective seller and potential wealth (current or deferred) for other family members. It's important to "do it right"—yet many owners have never sold a business before. As a result, many "deals" are turned down, buyers are frustrated, and the unsophisticated seller, who may be great at business but a novice at negotiating, loses time (and often money) in the delays that occur.

Sam, a 70-year-old businessman, owned a neon sign company and an advertising display manufacturing company. Sam's children were not active in the businesses; all were grown and had their own careers. Sam identified a buyer for the sign company, a long-time acquaintance in the same industry. He found another buyer for the display company, a parts manufacturer with whom Sam had enjoyed a vendor relationship for many years.

What did Sam do next? "Invited them in, showed them around, gave them the financials, and let them make an offer. Then we talked it over until we worked out a deal."

Seems reasonable, right? Wrong! The first mistake Sam made was to represent himself in the negotiations. Sam was too close emotionally to the transaction. The business represented 50 years of his life's work as well as his future financial security.

Sam was well aware of the risk. In fact, so much was riding on the transaction that he believed he was the only one who could handle it properly. He didn't trust anyone else to be involved. Just as artists are too close to their work to value it properly, so business owners need an intermediary working on their behalf.

Sam's lack of sophistication resulted in one buyer defaulting on promissory notes (while Sam was still personally liable on those notes to the bank). Sam had to come out of retirement three years later to take over his former company. The company had been mismanaged, assets and cash had been drained, and key employees had left. Sam had to rebuild his company so he could sell it again—otherwise, his retirement plans would be ruined. He did eventually sell the business again—for $1 million less. The sales proceeds just barely covered the indebtedness incurred to rebuild the business and the original bank debt on which Sam had remained personally liable. At 73 years old, Sam found his company and his retirement security gone.

Could this have been avoided with an intermediary? Perhaps Sam could have been released from his personal guarantees at the bank, or negotiated for stronger collateral and/or security devices built into the documents (described in Chapter 21). Most important, an intermediary would have balanced Sam's enthusiasm to "get the deal done."

Hire a Broker or an Investment Banker?

Who should represent the seller's interests? The choices are limited: brokers, investment bankers, or trusted advisers.

Business brokers generally work on small transactions—businesses between $100,000 and $3 million. They will usually "package the company" to be sold by developing pro formas of revenue and expenses, based on historical information, for a buyer to review. They will advertise the company in national and trade publications and screen prospective buyers. Fees tend to be a percentage of the selling price and are paid only if and when a transaction closes. The fee can be as high as 12 percent, and generally decreases inversely with the size of the deal.

Investment bankers fall into two broad categories: those who do financial transactions and those who do strategic transactions. Some do both. In a typical financial transaction, a buyer has capital (or access to it) but no direct expertise in the seller's business. The profit margins, earnings, and/or cashflow look attractive from a financial perspective, assuming management can be retained or brought in to maintain or enhance those earnings. The deal is based on "the numbers" alone.

A strategic transaction must also work from a financial perspective; yet generally there's a business "fit." For example, the seller controls a territory that the buyer wants to enter, or the seller manufactures a product that the buyer would like to sell (or vice versa). When two companies complement each other in a strategic manner, the match is called vertical or horizontal integration. For example, adding a production line of parts that fits into another company's products is one form of integration. Geographic complementarity is another.

Investment bankers have a wide network of contacts, and they bring sophistication to the bargaining table. They spend more time and effort than brokers do in "packaging" the company: researching trends, demographics, and industry data, and understanding the company's historical financial information so they can better explain opportunities and risks to a potential buyer. Investment bankers charge higher fees than brokers because of the additional services they perform. As a result, they tend to focus their activities on companies worth $50 million or more.

Many family businesses fall somewhere in the middle—the value is more than $1 million but less than $50 million. They are too sophisticated for a business broker, but sometimes not big enough for a full-service investment banking firm. These businesses have a number of options. One is to find a boutique investment banker that specializes in the industry in which the family business operates. Boutique bankers have a wide array of contacts and sources and are usually looking for ways to assemble or combine businesses for other clients. Family businesses should be cautious of firms that charge large, up-front appraisal fees before they identify prospective buyers.

An attorney, a family business consultant, or another trusted adviser who acts as an intermediary and who negotiates for the benefit of the seller is another option for medium-size businesses. Such negotiators step in only after the client identifies prospective buyers. The seller's representative will contact these prospective buyers to determine their interest. One benefit of this method is that fees tend to be substantially lower, since the seller is paying only for structuring and negotiating the deal—not for hunting for a buyer.

Industry acquisition firms should be included in the prospective pool of buyers. They are strategic buyers who are more likely to pay a premium than anyone else. They already operate in the seller's industry, and the family business may offer the buyer an intangible benefit: an expansion opportunity.

A few years ago, the Houston-based Service Corporation, Inc. (SCI), a funeral home acquisition company with more than 500 locations, expanded into the casket manufacturing business and the insurance business—selling annuities as a method of prefunding funerals.

After SCI targeted a potential new funeral home acquisition, it planned to sweeten its offer with additional money, if needed, to ward off any competitors trying to buy the seller's business. Besides the anticipated cashflow from the targeted seller's company, there were additional profits that SCI could realize. For example, the new acquisition could sell more units for the casket manufacturing division and could sell annuities for the insurance division. Thus SCI was a "better buyer" than other companies, because it factored these additional anticipated profits into its analyses and determined that it could pay more for the target company. Other acquisition firms had to increase their offers for a particular deal just to stay in; as a result, selling prices for funeral homes increased in general.

Unfortunately, the projected profits did not materialize, and after a couple of years SCI sold off its casket manufacturing division and its insurance business. As a result, the prices it paid for subsequent acquisitions dropped accordingly. The industry's inflated prices for businesses became more realistic.

The Seller's Role

The seller should do some homework before negotiation. Before any buyer is contacted, the seller and other family members, as appropriate, should define their financial requirements. It may help to go back and revisit Chapter 9. Obviously, there should be some type of reality check to keep the expectations of the sellers in line with what outside buyers are likely to offer. The best way to conduct this reality check is through cashflow analysis: Can the business afford to continue running, pay the sellers the price they expect, on terms that are acceptable, *and generate* a profit for the new owners? The analysis involves three key steps.

1. Begin by identifying industry expense norms—available through industry trade groups and/or business valuation firms that have statistical information on expenses identified by industry. Compare the family business's actual expenses against these norms. If expenses are higher than the norms, assume a new owner will reduce expenses to increase earnings. If actual expenses are lower than industry norms, use actual expenses in the projections. However, if rents to owners are below fair market commercial rates, the rents should be adjusted upward to fair market rates.

2. Using actual historical operating results, develop one or more 7- to 10-year pro formas (best case, worst case, middle of the road) indicating how the company *might perform* in the future under certain assumptions. If the seller can identify expenses that will change with a new owner, or if upgrades

SELLER INDUSTRIES, INC.							CASHFLOW PROJECTION	
			INCLUDING PLANNING CHANGES					
	Actual	Projected . . .						
	Last Year	19X1	19X2	19X3	19X4	19X5	19X6	19X7
% Increase in Sales								
– Middle Case Projection		6.00%	8.00%	0.00%	6.00%	8.00%	0.00%	6.00%
SALES	$12,400,000	$13,144,300	$14,195,604	$14,195,604	$15,047,720	$16,251,058	$16,251,058	$17,226,461
Cost of Sales	8,060,000	8,543,795	9,227,143	9,227,143	9,781,018	10,563,188	10,563,188	11,197,200
GROSS PROFIT	4,340,000	4,600,505	4,968,461	4,968,461	5,266,702	5,687,870	5,687,870	6,029,261
Operating Expenses								
Marketing and Sales	2,480,000	2,628,860	2,839,121	2,839,121	3,009,544	3,250,212	3,250,212	3,445,292
Administrative	1,240,000	1,314,430	1,419,560	1,419,560	1,504,772	1,625,106	1,625,106	1,722,646
Reduce Personnel Costs		(166,667)	(171,667)	(176,817)	(182,122)	(187,585)	(193,213)	(199,009)
Increase Rents		40,000	40,000	40,000	50,000	50,000	50,000	60,000
Total Operating Expenses	3,720,000	3,816,623	4,127,014	4,121,864	4,382,195	4,737,732	4,732,105	5,028,929
Operating Income	620,000	783,882	841,447	846,597	884,508	950,138	955,766	1,000,332
Income Taxes	(248,000)	(313,553)	(336,579)	(338,639)	(353,803)	(380,055)	(382,306)	(400,133)
NET INCOME	372,000	470,329	504,868	507,958	530,705	570,083	573,459	600,199
Cashflow Adjustments:								
+ depreciation	49,600	52,577	56,782	56,782	60,191	65,004	65,004	68,906
– equipment purchases	(100,000)	(100,000)	(100,000)	(100,000)	(100,000)	(100,000)	(100,000)	(100,000)
CASHFLOW PROJECTION AFTER PLANNING CHANGES	$321,600	$422,906	$461,651	$464,741	$490,895	$535,087	$538,464	$569,105

Figure 15-1.

or renovations are needed, they should be factored into the analysis (see Figure 15-1).

3. After projecting available cashflow from steps 1 and 2 above, superimpose the seller's desired outcome: price and terms. If projected company cashflow cannot cover the seller's demands *and* generate a return to the buyer of at least 20 percent a year, the seller should go back to the drawing board. Even though a buyer may offer cash, it's safe to assume there is a cost for the cash and that cost should be amortized over a 7- to 10-year period, with interest. In Figure 15-2, it is assumed that the transaction is for $2.5 million cash to the sellers, with the buyers borrowing the cash from their own lender but looking to the company to be able to repay the loan. It is also assumed that the company repays the $2.5 million loan over 7 years from future earnings.

The family and the current owner can save themselves a lot of aggravating negotiation time by reviewing cashflow availability and cashflow requirements and in essence structuring the transaction themselves, ahead of time, "to see if it will fly" for a buyer. This exercise also helps the current owner focus on and resolve some important issues before a buyer is brought to the table.

For example, one owner of eight grocery stores learned that her expected price was unrealistic because a new owner would need to spend $15 per square foot to refurbish the tired stores. After studying the situation, the seller

SELLER INDUSTRIES, INC.							CASHFLOW PROJECTION	
$2.5 MILLION CASH TO SELLER; FINANCED AT 9% FOR 7 YEARS.								
	Actual Last Year	Projected . . . 19X1	19X2	19X3	19X4	19X5	19X6	19X7
% Increase in Sales – Middle Case Projection		6.00%	8.00%	0.00%	6.00%	8.00%	0.00%	6.00%
SALES	$12,400,000	$13,144,300	$14,195,604	$14,195,604	$15,047,720	$16,251,058	$16,251,058	$17,226,461
Cost of Sales	8,060,000	8,543,795	9,227,143	9,227,143	9,781,018	10,563,188	10,563,188	11,197,200
GROSS PROFIT	4,340,000	4,600,505	4,968,461	4,968,461	5,266,702	5,687,870	5,687,870	6,029,261
Operating Expenses								
Marketing and Sales	2,480,000	2,628,860	2,839,121	2,839,121	3,009,544	3,250,212	3,250,212	3,445,292
Administrative	1,240,000	1,314,430	1,419,560	1,419,560	1,504,772	1,625,106	1,625,106	1,722,646
Reduce Personnel Costs		(166,667)	(171,667)	(176,817)	(182,122)	(187,585)	(193,213)	(199,009)
Increase Rents		40,000	40,000	40,000	50,000	50,000	50,000	60,000
Interest payments		214,000	189,000	161,000	131,000	98,000	63,000	23,000
Total Operating Expenses	3,720,000	4,030,623	4,316,014	4,282,864	4,513,195	4,835,732	4,795,105	5,051,929
Operating Income	620,000	569,882	652,447	685,597	753,508	852,138	892,766	977,332
Income Taxes	(248,000)	(227,953)	(260,979)	(274,239)	(301,403)	(340,855)	(357,106)	(390,933)
NET INCOME	372,000	341,929	391,468	411,358	452,105	511,283	535,659	586,399
Cashflow Adjustments:								
+ depreciation	49,600	52,577	56,782	56,782	60,191	65,004	65,004	68,906
– equipment purchases	(100,000)	(100,000)	(100,000)	(100,000)	(100,000)	(100,000)	(100,000)	(100,000)
– principal payments		(269,000)	(294,000)	(321,000)	(351,000)	(384,000)	(421,000)	(460,000)
CASHFLOW PROJECTION WITH LOAN PAYMENTS	$321,600	$25,506	$54,251	$47,141	$61,295	$92,287	$79,664	$95,305

Figure 15-2.

reduced her demands, and aligned her thinking more closely with industry valuation norms.

A seller should also plan to play "goodwill ambassador," promoting the company's intangibles, such as employees, distributors, and family heritage. However, the seller should not negotiate directly with the buyer on price, terms, or deal structure. These should be handled exclusively by the intermediary—keeping in mind that if all those involved in the sale have done their homework, the intermediary who represents the seller should have a pretty good idea how the transaction will be structured before the buyer begins negotiating.

An article in *Inc.* magazine underscores the need for the seller to have a clear-thinking intermediary. In it, a merger and acquisition specialist, acting as a buyer, admits how he uses the seller's emotional ties to the business:

> I want a seller who's 75 years old. I want him to have children who are artists and doctors and lawyers and who have no interest in the business. I want a guy who has no idea what his business is really worth and who doesn't even know what an investment banker is. If he does know, I want someone who hates investment bankers because he hates everyone associated with Wall Street. And I want to walk in there and get him to tell me about his business, take me to lunch, bring me home to meet his wife. I want someone who's selling something more important to him than his

wife, his children, his home. This isn't his business, this is his baby. He created it. And I want him to look at me and say, "I want *you* to own my business." Because once you've made this connection, money is no longer the most important thing to him. He's not going to turn around in the middle of the negotiations and sell his baby for a better price to some jerk from Wall Street.[2]

Many successful acquisition firms successfully employ a "good guy/bad guy" routine in buying businesses. The good guy comes in, shakes everybody's hand, and promises the owner and the family that everything will stay the way it always has been after the business is sold. In addition, he promises that the seller will realize top dollar for the business from the good guy's company, the current owner will be invited to be on the board of directors of the buyer's company, and, if that's not enough, he'll even marry the owner's daughter. Get the picture? A handshake seals the deal, and the family is euphoric.

The "bad guy," typically from the acquisition company's accounting department, comes in a few days later shaking his head and exclaiming in frustration how the "good guy" never should have promised this and never should have promised that. The "deal" begins to shrink, and the family business owner slowly falls off the acquisition cloud and sinks back to reality. Welcome to the world of negotiating over a family business.

Transaction Alternatives

One of the first items a seller should address with the intermediary as part of a negotiating strategy is whether the transaction will be arranged as a *sale of assets* or a *sale of stock*. Another consideration is whether the seller requires *immediate payment* (for example, all cash), *deferred payment*, or a combination of the two.

Finally, the seller should consider whether the transaction should be structured as a *taxable* sale or a *tax-free* transaction. Sellers should keep in mind that a tax-free transaction usually involves exchanging stock in the family business for stock of the acquiring corporation. Federal securities laws may require sellers to hold the stock for some period of time before they can sell it on the open market. The risk is that during this time the stock may fluctuate in value—up or down. The seller will not realize the value of the shares until they are sold. One owner exchanged her stock for stock in a public company; at the time the stock was trading at $22 per share. By the time she could legally sell her restricted shares, they were trading at $4 per share. Therefore, a tax-free transaction is not always the best deal for the owner and the family.

In a tax-free transaction (swapping stock for stock), any consideration paid in addition to the stock swap may be taxed as ordinary income. In a taxable transaction, the consideration is usually taxed as a capital gain; that is, the buyer purchases the stock for cash, a note, or both. If a sale of the family business is structured as a tax-free transaction, then sellers will be indifferent to whether the deal is structured as a sale of assets or of stock.

The tax-free stock swap is attractive when the seller believes that the stock of the buyer is a good long-term investment and the seller does not need all of the cash "up front." However, in a taxable transaction, sellers may prefer to sell stock because the capital gain treatment they receive results in a 28 percent tax compared with a 31 percent ordinary income tax rate. If the sellers receive deferred payments in installments, they can usually recognize their gain for tax purposes on the installment method.

Basis

For a seller, a stock's capital gain is always computed for tax purposes as the selling price in excess of basis. For many business owners, the tax basis in the stock of their company may be very low—for example, the $1000 (or less) that they originally put up to start the business.

Family members who receive stock through gifts have a carryover basis, which is the same as the donor's.

Stock transferred after the death of an owner can be structured to have a "stepped up" basis for heirs. This can be done through a shareholder's agreement (Chapter 20) or through the marital deduction (Chapter 24).

From the buyer's perspective, one advantage of a tax-free acquisition involving stock of the acquiring corporation is that issuing more shares will not drain the buyer's cash reserves. However, it may dilute earnings of the buyer. One benefit of a taxable transaction to the buyer is that, if debt is used, the resulting interest payments are deductible.

Stock or Asset Transactions

When the sale is taxable, sellers generally prefer a stock deal; buyers prefer an asset deal.

For a seller, an asset sale—selling assets from the corporate entity and retaining (or liquidating) the corporate shell—leads to double taxation. A gain on assets sold, or recapture of accelerated depreciation, would be taxed at the corporate level and then again at the shareholder level if the company is liquidated after the assets are sold. A combined 70 percent tax is possible when state taxes are figured in.

However, from the buyer's perspective, the asset transaction may be more favorable if the fair market value of the assets acquired is higher than the seller's basis: The buyer gets to *step up* its basis in the assets acquired. A new, higher basis in assets creates additional depreciation for the buyer, resulting in additional tax benefits. These tax benefits can be passed back to the seller through negotiation over price and terms.

If the seller's basis in assets is *higher* than their current fair market value, as has happened with land and buildings in the Southwest, the buyer may actually prefer a stock transaction. An asset deal here means the buyer would have to *step down* its basis and lose depreciation benefits. A stock deal here preserves for the buyer the seller's existing basis for tax purposes.

In a stock deal, the buyer acquires the corporation, with all its liabilities. If the liabilities can be identified, they can be factored into negotiations over the purchase price. If, however, the family business has unknown liabilities or contingent liabilities, it may be impossible to reflect them accurately in the stock price; buyers would be concerned about overpaying for the company if they assume the unknown liabilities.

Sellers can address such unknown liabilities by offering warranties and indemnifications in favor of buyers, but these may be difficult to enforce. Offset arrangements, whereby buyers reduce future payments to sellers as unknown or contingent liabilities appear, may not be an acceptable alternative when sellers depend on future cashflow for their retirement income.

An asset deal lets buyers acquire assets free of the selling corporation's unsecured liabilities. Generally an asset transaction poses fewer hidden or unknown liabilities for buyers. Another advantage for buyers in an asset transaction is that it eliminates having to deal with minority shareholders who may not agree to sell their stock. The minority shareholders may not be able to block a sale of the corporation's assets, if approved by the majority shareholders. The minority shareholders can still own their stock, but in a company that has sold its assets.

Environmental Issues

Among the "lurking liabilities" that can affect every transaction today are environmental hazards. Plants and offices built 30 or 40 years ago commonly used asbestos as a building material. Underground storage tanks used to fuel a fleet of trucks or cars, or certain tanks installed during the gas crisis of the 1970s, now pose hazards in terms of contamination to surrounding soil and underground water tables. Chemical treatment facilities that systematically dumped toxic residues into the ground face enormous cleanup costs. Companies that sold lead-based paint and casually dumped paint behind the store in the same place year after year have also created environmental hazards.

Family business owners who no longer use their underground storage tanks ("We haven't touched them in years") are often surprised to find that the tanks leaked in the past and left a residue in the soil. Whether the business is being sold to a third party or transferred to family members or key employees, it is helpful to have an EPA-soil test conducted by a qualified individual to determine if there is an environmental hazard.

Today, approval for the financing to buy a family business is contingent on a "clean" environmental test result. Even for an internal transaction, liabilities identified and projected cleanup costs can affect the valuation of the business. The family business owner should not wait to be surprised by a buyer's request, but should attempt to quantify potential financial exposure before negotiations begin.

Unwanted Assets

In some cases, selling the family business presents a problem when there are properties, assets, or wholly owned subsidiaries that are not attractive to the identified buyer. In a stock deal, these unwanted properties will make it difficult to consummate the transaction.

There are several strategies for separating unwanted pieces from those that can be sold. Two methods have negative tax consequences: (1) to distribute unwanted assets as dividends to shareholders and then sell the company; or (2) to sell unwanted assets off piecemeal, pay taxes, if required, at the corporate level, distribute the cash and/or installment notes as a dividend to the shareholders (taxed again), and then sell the family business.

Unwanted properties can, however, be separated in a nontaxable transaction, if the sellers can meet certain rules. For example, unwanted assets can be transferred to a controlled subsidiary. In such a spin-off, the family business distributes shares of the subsidiary tax-free to the existing stockholders. The existing stockholders do not surrender any of the original corporation's shares; they continue to own the same percentage of the family business—but now they own shares in two companies. After the spin-off, stockholders can proceed with selling the family business. Tax-free reorganizations are covered in more detail in Chapter 18.

Other Considerations

In many transactions, the price tag—for assets or stock—comes with employment agreements, noncompete agreements, or consulting arrangements. These concepts are addressed in Chapter 19. For now, the seller needs to know two things: What security will back a noncompete agreement? Will the buyer agree to triggers that would accelerate payment in the event of nonperformance?

When family members own real estate outside the business, and lease it back to the company, they may have additional opportunities for income shifting when negotiating the sale of the family business. If they do not, before looking to sell the business, the family should consider creating a family limited partnership to hold the business real estate. If the real estate is retained and leased to the new owners, the limited partnership provides a method to shift rental income to different members of the family while control of the property stays in the hands of the existing owners. Alternatively, putting the retained real estate into a grantor-retained annuity trust or dynasty trust creates opportunities for a family bank or for discounted transfers (see Chapter 26).

When lease payments and terms are negotiated, building in "puts" and "calls" at points in the future allows the property to be sold to the new owners on the basis of appraisals at the time of sale, preserves any property appreciation for the family, and guarantees a future market for the property.

From the buyer's perspective, purchasing the operating business and leasing the existing real estate "buys time" to pay off any debt related to the business acquisition. From the seller's perspective, it preserves an important piece of collateral in family hands: the business real estate. Giving the buyer a future option to acquire the real estate may improve the initial postacquisition cashflow of the business, thereby improving the business's chances for success.

What to Do After the Sale

After they sell the family business, the owner and spouse should literally *leave town*. Take a cruise, go to the beach, go anywhere. Just don't stay home. It's okay to come back in two or three months—after some mental and emotional distance has been created between the owner and the former company. Many clients have ignored this advice, even coming to work the day after the sale! And within 90 days, they've all agreed: They should have left the business for a while. Former owners often feel anxious, angry, and depressed at how the new owners treat them.

Summary

Selling the family business is stressful and can be detrimental to the employees and the company. Some research, however, indicates that there can be positive results for the company and its employees—depending on how the transaction is managed and communicated and, especially, on how well people are able to handle change.

Getting the business ready to be sold in order to realize maximum value and reduce personal stress takes time—sometimes several years. Cleaning up the financial statements and having them audited three to five years *before* the company is sold is an important factor. Negotiating the sale of a business can be both exciting and frustrating. It's exciting when a successful deal benefits both the family and the business. It's frustrating when a lack of preparation causes a "good deal" to fall through, to the detriment of the family and the business.

References

1. *Inc.*, vol. 12, no. 11 (November 1990), p. 7.
2. *Inc.*, vol. 13, no. 10 (October 1991), p. 11.

16

Option 4: Selling to an Inside Group

The fourth possibility is to sell the business to an inside group: active family members, long-term key employees, or a combination of the two. This option is undoubtedly the hardest, most complex, most gut-wrenching, and most soul-searching path to take. It is also (potentially) the most rewarding, loving, caring, enlightening, empowering, financially satisfying, goodwill-generating, inspiring, and courageous of the four options.

The Leveraged Buyout

Many of the problems associated with gifting and with transferring the business through the estate plan can be avoided with an internal leveraged buyout (LBO).

The internal LBO, in all its many permutations and combinations, enables the family business to pay the current owner the value of his or her stock. Ownership may actually be transferred via gift (combined with a stock redemption), via purchase, via trusts, or via stock bonus from the company. The key element is that the *transfer* of ownership and control can be one transaction; the value received by the former owner, in a combination of financial arrangements, can be a separate set of transactions.

The underlying assumption here is that if the business is worth $5 million, the current owner will accept total consideration of $5 million (even if it comes wrapped in different packages). Unbundling the change in control (i.e., the ownership transfer) from the consideration paid allows a transfer of ownership to family members, while payments can be made (and secured) by the family business, its assets, and future earnings. The internal LBO offers many additional advantages:

- The entrepreneur is able to realize full value for the business.
- Personal financial security for the withdrawing owner can be established in a manner that works both for the business and for all family members.
- The successors make the commitment that the current owner seeks by obligating themselves to make future payments.
- Strings are cut; it's a healthier environment when family members become differentiated.
- New family heroes can be created, and family culture and values can be perpetuated.
- The owner's estate can be frozen for estate tax purposes; value can actually disappear from the estate, perhaps saving millions in future estate taxes.
- Equalization and wealth transfer plans can be developed for all family members; estate planning gets unbundled from business succession planning. The process is less messy and more understandable to everyone.
- The transaction can be more easily tax-planned; dollars saved in income taxes (by using contracts, as described in Chapter 19) can be retained by the business, thereby improving its chances for success in the future.
- The withdrawing owner and spouse have new opportunities for personal growth and shared wisdom.
- An internal LBO can often "match" the price and terms of any offers the owner is considering from an outside party.
- If the LBO is properly structured, even if the deal fails, the former owner can quickly step in and sell the business to outside buyers.

In my experience, there are only three times when it is advantageous to sell the business to an outside party: (1) when the seller can get "all cash" or "near cash" and walk away; (2) when the seller has no psychological connection to the future of the business; or (3) when the strategic fit is right and selling the business is the best way to capitalize on growth opportunities.

Some owners mistakenly believe that there are limited financing opportunities for the future of their often undercapitalized business. As traditional sources of financing from banks become more and more difficult (some say impossible) to obtain, selling the business may seem like the only alternative for its survival. However, creative alternatives abound—from industry-supplier sources to other family businesses to partnering arrangements, as we'll see in later chapters.

Variables to Resolve

Besides future financing, an internal LBO will need to resolve a number of key variables.

1. *Who are the buyers?*   Are the kids active? Are they ready to take over? Will the buyer group be "appointed" by the current owners, or will they work out ownership issues among themselves? If active in-laws are key employees, can they participate as direct owners, or will ownership be reserved in a spouse's name? Are long-term, key nonfamily employees to be considered as "interim owners"? That is, will they have ownership until a predetermined date (say, age 65) and then be subject to a shareholder's agreement requiring them to sell their shares back to the company?

2. *Will multiple buyouts need to be considered?*   If the current owner's brother (or sister) owns stock but has no family members active in the business, will the "active" side of the family attempt to buy out their inactive cousins, aunts, or uncles? What if the inactives do not want to sell?

3. *At what price, and on what terms, will the current owner realize financial independence (and security)?*   Can the current value of the business support lifestyle requirements? Can the business cashflow support the seller's needs without jeopardizing viability and growth?

4. *How will personal guarantees on existing debt be addressed?*   Will collateral be released (or pledged)? Will note holders accept substitute guarantors? Will a change in ownership trigger demand clauses for payoffs of existing notes or working-capital lines? Will new or additional financing be required? How will the LBO debt incurred affect the company's balance sheet and debt-to-equity ratios?

5. *Can the valuation of the business support the transaction from a tax perspective?*   Will the value be managed to "get to the right numbers"? If so, how will that be supported for tax purposes?

6. *Will the current owner walk away as if the business had been sold to a third party?*   Or will the owner stay involved, and if so, in what role?

7. *Which family members will participate in addressing and resolving peripheral issues?*   The LBO will usually need to be coordinated with other family issues such as estate planning, wealth transfer, equalization for inactive children (or siblings), spousal maintenance, and possibly concerns about divorce. Will a family council be the forum to discuss and communicate these issues?

8. *Who will put the deal together?*   Will long-time existing advisers be used? Will they fairly represent all the diverse family interests? If a family business consultant is employed, what qualifications are required? Will the consultant have incentives to accomplish results? Will an interdisciplinary approach be used with multiple advisers, all involved in their own piece of the deal? Or will an integrated approach be used with someone to carry the ball and coordinate the legal, tax, personal, and business cashflows; family, emotional, and psychological requirements; and financing and estate-planning issues?

9. *Will security devices and protective covenants serve their purpose?*   Will they be triggered if, after the transaction closes, the company's profits and/or cash-flows deteriorate below acceptable levels? How will parents feel if they have to

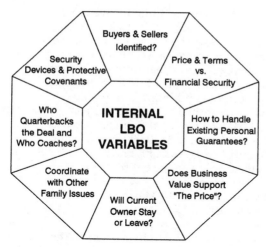

Figure 16-1.

foreclose on their son or daughter? What guarantees will be required and how financially stable is the guarantor?

The key to the internal LBO lies in the participants' ability to resolve the above issues. (See Figure 16-1.)

Case Study

John Kramer's recent success created his current dilemma. As a building materials distributor, he had seen his company's sales jump from $5 million to $20 million in five years. At age 60, John was pleased to discover he had attracted the attention of a larger, acquisition-minded distributor. After several visits, World Distributors offered John $4 million, an attractive price at 2.7 times book value.

Therein lay the problem. John's daughter, Carol, had been in the business for the past 10 years. In addition, his son-in-law (Carol's husband) and three other dedicated key employees had given John years of service. Although World had promised to retain all employees—and even provide attractive financial incentives to the key group—John wasn't sure what to do.

When he told Carol and the four others of the purchase offer, they indicated they would like to buy the business instead. John was pleased, but he wasn't sure they could manage a buyout. Even if they got financing, the loan might cripple the company's growth.

The employee group hired my firm to help them analyze and structure their proposal. They were surprised to learn they could do an LBO without any outside financing. Since World Distributors' offer was predicated on John's holding an installment note for $1.5 million, he agreed to do the same for the employee group.

John's accounting firm and the valuation department at my firm agreed that a redemption of John's stock (discussed in Chapter 17) in exchange for a $1.5 million note represented a fair market valuation of the stock; and that, on a per share basis, such a redemption was consistent with previous shareholder transactions and with industry comparables.

The balance of the $4 million was constructed with additional covenants wrapping tax-deductible compensation packages around the stock purchase agreement (described in Chapter 19). In John's case, the present value of the three offset contracts totaled $2.5 million: a noncompete agreement, a nonqualified supplemental pension plan, and a 5-year consulting contract at $150,000 per year (until John turns 65). The present value of the deal matched the $4 million that World Distributors had offered, although John would actually receive $5.75 million in total dollars over the life of the contracts.

The deal provided for John and his wife Martha personal financial security with long-term retirement income. John would receive $140,000 per year for 10 years (from age 60 to 70) from the noncompete agreement, and an additional $140,000 per year for 15 years (beginning at age 65) from the supplemental pension plan. Payments under these contracts would continue until the term of the contract ended, providing income to Martha in the event that John died before the end of the payment period.

For tax purposes, the payments for a noncompete agreement are considered ordinary income to the recipient and a deductible expense to the payer, amortized over the agreement's term. The acquisition of stock or company assets must be separate and distinct from the noncompete agreement. Compensation paid for the covenant not to compete must be distinguished from the price paid for the goodwill of the company, and must reflect economic reality in terms of the seller's age, knowledge, and ability to harm the new owners by competing with them.

Payments under the pension plans are deductible to the company, and subject to ordinary income tax treatment when received. Any funds informally set aside by the company usually remain an asset of the business and are reflected on the company's balance sheet. Benefits are expensed by the company as paid; therefore, this may be an effective way to provide an "off balance sheet" transaction and help preserve the financial ratios of the business.

Because the company no longer pays John's salary, the recovery of those funds helped redeem John's shares and pay for his other compensation packages. The tax benefits to the business (in a 34 percent bracket) created an additional savings for the company. The impact on the company's cashflow is affordable, and the bank is pleased that management continuity is intact.

Negotiating the Deal

While an internal LBO is being negotiated, the participants remain in an owner-employee relationship away from the bargaining table. The three to six months it takes to work through the issues identified earlier will put additional stress on all participants.

The owner will probably have some difficulty letting go as the closing approaches. He or she may seem to flip-flop on some issues and procrastinate on others. Family members and spouses need to be extra supportive and provide positive coaching during this period. Employees (family or nonfamily) should be especially sensitive to the owner's dilemmas, and should positively reinforce any progress that has been made. Often a spouse can indirectly be the key to getting a deal done—or not. If the spousal relationship is positive, and the spouse is in favor of the conceptual design, he or she can give strong support at home to the progress of the LBO at the business.

This is also an opportunity for prospective new owners to hone their team-building skills. Working with and gaining (or losing) respect for one another during the negotiating sessions will set the stage for their future relationships as owners.

Pricing the Deal

In some cases, like John Kramer's above, the internal LBO emerges as a response to an outside offer. "Matching" the outside deal becomes the main objective. In other cases, however, there is no offer to match. Both the seller and the buyer group begin with a minimum pricing approach, or floor, along with a ceiling, which is an opinion (usually from a business valuation firm or industry resource) of the fair market value of the business or the interests to be transferred (if less than 100 percent).

In another example illustrated in Figure 16-2, the *minimum* Jim and his wife Audrey need is $2 million as a present-value, after-tax amount at age 65 to support their desired standard of living for a projected 25 years. This "floor" would be equivalent to $2 million in cash, after taxes, by 65. However, that doesn't mean that's what they'll sell the business for and it doesn't reflect what the business is worth.

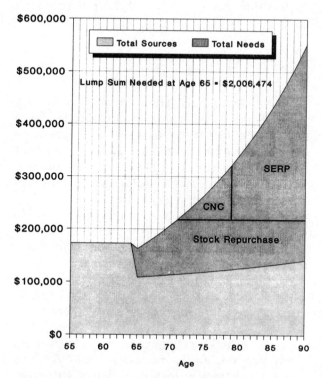

Figure 16-2. How much do Jim and Audrey need to retire? Building blocks to financial security.

If the business is worth only $1.5 million (below the floor), there's a problem. Why would anyone overpay for a business? On the other hand, if the business is worth $5 million (the ceiling), and Jim and Audrey need $2 million to live comfortably, then there are planning opportunities to address and resolve. For example, if through valuation engineering, the business is transferred to the next generation of owner-managers for $4 million, it would still represent a 20 percent discount off the "sale to an outsider" ceiling price. Jim and Audrey might direct the additional $2 million to inactive family members or to charity, or retain it for themselves as a well-deserved entrepreneurial reward. The discount given might reflect the past value contributed by the insider group that was now attempting to buy the business. In addition, it would represent Jim and Audrey's recognition of, and appreciation for, the dedication, loyalty, hard work, and success of that group.

One invaluable piece of advice to prospective buyers or new owners: *Always let the seller set the price if the buyer can set the terms.* That is, it's often psychologically important for the current owner to get his or her price. If the structure and terms of the deal can be established by the buyer, then the after-tax present value of the transaction can stay within the maximum limit that the buyer is willing to pay. For example, Jim and Audrey's "price" was $4 million, yet the business was valued at $3 million to $3.5 million (after the value was engineered). Pegging the transaction at $3 million and providing $1 million in additional covenants meets Jim and Audrey's "price," but keeps the buyer's cost at around $3.3 million.

Financing the Deal

Most family business transactions are leveraged. They involve borrowing money from an outside lender, the seller, or both. When an outside lender is involved, the money is usually loaned to the company, which uses the proceeds to buy the seller's stock under a stock redemption plan. The amount available is directly related to the ability of the company to borrow money. Existing company debt—lines of credit, inventory or equipment loans, long-term mortgages—will effect the company's borrowing capacity.

Lenders evaluate ownership succession loans more carefully than they do conventional credit decisions. They will want to know how a change in ownership affects existing management, and may view the transaction with some concern if they do not already know the future successors. If outside financing is a key part of the strategy, it pays to spend time in advance educating the lenders and letting them get to know the successors. Lenders should be involved in the strategy and planning; they are not likely to go along with a "done deal."

Most lenders use two basic criteria in making the credit decision to lend money: (1) ability of the borrower to generate sufficient cash to repay the loan during the term of the loan; and (2) availability to the lender of sufficient collateral to assure full recovery of the loan amount in the event of default.

Borrowers must present sufficient information to allow the lender to make a credit decision. The loan presentation usually consists of a business plan, which incorporates the previous discussions and concerns of the bank and describes how the new owners will address those concerns. The plan also outlines the proposed transaction and describes how the borrowers expect to repay the loan.

If the business value is comprised of intangible assets, the asset-based lender will need to be educated about how the valuation procedure calculated the intangibles' value. Many asset-based lenders often ignore intangible assets and focus solely on a borrower's tangible net worth. Intangible assets (such as trade names, favorable leases, and intellectual properties) may not be reflected on the company's balance sheet, even though they represent significant assets as part of an ongoing business or have value separate and apart from the business enterprise. A third-party valuation can help establish value for hidden intangible assets that can then be used as collateral in securing a loan.

If the sellers are willing to hold an installment note for some or all of the proceeds due, when there is already existing business debt, they will have to decide if they are willing to subordinate their position to the existing debtors. Cross-default provisions (as well as other security devices discussed in Chapter 21) can help protect sellers in a junior or subordinated position.

Some lenders ask sellers to subordinate any amounts due from nonqualified retirement plans and/or noncompete covenants *in addition to* the amount the sellers are willing to hold in an installment note. At that point it is probably wise to talk with another lender.

Many businesses attempt to obtain financing from the institution with which they have had an ongoing banking relationship. Although familiar lenders should be approached, there are often compelling reasons to consider multiple lenders as well. First, the company's regular bank may not be familiar with the successors; significant costs and delays can be incurred as the bank learns more about the proposed deal. Talking to several lenders at once allows each of the interested lenders to become familiar with the borrower at the same time and can reduce delays. Second, the regular bank may be having its own difficulties with banking regulators and so may be forced to offer less attractive pricing on the proposed loan. Finally, competition makes lenders hungrier. Lenders will often improve their proposed financing terms to obtain or retain the business of a mature, successful company.

Borrowers should not overlook nontraditional sources of financing: suppliers, manufacturers, and industry vendors may also be willing to act as lenders.

In one transaction involving key employees trying to buy out two elderly brothers, the key employees, a local CPA firm, and consultants from my firm made presentations to four banks in the midsize city where the business was located. The loan request was for $2 million, 50 percent of the $4 million deal. There was no long-term debt in the retail company; the key employees expected to sign personal guarantees and would even have agreed to salary "caps." The company's annual cashflow had been stable for the past eight years at about $700,000 a year.

Although the transaction, at roughly six times cashflow, may have seemed high, the key employees believed there was a lot of potential in this stable company that had been "coasting" for the past few years. Also, part of the $4 million was in tax-deductible compensation arrangements for the sellers, which brought the after-tax cost of the deal in line with industry norms. Three of the banks insisted that supplemental pension plans for the two sellers be subordinated to the bank loan and possibly not be paid out for seven years. The sellers had counted on that income to support their standard of living. In addition, the company would be required to maintain an annual cashflow of $840,000 (20 percent above its current level). Other restrictive covenants accompanied the loan offers.

This retail company ultimately sold its $3 million in receivables to a third party for 98 cents on the dollar and used the proceeds to pay $2 million to the sellers as down payment. The deal closed soon after. Selling the receivables proved to be prudent. Initially, the sellers had agreed to carry back a note and thought they would be in a subordinate position behind any of the banks used. But because the receivables were sold and no outside financing was needed, the sellers got their 50 percent down payment and were in a senior position on the note they held. The sellers and buyers also agreed on performance covenants as additional security behind the loan.

Timing

If there is sufficient time (five to seven years), the internal LBO can be substantially prefunded for the benefit of the withdrawing owner. Prefunding allows the company to set reserves aside specifically for the purpose of redeeming a shareholder's interest. Setting aside the reserves in advance provides the seller additional financial security—whether the funds are all paid out at retirement age or, more likely, paid out over a period of time. Funds not needed can continue to earn interest until paid out.

Often a grantor trust or rabbi trust (discussed in Chapter 10) can be an effective accumulation vehicle for this purpose. Corporate deposits to the trust are made with after-tax dollars, remain a corporate asset, and stay on the company's balance sheet. Deposits in the properly drafted rabbi trust are deductible to the company and taxable to the recipient as they are received.

The internal LBO takes approximately six months to complete when all conditions—motivated sellers and committed buyers—are right. It just may take five years for the conditions to be right.

Summary

The successful internal LBO uses a variety of different methods. Each method has different effects on the company's balance sheet. Maintaining the integrity of the balance sheet and reserving capital for growth are two determinants for choosing the proper method.

PART 4
Techniques of Ownership Transfer

17

Transfer Technique 1: Transfers of Stock

Significant tax consequences attach to the particular entity form chosen for a business. Although income taxes during the company's operating life generally drive a number of decisions, estate and gift tax considerations, especially during a change in ownership and control, are equally important.

A number of different entities are available to the family business owner: sole proprietorships, general or limited partnerships, C corporations, S corporations, and limited-liability companies.

The entity or entities chosen will depend on a number of factors—business considerations, banking requirements, personal and family income needs, estate-planning concerns, and, of course, income tax issues. In some cases, multiple entities can be effective in providing solutions to complex family problems. This chapter focuses on corporate forms of business ownership. (Partnerships are addressed in Chapter 22.)

Sole proprietors are treated for tax purposes as owning the assets of the business directly. From an estate-planning and succession-planning perspective, sole proprietorships do not provide any of the advantages that operating as a separate business entity provides. These advantages include:

- *Transferability.* Shares or units in an entity are easier to transfer; the "whole" may be worth more than the sum of its parts.

- *Management.* Decision making can be separated from ownership with voting and nonvoting shares, or with different classes of stock having different voting or distribution rights.

- *Bifurcation.* Family members' different needs can be addressed when different interests owned have different attributes. For example, growth interests can be separated from income interests.

- *Valuation.*   Lack of marketability and minority discounts may be used to reduce the value of the component divided interests, thereby reducing transfer taxes.

As we have seen, the corporate entity is more than the sum of its assets. The corporation is an entity with its own "life," reputation, and value.

Ownership of the corporation is evidenced through the issuance of stock certificates owned by shareholders. The stock certificates represent an increment, or a piece of the total value of the corporate entity. The value of that incremental piece of the total doesn't have a specific, fixed dollar amount. Even among publicly traded companies, share price changes daily as a result of variables such as earnings and the public's perception of the company's or industry's performance. Moreover, the value of corporate shares can change depending on whether they represent a minority interest in the company or a position of control. Marketability of shares, or the lack of it, also plays a role in the company's value.

The incremental pieces of the company (i.e., shares of stock) can be transferred one at a time or in large blocks. Most family business stock transfers have two objectives: to transfer a sufficient number of shares to the designated successor, or successors, in order to give them control of the business; and to compensate the current owner enough so that he or she can enjoy financial independence after the transfer.

The transfer of stock to the successor may *not* be the same transaction that creates financial independence for the retiring owner. For example, gifting stock can be one transaction; salary continuation payments to the retiring owner from the corporation through a nonqualified plan is a separate transaction. Together, however, they can satisfy the two objectives.

Common Corporate Forms

The general characteristics of a corporation that distinguish it from a partnership are continuity of life, centralization of management, liability for corporate debts limited to corporate property, and freely transferable interests.

Many family businesses operate as C corporations, commonly known as closely held corporations. Their income is subject to corporate income tax, and their earnings are distributed as dividends. A closely held corporation, for tax purposes, is defined as having 50 percent of its stock owned by five or fewer individuals. The corporation derives most of its income or revenues from business operations or activities.

If a closely held corporation derives 60 percent or more of its income from investment activities (such as dividends, interests, rents, or royalties), it is called a personal holding company. The personal holding company must distribute most of its income each year in the form of dividends to its stockholders; otherwise, it can be subject to a 28 percent penalty tax in addition to the general corporate tax.

An S corporation is defined as a small business corporation that:

- Has no more than 35 shareholders (U.S. citizens, resident individuals, estates, or certain types of trusts)
- Has only one class of stock, although the one class may be distinguished by voting and nonvoting rights
- Pays no corporate-level tax
- Taxes the shareholders directly on the income of the company whether or not the income is distributed

S corporation stock may be owned by qualifying trusts, including voting trusts. The newly created S corporation is exempt from the corporate general and penalty taxes that C corporations incur. Thus it may be an effective vehicle as a holding company for family investments.

Planning with S Corporations

The S corporation has less flexibility than the C corporation in allocating income, since it can distribute only one class of stock. However, through SERPs and other deferred compensation plans and sale-leaseback arrangements for business assets, some of these planning restrictions can be circumvented.

An S corporation can function as a family investment company or as a family office (discussed in Chapter 28). Figure 17-1 shows how an S corporation can coordinate with estate planning. Another method of using the S entity—as a corporate general partner in a family limited partnership—is illustrated in Figure 17-2.

When stock in an S corporation is placed in a grantor-retained annuity trust (discussed in Chapter 25), additional planning opportunities are created. The income from the S corporation is retained by the grantor for a number of years, while the value of the stock may not be subject to estate tax on the grantor's death.

Using an ESOP for Business Perpetuation

An ESOP (employee stock ownership plan) is a way for business owners to sell stock in their company to employees. The ESOP is an employee benefit plan designed to purchase stock from the company or its stockholders. As shown in Figure 17-3, the ESOP may or may not be leveraged. In a nonleveraged ESOP, the company establishes a trust fund and makes tax-deductible contributions of stock or cash, up to a maximum of 15 percent of payroll. If cash is deposited, the trust can then use the money to buy shares from existing stockholders.

Alternatively, in a leveraged ESOP the trust can borrow funds from a qualified lending institution and can use those funds to buy shares from existing shareholders. The company then makes tax-deductible contributions

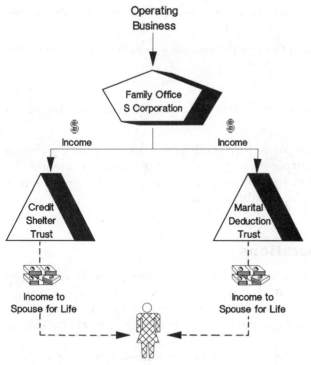

Figure 17-1. Using a family office S corporation for estate planning.

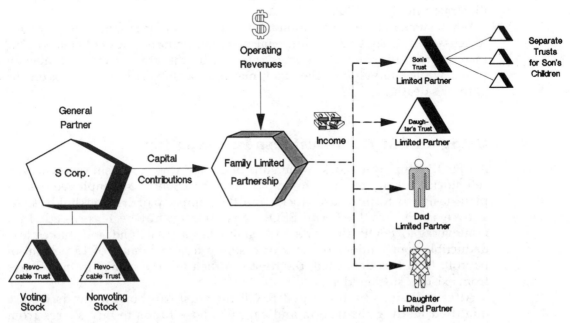

Figure 17-2. Using a family limited partnership for estate planning.

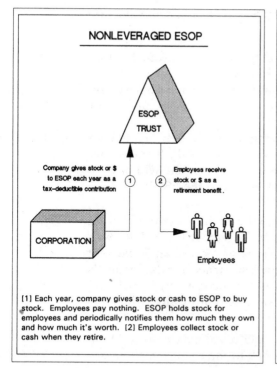

NONLEVERAGED ESOP

ESOP TRUST

Company gives stock or $
to ESOP each year as a
tax–deductible contribution (1)

(2) Employess receive
stock or $ as a
retirement benefit.

CORPORATION

Employees

[1] Each year, company gives stock or cash to ESOP to buy stock. Employees pay nothing. ESOP holds stock for employees and periodically notifies them how much they own and how much it's worth. [2] Employees collect stock or cash when they retire.

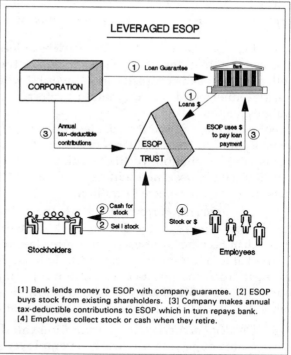

LEVERAGED ESOP

CORPORATION

(1) Loan Guarantee

Bank

(1) Loans $

(3) Annual
tax–deductible
contributions

ESOP TRUST

ESOP uses $
to pay loan (3)
payment

(2) Cash for
stock

(2) Sell stock

(4) Stock or $

Stockholders

Employees

[1] Bank lends money to ESOP with company guarantee. [2] ESOP buys stock from existing shareholders. [3] Company makes annual tax-deductible contributions to ESOP which in turn repays bank. [4] Employees collect stock or cash when they retire.

Figure 17-3. Comparing the mechanics of a nonleveraged ESOP to a leveraged ESOP.

to the trust, which uses the money to repay the loan. One of the most important features of an ESOP is the market it creates for shareholder stock.

The first step in considering an ESOP is to determine goals. An ESOP is a complicated transaction; when it "fits," it provides some unique solutions for family business problems, including substantial tax savings and a provision for shareholders to withdraw capital from their businesses in a tax-efficient manner. Often an ESOP stimulates a company to be more productive and efficient as employees become part owners. Key employees can be rewarded through an ESOP for helping the business succeed; this can sometimes serve to tie in key people who want an ownership incentive. But an ESOP doesn't always "fit," and many owners tell horror stories about their ESOP experience—usually indicating either that they didn't originally understand the ESOP or that it wasn't the right solution to the problem.

Important factors that influence the ESOP decision include:

- The number of shares that existing shareholders are willing to sell
- The ability of the company to obtain debt or other financing
- The ability of the company to service the ESOP debt and still grow
- The willingness of senior management to share ownership
- The size of the transaction as a percentage of gross payroll of the covered employees

The ESOP brings with it a number of tax incentives, including rollovers, tax-preferred borrowing, and dividend deductions.

1. *Tax-free rollovers.*   If the ESOP owns at least 30 percent of the outstanding shares after the transaction, the proceeds of the sale will not be taxable to the seller as long as the proceeds are reinvested within 12 months in a domestic security (either bonds or common or preferred stock of a qualifying private or public company).

For example, assume the business owner is trying to decide between having the corporation redeem shares or selling the shares to an ESOP. If the owner plans to sell $1 million worth of stock to the corporation, he or she will have to pay $300,000 in taxes and will net about $700,000. A sale to the ESOP, tax-free, nets the owner the entire $1 million.

2. *Tax-preferred borrowing.*   Both the principal and interest paid on an ESOP loan are tax-deductible to the borrower. Moreover, if the ESOP owns more than 50 percent of each corporate class of stock or more than 50 percent of the value of all outstanding stock, half the interest earned by the lender is exempt from income tax. If the lender shares the tax savings with the borrower, the ESOP loan will have a below-market rate. For example, in some cases the interest rate to the ESOP is 80 percent of prime.

3. *Dividend deduction.*   A corporation can deduct dividends paid to ESOP participants by paying dividends on employer stock to the trust, which passes them through to the participants.

An ESOP may indirectly change the way a company is managed. Employees must have the right to vote stock (allocated to their account) on major decisions: business merger, consolidation, recapitalization, liquidation, or sale of the business or substantially all of its assets. A board-appointed committee of employees normally votes the ESOP shares. With the ESOP shares representing a new ownership group, the original owners can no longer run the company for their benefit alone. The CEO shareholder may have to decide between no ESOP (with high salaries, perks, and benefits) and an ESOP. This means running a tight company and managing it for a higher stock value growth rate.

The ESOP provides a vehicle for the controlled sale of the business, either gradually or all at once. Ideally, it inspires increased employee loyalty and commitment to the company as well as higher productivity. Allocation of the company contribution is based on compensation, which means higher-paid managers usually wind up with the greatest number of employee-designated shares.

The ESOP is not for everyone. A major limitation is that it requires a corporate commitment to fund an increasing repurchase liability as the value of the employees' shares increase. On retirement, the employees can put the shares back to the trust, and the trust must be able to repurchase the shares. The ESOP causes a dilution of ownership for the existing shareholders. This dilution will affect sales and liquidation proceeds; the dilutive effect is somewhat offset by the increased earnings from the tax benefits of the plan. Finally, the ESOP may be expensive to set up and administer, since an annual valuation of the shares must be done by an outside party.

When an ESOP fits, however, it creates a ready market for an owner's shares and provides a tax-deductible method of transferring ownership to employees.

Stock Redemptions

A stock redemption occurs when the corporation repurchases shares held by a selling shareholder. The price should be at fair market value, determined by an appraisal or by formula, such as in a shareholder's agreement. The repurchase may be in cash, or the parties may decide to pay it over time.

In Figure 17-4, the corporation initially issued 100 shares, all owned by the sole shareholder. Over time, the sole shareholder's son came into the business and received a gift of 10 shares, so that Dad owned 90 percent and Son owned 10 percent.

Dad now wants to retire, provide for his retirement years, and turn control of the business over to Son. Dad enters into a stock redemption agreement, allowing the corporation to repurchase his 90 shares and retire them as treasury stock in the corporation. The 10 shares owned by Son prior to the redemption now comprise 100 percent of the outstanding shares of the corporation.

Dad's transaction was with the corporation and the corporation paid him for the stock. The payment may have been in cash, or it may have been a note. Either will provide Dad with an income stream.

The result is that Son has realized Dad's objective of transferring control and Dad has achieved value from the transfer of the shares. Since Dad is now no longer employed by the corporation, the corporation will no longer have to provide compensation and benefits for him. The corporation can use those dollars to fund the repurchase obligation to Dad.

As for tax consequences, Dad will recognize a gain equal to the redemption price minus the price Dad originally paid for the shares (his basis), if he can avoid the attribution problems discussed below. Son's basis will "carry over" and will be the basis that Dad had in acquiring the 10 shares in the corporation that he transferred to Son.

Direct Sale

If basis, or attribution, is an important consideration in the transaction, family business owners may want to consider a direct cross-purchase sale rather than a redemption. A direct sale of stock bypasses the corporation; stock is sold directly to an individual, as illustrated in the second part of Figure 17-4.

1.) Stock Redemption

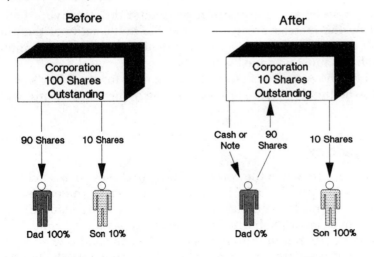

2.) Cross–Purchase

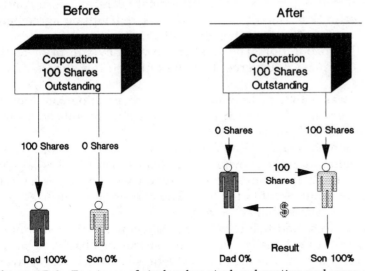

Figure 17-4. Two types of stock sales: stock redemption and cross-purchase.

In this example, the 100 shares that Dad owns are sold directly for their fair market value to Son, whose basis in those shares is equal to the price he paid. (If Son later sells those shares to a third party, his gain will only be the amount in excess of his purchase price.) Dad will recognize a gain equal to the price paid by Son minus the price he originally paid for the shares.

Figure 17-5 summarizes some of the pros and cons of various transfer methods.

	ESOP	REDEMPTION	CROSS–PURCHASE
Pros	Full transfer price is deductible.	Least complicated.	No dilution.
	Provides benefit and incentive to employees and may increase productivity.	Funds to buy stock are usually more readily available from the corporation.	Can be funded with life insurance without incurring corporate AMT.
	Stockholders can defer tax on gain from sale.	Can retain S status.	Can retain S status.
	Tax benefit of noncash contributions provides cashflow to the company.		
	Can make dividend payments deductible.		
Cons	Ownership of nonselling shareholders is diluted.	Attribution rules may cause sale to be taxed as a dividend.	Individual buyer may not have the necessary funds to buy.
	Family will have to answer to nonfamily stockholders.	Sale is fully taxable to the selling stockholder.	Sale is fully taxable to the selling stockholder.
	May be difficult to obtain ESOP financing.	No part of redemption payments is deductible.	No part of the purchase price is deductible.
	Repurchase liability grows as stock value increases.	Ownership of remaining shareholders may be unintentionally increased.	
	Relatively expensive to administer.	If funded with life insurance, proceeds may generate corporate AMT.	
	Will terminate S election.		

Figure 17-5. Comparison of three transfer methods: ESOP, redemption, and cross-purchase.

Avoiding Two Pitfalls

Accidental Dilution

When considering a stock redemption, a family business should be careful to avoid an accidental dilution of its stake and an enhancement of other shareholders' positions.

In a typical redemption transaction, the owner transfers some of his or her stock to a son or daughter, and then the corporation redeems the owner's shares, leaving the child as the outstanding shareholder, with 100 percent. Sometimes, however, a key employee or other family member has received shares throughout the years. In this case, the ramifications of a redemption must be considered carefully by all shareholders.

Assume that Dad started his company in 1935, and was originally issued 100 shares. Throughout the years, Dad transferred 10 shares to a key employee who provided valuable service. In the 1960s, Son joined the business and Dad

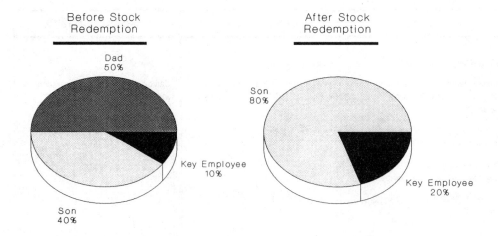

	Before Stock Redemption			After Stock Redemption	
Shares	Percent			Shares	Percent
90	90.0%	Family Ownership		40	80.0%
10	10.0%	Key Employee Ownership		10	20.0%
100	100.0%	Total		50	100.0%

Figure 17-6. Minority shareholder considerations in a stock redemption: beware of accidental enhancement or dilution.

transferred 40 of his shares to Son. The resulting ownership, before a stock redemption, left Dad with 50 percent, Son with 40 percent, and Key Employee with 10 percent. (See Figure 17-6.)

Dad died in 1978 and in order to provide income to Dad's wife, his stock was redeemed by the corporation. This arrangement seemed logical at the time, as the corporation had the necessary funds for the redemption.

However, one important feature was overlooked. After the redemption, Dad's 50 shares, having been repurchased by the corporation, were no longer outstanding and became treasury shares. Moreover, with those remaining 50 shares representing *all* the outstanding stock of the corporation, Son's 40 shares now represented 80 percent of the ownership and Key Employee's 10 shares represented 20 percent. Key Employee's ownership in the company had *doubled* through the redemption of the stock!

As noted earlier, a minority interest in a closely held company has limited value. How will the key employee realize value from the shares owned? Without a preexisting agreement, what's to prevent the key employee from transferring those shares to family members who are not active in the business? What is to prevent the key employee's spouse, after the death of key employee, from demanding dividends for the value of the shares from the company?

If the key employee received shares as an incentive, then a repurchase agreement for those shares *during the lifetime of the employee* should also be provided. Then the employee can be assured of realizing value from the shares, and the corporation and family members can be assured that they will not be involved with the key employee's spouse or children in the event of death, disability, or termination of the employee.

Attribution

Attribution among family members must also be considered and carefully analyzed to avoid unexpected tax consequences. Attribution is especially important when considering the estate tax implications of the transfer.

Section 302 of the Internal Revenue Code mandates that if a corporation redeems all its outstanding shares (so that the shareholders' interest in the corporation is terminated), the amount paid by the corporation to a shareholder or to his or her estate will be treated as an exchange for stock, not as a dividend. In other words, the redemption will be treated as a capital transaction for tax purposes.

The catch is that the corporation must redeem not only all shares actually owned by the original shareholder but also all shares *constructively* owned by his or her family. Shares owned by a beneficiary of the original shareholder are considered to be owned by the shareholder.

Assume that parents, Jack and Judy, each own 48 percent of the corporation's stock, and that daughter, Jean, owns 4 percent. Jack and Judy own Jean's shares for purposes of the attribution rules, so Jack and Judy's estate is deemed to own a total of 100 percent of the shares. Therefore, redemption of the 96 percent of the shares actually owned by Jack and Judy will be treated, not as a full redemption of stock, but as a partial redemption, subject to dividend treatment.

Under family attribution rules, shares owned by a spouse, children, grandchildren, or parents are deemed to be owned by the shareholder. A full redemption would be eligible for capital gain treatment; a partial redemption would be subject to dividend treatment. In either case, the corporation *cannot* deduct the price paid for the purchase of shares.

Since the IRS restored favorable capital gain treatment—28 percent versus ordinary income taxed at 31 percent—the impact of having the transaction viewed as a dividend versus a capital gain may be an important point.

Rules regarding *family attribution* therefore create a penalty provision if capital gains treatment is disallowed. This will be an important issue to consider in the future if capital gains continue to be taxed significantly differently than dividends.

There are three ways to avoid attribution of stock ownership among family members:

1. The shareholder must retain no interest in the corporation, except as a creditor, immediately after the redemption.

2. The shareholder cannot acquire any interest within 10 years after the date of redemption.

3. The shareholder must file a waiver agreement with the IRS that if a redeem-ing shareholder acquires a forbidden interest within the 10-year period, the IRS will be notified.

Be cautious of attribution through partnerships when shareholders are partners in other ventures with other shareholders of the family business. Although there are additional rules regarding family attribution, the primary issue with the IRS is to demonstrate that the redeeming shareholder's principal purpose was not to avoid federal income tax.

18

Transfer Technique 2: Asset Sales

In some cases, an asset sale can be used to split off growth assets or to separate operating assets from accumulated earnings of the company.

Which assets should be transferred in an ownership succession plan? The answer is operating assets—those used in the operation of the business. Which assets should be retained? Those that are not involved in the operation of the business: excess cash, receivables, real estate that may be leased to the new owners, and any other assets not used in the business on a daily basis.

Assume the objective is to transfer "the business" to family members. First, the new owners form a new corporation, probably a Subchapter S corporation. Their new corporation purchases operating assets from the current owner's C corporation. If the new owners have sufficient cash to put in their new company, they might pay cash for the assets they acquire. Precious cash, however, may be required for initial working capital, so it's more likely that the new owners will sign a note for the difference between the sale price of the assets acquired and a cash down payment. This installment note will produce income for the original corporation until the note is paid off.

Ownership of the family business has not changed. What has changed is that the operating assets have been sold. The name of the family business may also be transferred to the new owners, especially if it is important for the new company to use it. If the name of the corporation is transferred, then the "old" corporation must adopt a new name and record it with the state's corporation commissioner.

Note that *none* of the stock in the "old" corporation has changed hands. If Dad owned 100 shares prior to the sale of the assets, Dad will still own 100 shares after the sale of the assets. Figure 18-1 illustrates such a transfer. Prior to the transfer, Dad owned 1000 shares of Smith Steel Supply, Inc., and

ASSET SALE

BEFORE:

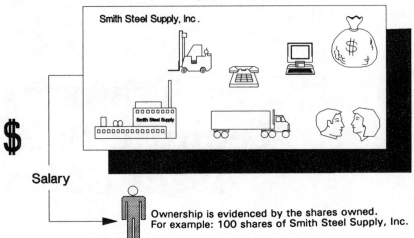

Family Business Corporation

Smith Steel Supply, Inc.

$

Salary

Ownership is evidenced by the shares owned.
For example: 100 shares of Smith Steel Supply, Inc.

AFTER:

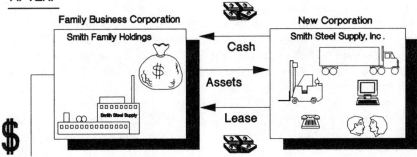

Family Business Corporation

Smith Family Holdings

New Corporation

Smith Steel Supply, Inc.

Cash

Assets

Lease

$

Revenues

Ownership in Smith Family Holdings
doesn't change, even though
the name changes. The current
shareholders still own
100 shares.

New owners own the shares
of the new corporation, which
may do business as
Smith Steel Supply, Inc.

Revenues: Management fees,
            dividends, etc.

Figure 18-1.

received a salary from the business. The corporation's assets included the office building and warehouse, business inventory, trucks and other rolling stock, cash in the bank, receivables, company personnel, and current work in progress.

Mom and Dad have determined that they are financially dependent on the business. The real estate owned by the corporation has probably appreciated in value since Dad bought it. Also, the company has accumulated excess cash, which has been retained as a corporate asset, currently in certificates of deposit. Dad believes that Son, his successor, won't need all the corporate assets, so he plans to retain the real estate and existing cash, as well as receivables from prior sales.

Son forms a new S corporation, which enters into a purchase agreement with Dad's company for its operating assets, including the rolling stock, inventory, all personnel, work in progress, and finally the name of the business, Smith Steel Supply.

Dad's newly named corporation—Smith Family Holdings—leases the real estate to Smith Steel Supply, and even gives it an option to purchase the real estate after the installment note for the assets has been paid off.

Financing the Asset Purchase

Son's purchase of the assets from Dad's business may be financed in one of two ways:

1. Son goes to the local banker, who is happy to see the family business continue in the community, but is cautious about establishing a banking relationship with Son. If the bank provides Son's new corporation with a loan to acquire the assets from Dad's corporation, it may also require that the parents guarantee the loan.

A note of caution: The parents' loan guarantee may, at best, subject them to a gift tax on the deemed value of the guarantee and, at worst, cause some adverse estate tax consequences. Son's company may ask the bank to extend it a working-capital loan to meet payroll costs until sufficient revenues come into the corporation. This arrangement, if acceptable, has two advantages: Son can cash out Dad's company, and Son begins to build a banking relationship and establish his identity in the community as a new business owner. Hopefully, the bank will only insist on guarantees or collateral pledges for a limited time.

2. Dad's corporation can act as the bank, selling assets to Son's company in exchange for a note from Son's corporation (and personally guaranteed by Son). Dad's company might also provide Son's company with the working-capital loan so Son can meet payroll. The notes, amortized over a period of years, and the rent Son pays for use of the business real estate provide an income stream to Dad's corporation.

Tax Treatment of Different Kinds of Assets

In an asset sale, *goodwill* represents the excess of purchase price over the value of the assets. Goodwill can neither be deducted nor depreciated by the buyer, although it does become part of basis. In the event that Son sells the assets to someone else, goodwill is added to basis and results in less capital gain for him. Generally, the buyer wants to allocate as little as possible to goodwill.

If Dad's company used accelerated methods of depreciation rather than straight-line depreciation, upon sale of its assets the "excess" depreciation will be "recaptured" as ordinary income by Dad's corporation and taxed accordingly.

Liabilities of the Seller

In an asset sale, unknown corporate liabilities (including environmental cleanup costs) usually remain with the corporation. Sometimes the buyer acquires specific liabilities, such as mortgages, as part of the transaction. Often, receivables and payables are not acquired, so the seller is responsible for collecting receivables and writing checks for existing payables.

One of the disadvantages of an asset sale is the potential for future lawsuits, which can still be brought against the owner of either corporation. Although indemnifications, representations, and warranties may protect the buyer and seller, they won't stop someone from suing.

Owner's Role After an Asset Sale

What is important after an asset sale is that ownership of the original corporation has not changed. Dad still owns the same 100 shares he owned prior to selling the assets. Figure 18-2 outlines the transaction and an allocation of the purchase price, and provides a brief summary of the tax treatment.

In Dad's new role as property manager for the real estate assets in the corporation, his corporate income is derived from collecting previous receivables, rent, payments on the note from Son's corporation, and interest on the corporation's certificates of deposit. Dad may even decide to make other investments on behalf of the corporation's other shareholders. To the extent that he is actively involved in the business ventures in which he invests, he may be able to draw an ongoing salary from the business.

With his former employees now working for Son's company, Dad's corporation is left with only one employee: Dad. If the income he draws is treated as compensation, Dad may also be eligible to shelter a portion of corporate revenues through tax-deductible deposits into a new defined-benefit retirement plan.

Let's say Dad has a five-year installment note to a newly formed corporation

	SMITH STEEL SUPPLY, INC.

	Fair Market Value		Allocation of $250,000 Purchase Price	Tax Treatment for Buyer – New Smith Steel Supply, Inc.
	Retained by Seller Smith Family Holdings	Sold to Son's New Company		
Cash and CDs	$500,000			
Accounts Receivable	70,000			
Inventory		$145,000	$145,000	Deducted When Sold
Land and Buildings	1,000,000			
Machinery and Equipment		100,000	100,000	Depreciable
Furniture and Fixtures		25,000	25,000	Depreciable
Vehicles		30,000	30,000	Depreciable
Goodwill			100,000	Nondeductible
	$1,570,000	$300,000	$400,000	

Figure 18-2. Elements of the asset sale.

owned by Son. Additional compensation is in a ten-year noncompetition agreement between Dad *personally* and Son's corporation. Son's corporation is paying $100,000 a year to Dad's corporation as rent for the use of business real estate. Dad's company is earning another $40,000 in interest on corporate cash which has been invested in certificates of deposit. The asset purchase note creates another $40,000 of annual income to the corporation for five years. There's no debt on the corporate real estate, so the total of $180,000 flowing into Dad's corporation is taxable income.

The accountant has agreed that, at age 60, Dad can reasonably expect his corporation to pay him a $30,000 salary for property management. Dad can live nicely on the noncompete payments he receives from Son's corporation, plus the $30,000 salary. He therefore wants to defer, on a pretax basis if possible, some of the excess corporate funds and let them accumulate, to be drawn in later years.

After the sale of assets, Dad's corporation establishes a new defined-benefit pension plan, designed to recognize his past years of service. Smith Steel Supply never had a pension plan while Dad was running the business. Therefore, according to actuarial tables, he will have to deposit approximately $100,000 a year for five years to provide a $55,000 annual pension benefit beginning when he turns 65. Dad's annual pension benefit will last for his and his spouse's expected lifetimes.

Dad's corporation takes a tax deduction for the contribution funded indirectly by the five-year interest-only installment note to his company. The note will be amortized in years 6 through 10. If Dad continues to work, he can continue to fund the pension plan beyond his age 65 by systematically continuing to deposit some of the corporate income into the plan. At the end of year 10, the plan will be funded to its maximum and Dad will have transferred additional corporate value to the pension plan on a tax-deductible basis. Dad will still need to do additional planning for the real estate and corporate CDs.

What about taxes on the $180,000 of corporate income? The corporation pays Dad a $30,000 salary and $100,000 gets deducted as a pension contribution; therefore, the corporation has $50,000 of annual taxable income, taxed at a 15 percent bracket.

The pension trust receives $100,000 annually and purchases more certificates of deposit in the pension plan's name; the interest compounds tax deferred inside the pension plan. Dad is trustee of his pension plan. Assuming the $100,000 earns 8 percent interest each year, by the end of year 10 there would be almost $1.5 million in the pension trust.

The $1.5 million can be paid out as a lump sum, as an annuity for life, or as a joint and survivor annuity for the remainder of Mom's and Dad's lives. Subject to an excess-accumulations tax, the pension funds left over after their death could be distributed to various family members through the estate.

The ability to install a new qualified plan may provide an attractive alternative to corporate liquidation after a sale of assets. The pension trust defers taxation while providing tax-free compounding. (See Figure 18-3.)

A Split-Off Can Solve Family Problems

Sometimes a split-off of assets can help conquer problems that threaten family unity. In a *split-off*, one owner retains a stake in the original company and no stock in the new company, while the other owner gives up all claims in the original company in exchange for shares of the new entity. The arrangement differs from a *spin-off*, in which the owners of the original company keep the same proportion of stock in the new entity as they had in the original.

A split-off can effectively solve family conflicts when the business has multiple locations, branch operations, or different operational components. The division can be especially attractive when there are several successors to the business who do not work well together. There are several requirements to keep in mind when a split-off is being considered:

- The division of the business must have a valid business purpose.
- Immediately after the division, both corporations must actively conduct a trade or business.
- The business being divided must have been actively conducted for five years before the distribution is made.

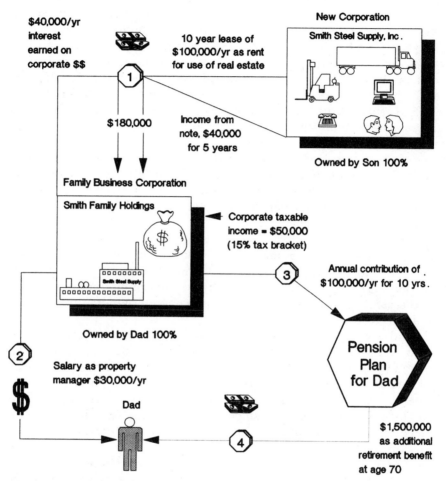

Figure 18-3. Alternative to liquidation after an asset sale.

- The parent corporation must distribute all its stock in the newly formed corporation.
- The distribution of stock from the new corporate division must not be a device for distributing earnings and profits.

David Boyd recently learned the value of a split-off in preserving family harmony. His younger son, Kevin, had been managing the family's building-materials distribution business for seven years. David's older son, Steve, had wandered through a variety of jobs and still had not quite found himself. David worried about Steve and invited him to join the family business. Steve accepted.

Kevin, who considered the business his company, resented his older brother's new involvement and found numerous reasons to criticize his behavior. Steve, on the other hand, resented Kevin's favorite-son status. Kevin was further dismayed when, a year later, Dad began to consider transferring the business in equal parts to his two sons. Previously, he had made a gift of 20 percent to Kevin and 10 percent to Steve and retained the rest of the stock.

Dad had noticed the boys' increasing sniping at family meetings and wondered if the business's recent downturn in sales was the result of their arguments. They seemed committed to sabotaging each other. Dad's temporary solution: Appoint each son as manager of one of his two warehouses, located about 45 miles apart. Outside consultants were then called in to design a more permanent solution.

After extensive interviews with family members, the consultants recommended dividing the business through a tax-free split-off, or corporate division. Even though the division created operational inefficiencies for the Boyds, it was less costly than a partnership, which would have allowed the sons' bickering to hurt the business.

The division involved an exchange of some assets of the corporate parent (Brother's, Inc.) for the stock of a new, wholly owned subsidiary (call it Other Brother's) created to acquire those assets. Existing assets were allocated between the parent company and the subsidiary. A determination of value for each set of the assets helped determine the percentage ownership each son would have in his respective company.

Steve surrendered his 10 percent of the stock in the parent company in exchange for new shares of Other Brother's. Dad surrendered half his 70 percent stake in the parent for shares of Other Brother's. Steve then owned 22 percent and Dad 78 percent of Other Brother's. The parent corporation is now owned 36 percent by Kevin and 64 percent by Dad. The exchange by the parent company of Dad's and Steve's stock for their interest in Other Brother's was a tax-free transaction under Section 355(a)(1) of the Internal Revenue Code. (See Figure 18-4.)

Under the Boyds' plan, each son can run his respective company without interference from the other brother. However, if the boys ever decide to put the two companies back together, they can. Dad is now free to proceed with his retirement planning. He can use different timing for each son to take over his respective company, and can structure a redemption of his shares in the two companies if he chooses, pegged to each son's readiness to assume full ownership.

In addition, the impact of dividing the business into fractional parts can reduce future estate taxes when Dad becomes a minority shareholder in the divided corporations. The value of stock of a minority shareholder may be discounted, resulting in a lower valuation in the estate and a reduced estate tax liability.

Now that both sons realize they will own their entire company eventually, they have a renewed sense of commitment to their corporation. Today family get-togethers are much more harmonious. As David's wife says, "We feel like a family again."

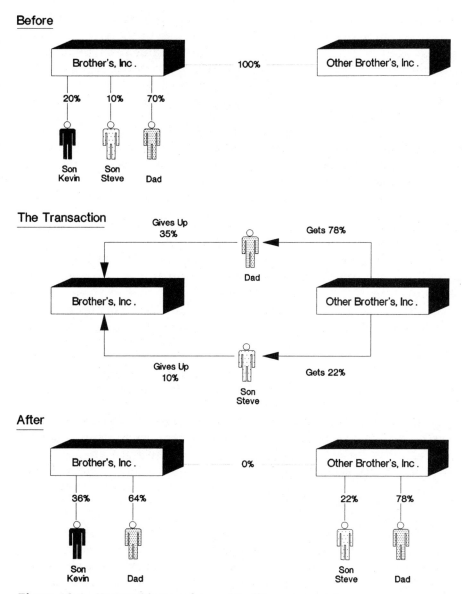

Figure 18-4. Nontaxable transfers: split-off (non-pro rata).

Liquidation Traps and Tricks

The Tax Reform Act of 1986 repealed a 1935 law known as the "general utilities rule." For 50 years the rule had provided a method of selling corporate assets, simultaneously liquidating the corporation, and recognizing a gain for tax purposes only once—at the shareholder level. The 1986 provisions recognize (and tax) gains (or losses) at the corporate level, whether or not a simultaneous liquidation occurs. On liquidation, the gain (or loss) is recognized again at the shareholder level.

The *corporate* gain from an asset sale at fair market value can now be taxed at a maximum federal corporate rate of 39 percent. Recaptures of accelerated methods of depreciation are taxed when the depreciated assets are sold. If a liquidation of the corporation occurs, the shareholders have to pay taxes on the corporate assets, in excess of their basis in the corporate stock. The combined federal and state corporate and personal income taxes could be well over 70 percent! Estate taxes at death could claim 55 percent of whatever is left. Understandably, shareholders are likely to look for ways to maintain the corporation after assets are sold. The routes are many.

One method, if the corporation can qualify as an operating business, is to elect to be taxed as an S corporation rather than a C corporation (see Chapter 17). If the corporation's only asset is a portfolio of marketable securities which are actively managed, a newly created S corporation may be an attractive means of avoiding the personal holding company tax. The 1991 Tax Simplification Act permits certain tax-free liquidations into parent S corporations.

Another alternative is to contribute the stock of the C corporation to a charitable remainder trust. The trust can subsequently liquidate the corporation (and pay tax once, at the corporate level). As we'll see in Chapter 26, the shareholders receive a charitable contribution tax deduction when the stock is placed in the trust, and can receive an income from the trust for the remainder of their (and their spouses') lives. At their death, the trust donates the principal to a charity.

A third alternative to liquidation is to use nonqualified plans, as described in Chapter 10. SERPs are especially flexible and can provide supplemental retirement benefits for key, long-term employees in both an S and a C corporation. In the above example, in addition to or in lieu of the defined-benefit plan, the SERP can provide another avenue for distributing tax-deductible corporate assets (at the corporate level).

For example, assume Dad's corporation's sole asset is real estate, which can be sold on an installment note to Daughter. (Daughter would raise the installment note payments by leasing her newly purchased real estate to her corporation.) Daughter's payments to Dad's corporation could be coordinated with a SERP in Dad's company. As Dad's company collected principal and interest from Daughter, it would offset (for tax purposes) that income by paying Dad a benefit established by the SERP plan.

Or Dad could use his C corporation as general partner in establishing a family limited partnership. The remaining assets in the C corporation could be used as a capital contribution to fund the limited partnership. The limited partners could be other family members or trusts established for family members. The partnership shifts partnership income (in this case, the rents received from the real estate that Dad used to capitalize the partnership) to other family members, shields assets from creditors, and possibly reduces the value of Dad's stock in his C corporation for estate tax purposes.

Tax-Free Exchange

Another possibility emerged for a business owner who sold her assets to a publicly traded corporation and retained the real estate. Karen entered into a 10-year lease with the acquisition company for the use of the property, installed the pension plan as described above, and provided herself with an effective tax immunization tool.

At the end of 10 years, Karen plans to exchange the stock in her corporation for stock in the acquisition company on a tax-free basis. Also, at the end of 10 years, she should have drained all the cash out of her corporation, leaving real estate as its only asset. By effecting a tax-free exchange with a publicly held company, Karen will avoid recognizing capital gains on the sale of real estate, and further avoid the double taxation on liquidation of her closely held business.

The tax-free exchange with the publicly held company may result in Karen's receiving unrestricted stock which can be sold at any time. Or she can elect to hold the stock and receive dividends. If she decides to sell the stock, her basis will be the very low basis in the stock of her own closely held company. Therefore, on a sale of stock, almost the entire sale price will be taxable. It will be up to Karen to decide if, when, and how she wants to sell the stock. In the event she dies with the stock in her estate, the estate will receive a "stepped-up basis" and Karen's spouse could then sell the stock with *no capital gain treatment* whatsoever.

As this example illustrates, a number of alternatives are available for liquidating a closely held business. Tax, pension, and estate implications vary widely, so owners must be sure to consider the impact their decision can have on their own future and that of their family.

A Spin-Off of Growth Assets

In some cases the tax-free reorganization of corporate assets, through either a split-off or a spin-off, can kill two birds with one stone: succession planning for active family members and wealth transfer and estate planning for parents.

A split-off or spin-off can be useful for more than resolving family disputes. Here are a number of possible scenarios: Assume the family's long-time core business, TE Inc., is an advertising and public relations firm. The company has been relatively stable—some would say flat, no growth. Business revenues and earnings, however, have been growing rapidly—through acquisition of other advertising and PR firms, primarily on the East Coast. Son and Daughter, both active, are highly successful in operating TE/NY, the new East Coast acquisition group. Dad doesn't want to "let go," as he believes he'll live forever. His primary interest, though, is in the original core business; he takes little interest in the new acquisitions. Mom is concerned with how the inactive children will be treated, since the business value represents most of Mom and Dad's estate. The active kids worry about estate taxes as they continue to succeed and build the business. They know Uncle Sam may claim up to 55 percent of the value they create.

A likely solution here—one that allows Dad to stay in control of the core business—is a spin-off in which the "growth" subsidiary is separated from its "no growth" parent. (See Figure 18-5.) Mom and Dad's percentage ownership in the two companies is identical following the spin-off. Mom and Dad can then gift the low-value stock in the fast-growing TE/NY to their kids. Maximum estate tax savings can be generated by gifting all Mom and Dad's stock to the kids shortly after the spin-off is completed (using unified credits to reduce or eliminate gift taxes).

Before

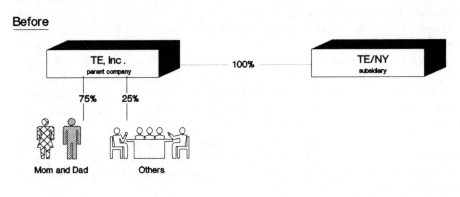

The Transaction

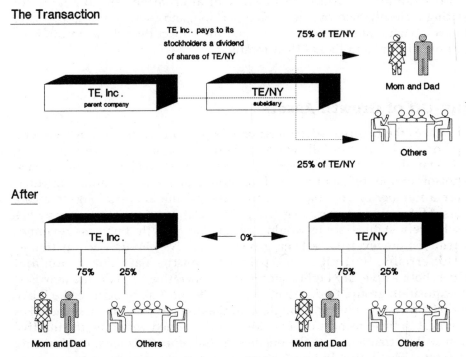

Figure 18-5. Nontaxable transfers: spin-off (pro rata).

Mom and Dad continue to control the original core business, which satisfies Dad's desire to stay active, but the parent company does not generate growth in the taxable estate. The kids now control the growth company, and can pursue their growth and acquisition plans without Uncle Sam's estate tax representative peering over their shoulders. And if stock is gifted to inactive as well as active kids, the inactive children can receive dividends from TE/NY, which will satisfy Mom's concerns.

Finally, a rapidly growing asset has been removed from the taxable estate. The results of estate planning centered around the spin-off are shown in Figure 18-6.

Dad's original no-growth company could provide services to, and receive fees from, the growth company. As an alternative, the no-growth company could be recapitalized into common shares (gifted to the children) and preferred shares (which Dad retains), so that the effects of inflation would be kept out of Dad's estate as well. If recapitalized, the no-growth company could enter into a stock purchase agreement with Dad for his preferred shares at death. The common stock (in no-growth) could be owned by all children, perhaps some with voting and others with nonvoting shares. Or the common stock could be owned in trust for the children, and the grandchildren, so the family enterprise could be perpetuated for many years.

If the stock purchase agreement were funded with insurance, Mom would

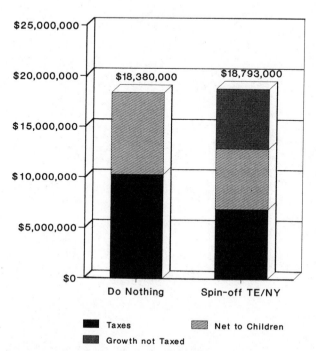

Figure 18-6. Estate tax comparison 10 years from now: the plan results in tax savings of $3.4 million.

receive the insurance proceeds (or interest from those proceeds for her lifetime) for Dad's preferred stock. The no-growth company could be managed by the active kids or by professional managers as a family enterprise for active and inactive members. The active children may be busy with their growth company, so the family enterprise provides a mechanism to treat all children equally and fairly.

Opportunities abound here for valuation engineering prior to the spin-off and for substantial additional estate tax savings. The original objective, spinning off growth assets, spawns other family benefits as well.

Summary

Tax-free asset reorganizations via split-offs and spin-offs provide numerous creative opportunities for solving the more difficult issues associated with succession planning. The asset-based transaction creates a stepped-up basis for the purchaser, providing a method to depreciate the assets as if they were newly purchased. Also, by selling certain assets and retaining others, business owners can create a flow of income to provide future security. At the same time, the transaction can be structured so that it is affordable to the successors.

For tax purposes, owners can defer receipt of some income and provide supplemental pension benefits for themselves and their family in the future.

19

Transfer Technique 3: Additional Covenants

Negotiating the sale of a business involves more than determining the purchase price and terms. Another consideration is whether the deal will come with any additional covenants, such as a noncompete agreement, a salary continuation agreement, a consulting or employment contract, supplemental retirement benefits, and royalties or licensing fees. If so, the buyer and seller must also negotiate the value and terms of the additional covenants.

Typically, these arrangements are called *offsets* (made to satisfy discrepancies between seller's perceived value and buyer's willing purchase price of the company) or *add-ons* (tacked on to the business's fair market value to "sweeten" the deal for the seller). Both terms have dangerous tax implications, however, because they imply a partial compensation for the business. A buyer is permitted to deduct (as a business expense) the cost of such additional agreements as long as the IRS is convinced they are not in any way linked to the purchase price. If the IRS believes otherwise, it will disallow the deduction, which can mean $15,000 to $34,000 in unexpected taxes for each $100,000 worth of covenants. To avoid this unfortunate impression, I use the term *additional covenants* to describe such arrangements.

With comprehensive planning, a substantial part of the business's financial obligations to the exiting owners can be completed in 7 to 10 years. Additional covenants can be "wrapped around" traditional installment obligations (for stock or assets). Properly timed and funded, the 7- to 10-year business obligation can create a 20-year (or longer) income stream to the former owners.

Supplemental Retirement Benefits

A nonqualified supplemental pension plan can be informally funded by the business making deposits into a corporate-established grantor trust for a 7- to 10-year period. These funds, if invested in specially designed insurance products, can continue to grow tax-free inside the trust while other obligations (e.g., installment notes and noncompete agreements) are being paid off. Then, when those contracts are completed, the funded pension plan can begin to make distributions by taking withdrawals from the insurance product. Since the participant in the pension plan is not taxed until he or she begins to receive benefits, the tax deferral can provide an inflation hedge while simultaneously ensuring the participant a secure retirement income.

Consulting agreements, noncompete agreements, and royalties or licensing fees may complete the additional covenants "package." These agreements may be paid out in the "early" years after the transfer, while the supplemental plan is being funded. Or the supplemental plan can be funded on a "pay as you go" basis out of future earnings of the business. The resulting change in ownership—whether through an asset sale or a stock redemption—may be more efficiently completed by the buyers if (1) it is prefunded by the business before the former owner needs it, and (2) a portion is tax-deductible.

Tax deductions to the buyer can reduce the cashflow impact of the overall transaction costs. The deductions recover part of the transfer expenses through tax savings that can range from 15 percent to 34 percent. Payments made under a supplemental retirement plan must be reasonable and should take into account benefits due from other qualified or company-sponsored retirement programs.

A variation is to calculate actuarially the value of the supplemental pension benefits due as a "lost wages" package. That is, many business owners in the "early days" worked long hours and usually were underpaid for their work. Current compensation levels may be a relatively recent event. The value of the wages that the owner "should have" been paid (but wasn't) over a 30- to 40-year period can be calculated as the basis for determining amounts due under a supplemental retirement plan.

The value of the tax savings to the buyer (or to the business) may be an important part of a negotiation strategy. Sometimes the value created by the tax savings can allow the buyer to provide the extra dollars that the seller needs to meet standard-of-living requirements while balancing conflicting demands: satisfying the buyer's own requirements not to "overpay" while meeting the seller's "price." If the corporation is in a 34 percent tax bracket, for every $1 that is paid and deducted, Uncle Sam gives the business a 34-cent refund—that is, a $340,000 refund for every $1 million invested.

Figure 19-1 shows how the transaction of Seller Industries (discussed in Chapter 15) could have been structured so that key employees or family members could "match" the offer from the outside party.

One advantage of the supplemental pension plan (discussed in Chapter 10) is that recording the present value of the unfunded liability due on the

	Purchased by Third Party	Purchased by Key Employees	Purchased by the Kids
Cash	$2,500,000	$1,500,000	$500,000
	Paid to Seller, borrowed from bank and repaid at 9% over 7 years.		
Note Payable to Sellers			500,000
			Interest only for 5 yrs, then amortized over 5 yrs
Total for Stock	2,500,000	1,500,000	1,000,000
Noncompete Agreement		500,000	500,000
		To be paid monthly for 5 years.	
Supplemental Pension		500,000	1,000,000
		$50,000/yr for 10 yrs beginning in 6 yrs	*$100,000/yr for 10 yr beginning in 11 yrs*
Total Other Covenants	0	1,000,000	1,500,000
TOTAL DOLLARS TO JIM and AUDREY SELLER	**$2,500,000**	**$2,500,000**	**$2,500,000**
COST TO THE BUYERS (Present Value at 9%)	**$2,500,000**	**$2,097,517**	**$1,660,054**

Figure 19-1. Three possible sales: All three sales generate the same total dollars to Jim and Audrey Seller. But the terms are different, and the cost to the buyer is lower with favorable terms.

company's financial statements can serve to reduce the fair market value of the business by the amount of the unfunded liability. It is important in establishing the supplemental pension plan that it not be linked to an ownership transfer. For example, if the supplemental pension plan was established on Tuesday, and the same individual's stock was redeemed by the company on Wednesday, the IRS would (correctly) claim that the plan was a sham transaction, and the company's deductions when paying plan benefits would be disallowed.

As part of a long-range succession plan, however, the supplemental pension plan can be established to provide additional retirement benefits. Setting up the plan one to two years (or sooner) before an ownership transfer occurs is advisable; a planning maxim—the sooner you begin, the easier it is—holds here also in regard to an IRS challenge.

Covenant Not to Compete

When a business is sold, the parties involved frequently enter into a noncompetition agreement which restricts the seller or the shareholders employed by the corporation from competing with the purchaser. For tax purposes, an arm's length payment for a noncompetition covenant is considered ordinary income to the seller and a deductible expense to the buyer, amortized over the term of the noncompete agreement.

The Internal Revenue Service may question whether noncompete payments are really part of the purchase price of the business. In addition, the value assigned to a covenant may be called into question. If the IRS is successful in arguing that the covenant is a disguised part of the purchase price, deductions for the buyer will be disallowed.

The courts have applied at least four tests to determine whether an amount may be separately allocated to a covenant. The first test focuses on "whether compensation paid for a covenant is separable from the price paid for the goodwill."[1] That is, the noncompete covenant should have independent value, one that can be supported by an outside opinion or appraisal.

The second court test considers whether the tax effect of the covenant was included as part of the allocable price in setting the value on the transfer. The third test questions the existence of a mutual intent by both parties to assign some portion of the purchase price to the covenant not to compete. Both the buyer and the seller should allocate a value to the noncompete agreement that is independent of the value of the company.

The fourth test ascertains whether the covenant is economically valid. The courts have ruled that the covenant must have some independent basis or arguable relationship with business reality, such that "reasonable men, genuinely concerned with their economic future, might bargain for such an agreement."[2] That is, the seller must actually pose a competitive threat to the buyer. The amount allocated to a covenant should be reasonable and should take into account the age of the seller and his or her knowledge of the industry and effectiveness in having a negative competitive impact on the new buyer, thereby reducing the value of the company.

If the four tests can be met, the noncompete agreement provides tax deductions to the buyer and a method of compensating the seller for assurances that he or she will not compete with the business in the future.

The value attributable to a noncompete agreement should be supported with a valuation report, and it should be established through negotiation separate from the employment or sale agreement. If the IRS contends that amounts paid under the noncompete agreement, or an employment agreement, are disguised payments of the purchase price, it will attempt to disallow the corporate deduction. Under current tax law, a single selling shareholder is only marginally affected (by 3 percent), but the resulting loss of deductions to the purchaser can be a sizable blow.[3]

If there is more than one selling shareholder, the downside can be worse—the selling shareholders can be affected in a second way by a reallocation. Unless each shareholder's noncompete agreement is proportional to his or her former ownership percentage (which would invite an IRS challenge anyway), a reallocation of the noncompete could be construed to have been a gift from the shareholders who did not receive the noncompete to the one who did!

For example, Linda and her brother, Tom, each sold 50 percent of the stock of the family business. In addition, Linda received a $1 million noncompete payment; Tom received no payment. If the IRS deemed the noncompete invalid, then the $1 million would be reallocated to the value of the business. Each seller should have received 50 percent of the $1 million, or $500,000. The IRS may consider Linda's $1 million to be her own $500,000 plus a $500,000 gift from Tom. Tom would pay gift taxes on the $500,000 he "gifted" to Linda.

The caution is clear: Be sure that the noncompete agreement has substance and that it is reasonably valued.

Consulting and Employment Agreements

Barring personality conflicts or hostility during the change of ownership, the owner may want to remain active in the business after the transfer in order to receive future compensation. In this case, the owner might consider an employment or consulting agreement providing compensation for future services—in addition to the purchase price received for selling the business.

The consulting or employment agreement provides for specific duties. Someone else will be running the business; the former owner will be an employee. The buyer may need the former owner's services in order to take advantage of community and industry reputation and relationships. The owner's willingness and ability to provide expertise and knowledge to the new owner could be an important factor in determining the business's future success.

Keep in mind, however, that any consulting fees or employment contracts in excess of Social Security earnings limits will preclude the owner from receiving any Social Security benefits until age 70. (See Figure 19-2.) Also, former owners must be available to provide services in order for the agreement to meet the Internal Revenue Service requirements and provide a deduction to the corporation.

Future social security benefits are limited for recipients with excess earnings. This can be helpful if you're planning to retire soon:

	Earnings Limitation				
	1992	1993	1994	1995	1996
From ages 62 – 65	$ 7,320	$ 7,680	$ 8,160	$ 8,640	$ 9,120
From ages 65 – 70	10,080	10,560	11,280	12,000	12,720

Those ages 62 to 65 lose $1 in benefits for each $2 earned over the limit.
Cutback is $1 for each $3 in excess earnings for recipients ages 65 to 70.

Figure 19-2.

An employment agreement generally is a contract for full-time services and provides for a continuation of salary and benefits. The value of the employment contract is usually over and above the value received for the business. The compensation received for future efforts on behalf of the business is separate and distinct from the sale price. The sale price represents the value created up to a certain point in time. Additional efforts are entitled to additional compensation. Sometimes incentive compensation, contingent on future business results, can be part of the package.

If family members will become, or will continue to be, stockholders, and the business plans to acquire some or all of the exiting owner's shares through a stock redemption plan, the consulting agreement is preferable to an employment contract. As discussed in Chapter 17, stock attribution among family members can be waived as long as there is no ongoing employer-employee relationship between the company and the exiting shareholder. In this way, the company preserves the ability to deduct interest payments on installment notes held by the shareholder (acquired when the stock was sold back to the company), as long as the attribution rules are waived. Some attorneys believe that even a consulting relationship violates the attribution rules. In that case, the supplemental pension plan may be a preferred alternative.

A consulting agreement is philosophically different from an employment agreement. Past experience qualifies the owner to consult with the business on a part-time or "as needed" basis for a monthly or annual retainer. The IRS has well-established guidelines that distinguish a consultant—an independent contractor—from an employee. Compensation paid under either an employment agreement or a consulting agreement is fully deductible by the company and is received as ordinary income by the recipient.

Figures 19-3 and 19-4 show how the transfer of ownership of Seller Industries (discussed in Chapter 15) might have looked from a cashflow perspective of the company.

Royalties or Licensing Fees

Another opportunity for additional covenants occurs when extraordinary relationships exist among the owner, the business, and/or suppliers. Such relationships must be ascertainable and exist outside the scope of a normal employment relationship. Royalties on products created by the owner and distributed by the company, fees for license agreements which provide access to trade names, and brokerage agreements for special services are three examples.

Royalties can be paid as a flat amount (e.g., 5 cents per unit sold) or as a percentage of gross dollars received on a particular line of products, or block of business, created by the founder.

When license or franchise agreements are required for access to brand-name or proprietary products and require the former owner's continued involvement with the licenser or franchiser, license fees can be paid in consideration for the exiting owner's efforts to maintain those agreements. In

SELLER INDUSTRIES, INC.								CASHFLOW PROJECTION
	Actual Last Year	Projected ... 19X1	19X2	19X3	19X4	19X5	19X6	19X7
% Increase in Sales – Middle Case Projection		6.00%	8.00%	0.00%	6.00%	8.00%	0.00%	6.00%
SALES	$12,400,000	$13,144,300	$14,195,604	$14,195,604	$15,047,720	$16,251,058	$16,251,058	$17,226,461
Cost of Sales	8,060,000	8,543,795	9,227,143	9,227,143	9,781,018	10,563,188	10,563,188	11,197,200
GROSS PROFIT	4,340,000	4,600,505	4,968,461	4,968,461	5,266,702	5,687,870	5,687,870	6,029,261
Operating Expenses								
Marketing and Sales	2,480,000	2,628,860	2,839,121	2,839,121	3,009,544	3,250,212	3,250,212	3,445,292
Administrative	1,240,000	1,314,430	1,419,560	1,419,560	1,504,772	1,625,106	1,625,106	1,722,646
Reduce Personnel Costs		(166,667)	(171,667)	(176,817)	(182,122)	(187,585)	(193,213)	(199,009)
Increase Rents		40,000	40,000	40,000	50,000	50,000	50,000	60,000
Interest Pmts to Bank		43,000	38,000	32,000	26,000	20,000	12,000	5,000
Interest Pmts to Parents		45,000	45,000	45,000	45,000	45,000	42,000	34,000
Noncompete Payments		100,000	100,000	100,000	100,000	100,000	0	0
Supplemental Pension		0	0	0	0	0	0	0
Total Operating Expenses	3,720,000	4,004,623	4,310,014	4,298,864	4,553,195	4,902,732	4,786,105	5,067,929
Operating Income	620,000	595,882	658,447	669,597	713,508	785,138	901,766	961,332
Income Taxes	(248,000)	(238,353)	(263,379)	(267,839)	(285,403)	(314,055)	(360,706)	(384,533)
NET INCOME	372,000	357,529	395,068	401,758	428,105	471,083	541,059	576,799
Cashflow Adjustments:								
+ depreciation	49,600	52,577	56,782	56,782	60,191	65,004	65,004	68,906
– equipment purchases	(100,000)	(100,000)	(100,000)	(100,000)	(100,000)	(100,000)	(100,000)	(100,000)
– principal pmts – bank		(54,000)	(59,000)	(64,000)	(70,000)	(77,000)	(84,000)	(92,000)
– principal pmts – parents		0	0	0	0	0	(83,000)	(91,000)
CASHFLOW PROJECTION WITH LOAN PAYMENTS	$321,600	$256,106	$292,851	$294,541	$318,295	$359,087	$339,064	$362,705

Figure 19-3. Cashflow projection assuming a purchase by the kids.

some cases, licenser or franchiser agreements cannot be assigned to a successor without a substantial change in their terms, usually to the detriment of the family business. This further supports a fee arrangement with the owner to maintain the "grandfathered" agreements.

Brokerage agreements, which pay commissions, provide another opportunity. One family business owner in the construction industry also had a paving company. Each year he would negotiate to purchase asphalt at the best price he could find. The company paid him a commission as an asphalt broker. The fact that he planned to continue acting as the company's asphalt broker made transfer of ownership easier. The supplemental income provided by the brokerage commissions allowed him to be more flexible when negotiating with his son over the price and terms of the business transfer.

Leases and Purchase Options

Planning opportunities may exist when operating equipment and real estate (equipment, buildings, land) are owned outside of the business and leased

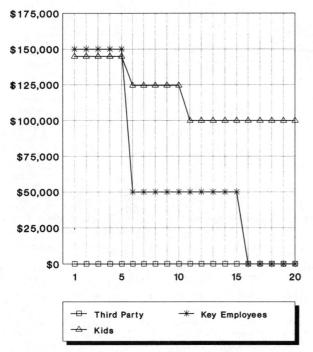

Figure 19-4. Cashflow to parents (after a cash down payment) from three possible sales: sale to the kids, sale to key employees, or sale to a third party.

back to the company. Generally there is a "range" that defines a fair market rental rate. Many family business owners may be at the low end of this range, or even well below fair market value rents. The logic in paying a below-market rent is to retain needed working capital in the company.

Leasing arrangements should be reconsidered when a change in ownership is contemplated. Increased rents (to the high end of the fair market range) could be supported, especially if the possibility exists that additional land for business expansion may be acquired at some point in the foreseeable future. In some cases, and where justified, increased rents can be used to accelerate and pay off any mortgage obligations on business real estate owned outside the company. Continued rents, after retirement and after mortgage indebtedness is paid off, become an additional source of income.

Purchase options, paid by the company or the individual, active shareholders, can also be used to "lock in" a current price for the property or just to lock in an option to buy the property at some point in the future. Exercised in the future, the option automatically triggers a sale of the real estate. For example, assume the stock of the business is sold back to the company on a 10-year note so that Mom and Dad collect their installment payments and continue to receive rent for the 10-year period. The new owners have a purchase option—say, a 90-day window at the end of the tenth year—to acquire the property. They exercise the option and acquire the property on the basis of an appraisal at that time. They can either get a new mortgage and pay cash for the property—using their rents to make mortgage payments—or sell the real estate on a 10- to 15-year note, thereby gaining a further income stream.

Alternatively, a value-shifting technique can be used by transferring the property to a grantor-retained annuity trust (GRAT), as described in Chapter 25. The income would be reserved for Mom and Dad for the term of the trust. At the end of the trust term (say, 10 years), the property would automatically be discounted and transferred to the next generation.

Summary

Sometimes the owner's cost of "financial independence," or the perception of the company's worth, is substantially greater than what the buyer believes is the fair market value of the corporation. An "offset" arrangement, using additional covenants, can sometimes bring the two sides to an agreement. The additional covenants described in this chapter are invaluable for bridging "gaps" between the seller's expectations and the buyer's willingness to purchase.

The timing of the payment of additional covenants is equally important. Since covenants, by definition, do not accrue interest when paid over time (like installment notes do), a buyer often wants to push the term of a fixed covenant out as long as possible—it is equivalent to an interest-free loan from the seller. Sellers, however, prefer to get covenants paid off as quickly as possible. Negotiating acceptable terms for a covenant, along with the price paid, is a key issue to be resolved in the transfer process.

References

1. *Ullman v. Commissioner* (2nd Cir. 1959).
2. *Schulz v. Commissioner* (9th Cir. 1961).
3. See Freeport Transportation, Inc., 63 TC 107 (1974).

PART 5

Tying the
Deal Together

20
Shareholder Agreements

Many family businesses have wisely drafted shareholder or buy-sell agreements between the business and its shareholders describing what happens to family business stock in the event of a stockholder's death. More sophisticated agreements also cover what happens in the event of a disability or termination (voluntary or involuntary) from the business.

These agreements ensure that shares will not fall into the hands of outsiders. Restrictive covenants prevent a stockholder from selling, pledging, or disposing of his or her stock against the wishes of the other stockholders. They also serve to ensure stockholders and their families that in the event of death each stockholder's investment in the family business will be converted into a liquid asset. Cash or a note, paid in consideration for the stock, provides money to pay estate taxes and/or an income stream for the shareholder's survivors.

Valuation Methods

Valuation clauses in these agreements describe how family business stock will be valued, and how that value will be paid. In the past, a properly drawn buy-sell agreement effectively fixed the value of stock for federal estate tax purposes on the death of a shareholder. However, the 1990 Tax Act provides many opportunities for the IRS to question the valuation method of a buy-sell agreement for estate tax purposes.

Imagine this scenario: George and Harold were brothers as well as model business partners. Each brother owned 50 percent of a $7 million (annual revenue) publishing company. Their buy-sell agreement, drafted 10 years earlier, included a valuation clause specifying a book value calculation of their stock in the event of death. Both brothers thought book value, currently at $2 million, was a fair price for their stock, if they died. Each brother had a $1 million life insurance policy that would be used to fund the agreement: It would be paid to the surviving brother, who would use the proceeds to acquire stock from his deceased brother's spouse.

Not long ago, George and Harold had turned down a $7 million offer for their company from a larger publisher. They weren't ready to sell the family business. The offer, at one times gross revenue, was based on a common valuation rule of thumb in the publishing industry at that time.

Although the brothers knew the business was worth more than their buy-sell agreement price, they were concerned that putting their own agreement at a level close to gross revenue would burden the company financially and jeopardize its future. They believed their spouses would be financially protected with the existing agreement, since they each had other assets outside the business interests which would provide their spouses with financial security.

A few months later, George and his wife were tragically killed in a drive-by shooting. The insurance proceeds were paid to Harold, who used the money as the agreement specified. The attorney for George's estate listed the value of George's interest on the estate tax return at $1 million.

The IRS audited the return and claimed that the fair market value of George's business interest was $3.5 million—George's 50 percent share of the amount he and Harold had turned down prior to his death. Additional estate taxes of $1,375,000 (55 percent of the value over the $1 million claimed) were due.

George's attorney, protesting that the valuation provision in the buy-sell agreement should establish the publishing company's value for estate tax purposes, found that the IRS was reading from a different book. Chapter 14 (of the IRS book) reads that *a stock purchase agreement does not conclusively establish the estate tax value* unless each of the following requirements are met:[1]

1. The agreement is a bona fide business arrangement.

2. It is not a device to transfer the family business (or other property) to a family member for less than full consideration.

3. The agreement is comparable to similar arrangements entered into in an arm's-length transaction.

The IRS recognizes that there may be several different, generally accepted, valuation methods within a particular industry. In George and Harold's case, however, the IRS concluded that their particular valuation method was a tax-avoidance device and therefore invalid for establishing the federal estate tax value of George's shares.

There was a way George and Harold could have given weight to fixing the value for estate tax purposes: with a restriction on *lifetime stock transfers,* using the same valuation calculation as a transfer at death. The IRS acknowledges that when the value of lifetime transfers is restricted, it will not contest estate tax valuation clauses as long as those same valuation clauses apply to lifetime transfers.

The above requirements also apply to family members of the owners of a business. The IRS defines "family" as an individual's spouse or ancestor, or a lineal descendent of the individual or spouse, the individual's brother or sister, or the spouse of any of these. In IRS prose: "the natural objects of one's bounty."[2]

Any agreement signed prior to October 1990 is not subject to the above provisions, unless the family has substantially modified, or plans to modify, the agreement after that time. Adding more family members is viewed as a substantial modification to the agreement. That is, if an existing valuation provision in an "old" agreement contains an annual valuation update mechanism, the IRS will allow the agreement to establish the estate tax value of the stock—as long as the stock is revalued *each year* under that provision. If the stock is not periodically revalued, or the agreement has a "fallback" valuation clause (e.g., "stock should be valued at X times earnings, but if the stockholders neglect to formally establish the value in the company's minutes, then book value will be used"), then the "old" agreement is no longer protected.

Establishing the Buy-Sell Agreement Price

Orville Lefko notes in the *Michigan State Bar Journal:* "Almost by definition, the setting of a value for a business to be covered by a buy/sell agreement is an essential feature of that agreement. Too often it is also the most neglected feature of the agreement, set in an arbitrary, unprofessional manner—almost as an afterthought."[3] An additional difficulty in setting a value for a buy-sell agreement is that no one knows when an event which triggers the agreement will occur.

There are three basic approaches to developing a fair market value in a buy-sell agreement:

1. Negotiation among the parties.
2. Some type of formula based on the financial statements. This could be book value, adjusted book value, capitalization of earnings, or some combination of those variables, consistent with industry formulas and capitalization rates.
3. Independent outside appraisal.

The formula approach is not difficult to use; once the formula is established, however, it is frequently not reviewed for accuracy in later years. Business conditions can change, as can capitalization rates. Years can pass until some event triggers a redemption. Then, if the formula is not reviewed, the dismayed shareholders find that the price established does not reflect the original intent of those who developed the agreement. The formula should be tested annually by the shareholders to make sure that the pricing mechanism is fair to all parties.

Another common problem in valuation agreements is the lack of clear definition. Even when the agreements specify the purchase price at book value, it may be difficult to define book value. For example, is book value calculated as of the date of death, the end of the month preceding death, the last regular accounting period, or the end of the fiscal year of the entity?

Whose Arm Is Measured in Determining Arm's Length?

Meanwhile, the 1990 Tax Act, which may come to be called the Appraiser's Full Employment Act, established that a valuation method must be comparable to similar arrangements entered into by persons in an arm's-length transaction:

> Such determination would entail consideration of such factors as the expected term of the agreement, the present value of the property,...It is not met simply by showing isolated comparables but requires a demonstration of the general practice of unrelated parties. Expert testimony would be evidence of such practice. In unusual cases where comparables [are] difficult to find because the taxpayer owns a unique business the taxpayer can use comparables from similar businesses.[4]

One potential problem these provisions create is a liability for increased taxes. If a buy-sell agreement provides for a certain valuation but the estate is required to value the shares at a higher rate, who is liable for the unanticipated estate taxes attributable to the increase? Another problem concerns marital deductions. If the estate sells a family business interest (e.g., stock) for less than the estate tax value, what happens if the excess estate tax value won't qualify for the marital deduction (because it didn't pass to the spouse)? Finally, what if the fiduciary for the estate concludes that he or she has an obligation to contest the agreement?

It seems clear that a fair market value determination is the intent of the 1990 Tax Act provisions. Defining fair market value may be easier said than done. All parties to family business shareholder agreements that have been drafted or modified since October 1990 should review their valuation formulas against these new provisions.

To Cross-Purchase or Not?

Other provisions in existing agreements also merit periodic review. The three basic types of shareholder agreements are as follows:

1. *Redemption agreements.*   These are also called entity purchase agreements, or stock repurchase agreements. The issuing corporation buys the interest from the withdrawing party or from the estate of the deceased individual. A number of events can trigger redemption. (See Figure 20-1.)
2. *Cross-purchase agreements.*   Two or more individuals or entities buy the

TRIGGERING EVENTS	Type of Provision					Valuation Method			Funding			Terms		
	Option		Mandatory		Wait		Apprai-			Sinking			Cash &	
	Co.	S/H	Co.	S/H	& See	Formula	sal	Book	Ins.	Fund	None	Cash	Note	Note
Death														
Disability														
Retirement														
Resignation														
Involuntary Termination														
Gift														
Sale to Third Party														
Divorce														

Figure 20-1. Stock redemption matrix.

interest directly from the withdrawing party or from the estate of the deceased individual.

3. *Hybrid agreements.* These provide for either a repurchase by the business or a cross-purchase, in which case the entity and/or the individual shareholders determine at the time the event is triggered who (business or individuals) will acquire the shares being transferred. (See Figure 20-2.)

Here's how a hybrid agreement might work: Shareholders grant a "first option" to the corporation to redeem all or any portion of a deceased, disabled, or retiring shareholder's stock. A "second option" is then granted to remaining shareholders to cross-purchase the shares tendered by the exiting shareholder or his or her estate. A final mandatory provision requires the corporation to redeem any shares not picked up under the first or second option. Such an arrangement, sometimes referred to as a wait-and-see agreement, provides flexibility in selecting the buyout method most advantageous to all parties at the time of the actual transaction.

The provisions in the agreement need not be applied equally to all the shareholders. They may be mandatory and binding on all parties, or they may

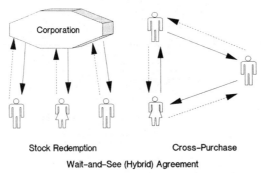

Stock Redemption   Cross-Purchase

Wait-and-See (Hybrid) Agreement

Advantages of Hybrid Agreement

- Avoids AMT on corporate-owned life insurance

- Provides opportunity for surviving shareholders to elect a step-up in the basis of the stock acquired

- Split-dollar agreements can provide income-tax-free cash to individuals to fund buyout

- Disability or retirement buyout can be funded by corporation

Figure 20-2. Hybrid shareholder agreement.

be optional on the part of one of the parties to the agreement. For example, if a key nonfamily employee has an ownership interest, the agreement may provide for a mandatory repurchase when that employee reaches age 65, while allowing other shareholders to freely transfer their shares via gift or other means among family members active in the business.

For S corporations, a restrictive provision in the shareholder agreement should prevent stock from going to an ineligible shareholder—such as the bypass trust of the deceased—or else an unintended termination of the S election may be an unexpected surprise.

Advantages and Disadvantages of Different Agreements

There are income tax as well as practical considerations in choosing the right agreement.

Cross-Purchase Agreements: Advantages

- Surviving shareholder-purchaser gets stepped-up tax basis on stock purchased. If a subsequent sale of the business is contemplated, this is a significant benefit.

- Corporate assets may be subject to creditor's claims; if insurance is paid outside of corporation (e.g., to surviving shareholder), proceeds are outside the reach of creditors.

- The alternative minimum tax on life insurance proceeds used to fund the agreement is avoided.
- Individual survivors are personally liable to satisfy the terms of agreement.

Cross-Purchase Agreements: Disadvantages
- Individuals may be in a higher tax bracket than the corporation.
- It may be difficult to enforce the obligation on a surviving shareholder to collect the amount due on stock price in excess of the insurance proceeds received.
- The agreement can become complex when there are multiple shareholders.

Stock Redemption Agreements: Advantages
- It is easier for an attorney to draft, and for shareholders to understand, the terms of redemption.
- Corporate assets are available as collateral to secure amounts due, or when insurance proceeds are insufficient.
- Redemption may qualify the selling shareholder for capital gains treatment.

Stock Redemption Agreements: Disadvantages
- Surviving shareholders retain their existing basis in their stock.
- Potential unwanted dilutive effects: Dad owns 50 percent and his brother owns 20 percent. Dad's son and daughter own 15 percent each. Dad dies and corporation redeems Dad's stock. Brother's ownership *automatically* increases to 40 percent after the redemption.
- Corporate-owned insurance may be subject to an alternative minimum income tax of 20 percent.
- Insurance proceeds are subject to claims of creditors.
- If attribution rules are not followed, a redemption may be treated as a taxable dividend.

The hybrid (or wait-and-see) agreement may be the best solution. For example, it could provide for a redemption in the event of retirement or disability, and a cross-purchase at death. (See Figure 20-3.)

Funding the Agreement

Most state statutes allow a corporation to reacquire its own stock, although a company's ability to do so is usually limited to its retained earnings. If and when shareholders modify their agreement's valuation formula to comply with the 1990 Tax Act, most family businesses will find a built-in "Catch-22": The retained earnings limitation (i.e., book value) allowed for stock redemption

	FAVORS REDEMPTION	FAVORS CROSS-PURCHASE
Life insurance used		X
Family attribution rules apply		X
More than 2 or 3 shareholders	X	
Buyout funded by existing assets	X	
Funded by future income	X	
Ease of drafting and administration	X	
Step-up in basis for survivor		X
Estate tax values		X
Source of funds for payout	X	
Combined with restrictive covenant to enable payments to be deducted	X	
Constructive dividend to survivor		X
Corporate creditors reaching life insurance values		X
Assurance that premiums will be paid	X	
Payments would render corporation insolvent		X

Figure 20-3. This schedule can be used to decide which arrangement (redemption or cross-purchase) is preferable.

under state statutes (using a stock redemption agreement) may be significantly less than the fair market value as determined by the 1990 federal law.

Additional funding over and above the company's available working capital will often be required to satisfy obligations of these agreements. Traditional financing may not be available when it is needed—for example, upon the death or disability of a shareholder who is also the most valuable key employee.

Insurance funding mechanisms offer inexpensive alternatives, provided they are properly structured. Placing the wrong owner or beneficiary on the insurance application can inadvertently unravel the most sophisticated redemption plan. For example, a $1 million key employee policy paid to the corporation may trigger an alternative minimum tax of $200,000. If the insurance proceeds instead were paid to the surviving shareholder, the surviving shareholder could loan, or contribute, the proceeds to the business to satisfy a stock redemption obligation and avoid the alternative minimum tax liability.

Cross-purchase agreements funded with life insurance require each shareholder to own a policy on the other shareholders. If there are five shareholders, 20 policies will be required with a cross-purchase agreement. Using an escrow agent to hold all stock certificates may simplify matters, since the escrow agent could also be the assignee of the insurance proceeds.

By contrast, with a stock redemption agreement, the corporation takes out one policy on the life of each shareholder (five policies are required with five shareholders).

Split-dollar arrangements (discussed in Chapter 27) can be used to fund hybrid agreements. For example, the corporation can own cash values and use them for retirement or disability buyouts. Death benefits can be paid to individual shareholder(s), providing a cross-purchase option at death. Another alternative is a disability buyout policy that provides disability benefits (payable in a lump sum or over five years) equal to the value of the disabled shareholder's business interest.

Using life insurance to fund stock redemption agreements can trigger unexpected taxes. The valuation clause in the agreement may stipulate that "the value to be paid is the *higher of* the insurance proceeds received or the value determined by formula." If the insurance proceeds are higher, the *excess* over the formula calculation may be subject to income tax and an estate tax in the estate of the decedent. Also, transfer-for-value rules limit how life insurance ownership provisions can be changed. Breaking these rules means that policy proceeds at death are subject to income tax (normally life insurance proceeds are tax-free).

Properly structured, life and disability insurance products can effectively fund shareholder obligations and prevent a cash drain on the family business when death, disability, or termination occurs.

Agreement Provisions

Four often overlooked provisions should be considered in every shareholder agreement: disability, termination, windfall profit, and deadlock. Many agreements neglect to include provisions to address such events. As noted above, for an agreement to be binding for estate tax purposes, it must include a pricing mechanism for lifetime transfers as well.

Disability

It is important to provide for disability in the purchase agreement, as a disabled shareholder may need additional income, which the value of his or her shares could provide. A disability provision should address several crucial questions. When will a disability buyout occur? Usually 12 to 24 months after the disability begins gives the disabled shareholder a chance to recover before buy-sell provisions mandate a sale of stock. How does the agreement define disability? Will compensation be continued for a disabled shareholder? If so, for how long? What if the disabled shareholder recovers after the buyout? Can he or she reacquire those shares?

If compensation continues, the IRS is likely to construe it as a dividend and disallow the deduction to the corporation. A disability salary continuation agreement, however, could provide a continuation of income to a disabled shareholder for a specified period—until the date at which a disability buyout provision would require other shareholders or the corporation to purchase the disabled shareholder's stock. A disability salary continuation agreement may cover one individual or a selected group without including all employees.

Termination

One method of deterring a key shareholder from leaving the company is for the agreement to require a shareholder who wants to quit to sell his or her stock to other shareholders—at a specified discount.

Involuntary termination should also be addressed in the agreement. Moral turpitude, felony or criminal charges, loss of required professional or business licenses, personal bankruptcy, drug or alcohol abuse—all could be triggering events causing an involuntary termination and a sale of shares held.

Windfall Profit

Consider this scenario: (1) Dad dies, becomes disabled, or leaves the business, (2) his or his family's stock is purchased under a previously determined formula valuation clause, and (3) soon thereafter the family business is sold to a third party for substantially more than Dad received for his pro rata interest. The possibility of a future sale often keeps shareholders "in" longer than they want or creates intense family animosity when the above scenario plays out.

A windfall-profit provision specifies a formula that the business must follow for sharing some of the "excess" amounts with a former shareholder in a subsequent sale of the business. Generally the provision has a finite life— five to ten years, and provides a downward-sliding pro rata percentage. For example:

If the business is sold in the following period after redemption	the former shareholder's pro rata share of the sale proceeds in excess of amounts received for the stock would be
Months 1–12	100%
13–24	80%
25–36	60%
37–48	40%
49–60	20%
61 and over	0%

This clause may not prevent family feuds, but at least it provides an opportunity for fair play.

Deadlock

A conflict-resolving provision in a shareholder's agreement can be effective if all communication breaks down. Sometimes a deadlock provision can motivate unhappy shareholders to compromise their personal positions.

Deadlock is generally defined as a persistent disagreement between shareholders concerning the affairs or direction of the corporation. It typically occurs when two shareholders (or groups) with equal voting power disagree on fundamental issues. Deadlock can also occur when minority shareholders exercise a veto power, or when there is a supermajority requirement for certain business decisions.

A simple way to avoid deadlock is to control voting power by: issuing two classes of stock, one voting and the other nonvoting. For example, retiring shareholders who aren't compelled to sell shares would convert their voting shares to nonvoting shares at retirement so that only active shareholders would hold voting stock.

If deadlock occurs, the shareholder agreement or the corporate bylaws can require a liquidation or sale of the corporation. In this case, only major corporate decisions (e.g., sale of the business, reorganization, recapitalization) would be defined as deadlocking issues forcing a liquidation. Another alternative is to provide in the business charter that the company's existence will expire after a specified period of time, requiring unanimous consent of future shareholders to keep the company going and avoid liquidation or sale.

Other remedies involve predetermined buyout clauses if deadlock occurs. An example is the Dutch auction—also known as closed auction—in which each shareholder submits one price at which he or she agrees to either buy or sell. High bid wins. Another buyout remedy is a coin toss to determine who leaves and who stays.

Mediation, discussed in Chapter 5, may be an answer, but it requires a willingness on everyone's part to want to reach an acceptable solution. A split-off, described in Chapter 18, is often effective when siblings' management styles and goals are miles apart.

References

1. IRC Sec. 2703(a),(b).
2. IRC Sec. 2704(c)(2). Prop. Reg. Sec. 25.27032-1(b)(ii).
3. Orville B. Lefko, "Buy/Sell Agreements and Appraisals," *Michigan State Bar Journal,* February 1976, p. 116.
4. Senate explanation of IRC Sec. 2703(b)(3).

21
Security Devices and Triggers to Protect Sellers

"Trust in God, but tie your camel first," is an old Sufi proverb that family business owners should heed when considering an ownership transfer. Whether the buyer is a third party, a long-time trusted key employee, or a son or daughter, a number of protective devices should be negotiated early on in the succession plan to protect every seller of a family business.

Most ownership transfer plans involve some form of deferred payout, which creates a risk that promised and expected funds may not be collected. A business owner facing retirement wants security, not risk. The deferral may come from the seller transferring stock in exchange for an interest-bearing installment note. Or it may come from a supplemental pension plan with payments funded by future earnings of the family business. Unless the transaction is for "all cash," sellers take on some risk.

There are a number of security measures that sellers can insist on to legally ensure that the proceeds from a sale or income from a pension will not be interrupted. The hard call is how far you go in protecting the seller without strangling the golden goose.

Putting liens on all business assets to secure collateral may defeat the seller's purpose in perpetuating the business. Liens might restrict the company's ability to obtain needed operating capital.

Because a lease is tied to a specific property, and because lessors do not convey ownership rights, it is fairly simple to describe what happens when a lease is in default: The lessee loses the ability to use the property. Whether it's a building, a piece of land, or a forklift truck, the property owner reclaims it.

Protecting the seller after family business ownership rights have been transferred is more complex. The seller's rights to reclaim assets in the business may be secondary to rights of other creditors such as the company's banks. As discussed earlier, conveying ownership rights to the next generation is psychologically good for the heirs, the family, and most likely the business itself. But whether former owners convey those rights by gift or sale, they often leave themselves *dependent* on someone else for their future income. Prefunding the transaction, with enough advance planning, can reduce or eliminate risk by giving the owner some time to begin setting corporate cash aside for himself. Lead times of five to seven years can also help the owner assemble and groom the next generation of owner-managers.

A supplemental pension plan used in conjunction with a rabbi trust (see Chapter 10) is one way to prefund the arrangement. Corporate funds deposited in a grantor or rabbi trust remain a corporate asset, but are earmarked and actually set aside for the benefit of the participants. Although the funds are subject to corporate creditor's claims, a "call-down" provision may be negotiated with participants to protect their benefits. The pension plan document would establish performance measures for the company and tie them to the debt-to-equity ratios and cashflow coverage requirements described below. If the company were to fall below the established norm, the participant in the supplemental pension plan would have a right to "call down" the present value of all benefits due in a lump sum. (The participant would forfeit 5 to 10 percent of the benefits to exercise this call-down right.) If the family business funded $100,000 per year and earned 8.5 percent interest for the entire period, at the end of the seventh year, the business would have accumulated approximately $1 million in the trust for the benefit of the current owner.

Most family business owners, unfortunately, are not that farsighted. Or they find better things to do with business funds that, at the time, seem wiser investments for the business. But when owners are tired and ready to let go, they'll find all the birds in the bush, so to speak, and none in the hand.

Many of the following security devices, available to any business owner who acts as "lender," are the same ones that local bankers might use. (See Figure 21-1.)

Guarantees, Caps, and Dividend Limitations

If buyers are not willing to put up the house, the car, and the kids as collateral, then they're not ready to be strategic entrepreneurs. One 63-year-old owner was at her attorney's office ready to sign papers—she was selling her business to her son with a long-term note. The son had put no money down. When Mom insisted that her son sign a personal guarantee, he refused and "walked the deal." Mom later confided that she was glad to know early on that her son did not have the needed commitment, because she would have been dependent on him for retirement income. Instead Mom sold the business to a third party: half for cash and half in a secured installment note.

The first two or three years will be the toughest for the new owners. Are they taking over the company because they want the former owners' income

These typical devices . . .

- Personal guarantees
- Compensation/bonus "caps"
- Restrictions on dividends during deferred payout period
- Restrictions on additional financing which subordinates the seller to a junior position
- Cashflow coverage requirements (typically 1.1 to 1.25) during deferred payout period
- Periodic financial information provided to third party for review
- Balance sheet requirements; i.e., acceptable debt to equity ratios per industry norms
- Third-party escrow agent to "hold" stock during deferred payout period
- Letters of credit

. . . Can be applied to any of these

- Installment notes
- Noncompete covenants
- Consulting arrangements
- Royalty fees
- Supplemental pension nonqualified arrangements

Figure 21-1. Security devices which protect sellers in deferred payout transactions.

and lifestyle? To keep sufficient cash in the company and make sure that new owners have a long-term view, exiting owners can require their successors to maintain existing compensation levels (if fair for the job they have been doing, plus extra compensation to cover their new responsibilities) for two or three years and/or restrict bonuses and other perks.

If the family business is a C corporation, it's unlikely that dividends will be paid. However, if the business is an S corporation, distributions should be limited to the amount needed to pay income taxes until the new owners have completed all obligations.

Restrictions on Additional Financing

Different deferral methods have different priorities (in the event of default) on business assets. For example, a holder of an installment note, secured with collateral, would typically be in a more senior position to collect money owed than a general creditor (such as the participant in a supplemental pension plan) in the event of default. Preexisting banking relationships may require the company to maintain a specific debt-to-equity ratio, in order to avoid having the bank call inventory loans, working-capital loans, or other loans.

If the ownership plan is structured as a long-term installment note, this additional debt may tip the debt-to-equity ratio into an unacceptable position and generate a not-too-friendly visit from the banker. Bankers view obligations promised through a supplemental pension plan as junior obligations, subordinated to their loan. For their debt-to-equity calculations, they often treat such obligations as "above the line" equity instead of long-term debt. The owner's choice here is the less secure nonqualified pension plan that helps the company remain viable and maintain banking relationships.

Typical restrictions include a pledge from the new owner that existing lines of credit will not be expanded without the former owner's consent (for as long as the former owner is a creditor of the company), and there will be no additional indebtedness that further subordinates the seller—to a third or fourth position—on collateral. A cross-default provision whereby a default on *any* obligation throws *all* obligations into default is another sound, safety feature.

If the former owner still has personal guarantees on any corporate indebtedness, those guarantees should be removed before, or concurrent with, a change in ownership. If for some reason the guarantees cannot be removed, the new owner should provide indemnifications to the seller (even though they may be difficult to enforce). Caveat: Don't expect the bank to accept the new owner's substitute guarantees automatically. It may take several years, and many visits, for the banker to develop a comfort level for the proposed change.

Cashflow and Balance Sheet Requirements

The business's accountants can determine the company's historical cashflow—even if the company is in a cyclical industry, they can spot trends. Cashflow is generally defined as earnings *before* depreciation, interest, and taxes—EBDIT. The company should maintain at least a 1.0 times EBDIT coverage during the deferred payout period. For greater security, the factor increases. Some banks and other lenders require 1.25 to 1.5 times EBDIT. If the business's cashflow were to fall below a mutually agreed-upon coverage requirement, it would constitute a default by the buyers. Low seasonal cashflow can accidentally trigger a default. A solution is to test the coverage periodically over a period of time (quarterly, for example) and establish a default as four or more quarters below the norm.

For example, if a company's historical annual cashflow is $500,000, a 1.25 coverage would require the company to improve its cashflow to a minimum of $625,000. In order to maintain the required cashflow coverage, the company may have to delay expansion activities such as new locations or new equipment. The seller's objective of perpetuating a competitive business has to be balanced with concerns over personal financial security during the deferred payout period. Also, any cashflow coverage requirements would normally factor in the effect of obligations to sellers (e.g., in the debt amortization portion of the calculation). Lower principal indebtedness—by paying more to sellers as tax-deductible expenses (noncompetes, royalties, consulting fees, SERPs)—improves the cashflow picture.

Keep in mind that the purpose of a cashflow coverage requirement is not to make business operation so tough that new owners will fail. The purpose is to ensure that, if new owners do fail, former owners can get their company back before it's wrecked and then sell it to another party.

If an existing lender requires debt-to-equity ratios to be maintained, along with current and quick ratios, these same requirements should be written into the seller's agreements—along with supplemental pension plans and noncompete covenants (see below).

The remedies in the event of default or cross-default may be different in each agreement. With an installment note, a breach could cause foreclosure on collateral. With a supplemental pension plan, a breach may trigger a call-down provision through the rabbi trust, if it was funded (even an unfunded trust can have a "springing" provision for funds to be deposited). With the noncompete agreement, a breach of financial standards might void the covenant without providing any monetary reward.

Third-Party Security Measures

An outside accounting firm, along with the former owners, should review internal monthly and annual statements. Industry norms (ratios, expenses) should be tracked and compared with the family business. Default provisions may be expanded to include nonperformance on other measurements important for industry success—for example, managing receivables and maintaining discounts on payables.

Although it is standard practice for a third party to hold transferred stock certificates until debts related to the buyout have been paid off, new owners are not restricted from dramatically changing the financial condition and nature of the business. Also, a stock pledge works only when there's indebtedness tied to stock acquired. If stock was gifted and the income stream to the former owners was provided through nonqualified retirement plans, this security device would have no value. Another problem with the stock pledge is that by the time the former owners take back the stock, it may be too late to save the company.

Letters of credit are commonly used when there is a third-party buyer. In essence, a financial institution issues a letter of credit stating that the obligor is creditworthy and the financial institution guarantees the loan. This device has a number of drawbacks with internal transactions involving family or key employees. First, letters of credit are expensive for the company—1 percent to 2 percent per year of the amount being guaranteed. Second, letters of credit are usually good for only one year at a time; they don't cover the entire period of indebtedness. Finally, and probably most important, the guarantor may require the company to set aside a portion of its available, existing line of credit as collateral to secure the guarantor's letter of credit. For the family business dependent on existing credit lines, this could be a disaster.

Other Safeguards

Noncompete covenants from new owners are an important safeguard. If the business doesn't succeed, a new owner should not be able to gain experience at the former owner's expense, and then leave to set up shop elsewhere.

Similarly, restrictions on the sale of assets, acquisitions, and expansions can help ensure that former owners receive their entire payout. An internal buyout should keep new owners focused on productively using assets acquired, not spinning them off for quick profit. The same goes for acquisitions and expansion. If former owners approve, then caveat emptor. However, risk-averse former owners should ensure that new owners pay them off before embarking on any expansion or acquisition program.

One client established this as a triggering device. That is, if his daughter wanted to do an acquisition, she could. It's just that all amounts due Dad would accelerate and have to be paid up. Daughter found an acquisition that was sufficiently attractive to pursue, and closed it, triggering Dad's payoff. Everyone was pleased—Dad got his money earlier than expected, Daughter bought a new company, and the new company's cashflow helped pay off the debt that Daughter incurred when she cashed Dad out.

Finally, if a new owner is disabled or killed, the former owner may have to step back in. Here life and disability insurance on the new owner is a valuable security device. With the proceeds of insurance that has been collaterally assigned to them, the former owner can be assured of collecting any amounts due. Insurance thus prevents one tragedy (the new owner's death) from becoming two tragedies (the former owner's losing everything as well).

Down-the-Line Protection

This discussion of security devices, though not exhaustive, underscores the importance of the seller getting upfront protection for the period *after* the transaction is completed. Voting rights restrictions, liquidation rights, and veto rights take down-the-line protection a step further. For example, the seller could amend the company's bylaws to include a "supermajority" provision that requires more than a simple majority for approval of changes in the direction of the business. If Dad retained 20 percent of the stock, a supermajority provision could require a vote of at least 81 percent of all stockholders for major decisions. Such a provision could, in effect, give minority shareholders a veto over a sale, merger, recapitalization, refinancing, or other major decision.

It may be, however, that if the seller feels the need for such restrictive guarantees, the seller or buyer isn't ready for the transaction. The process of negotiating these security devices often brings out hidden concerns on both sides.

To perpetuate the family business, some strings need to be cut. There's a fine line between security-driven covenants that protect aging former owners and those that enable owners not to let go.

22

Creating Options When There's Uncertainty over Who the Successors Will Be

Many business owners know that they should begin planning, but they cannot decide who the successors should be because (1) the children aren't grown; (2) there is no key management group and no key employees whom the owner trusts; or (3) the owner still enjoys the business and is not ready to sell and retire.

At this stage, a contingency plan is needed (see Chapter 14). It also helps if the owner understands the many options available.

Prefunding the Business

One client, Roger, is 57, a Stanford-trained MBA, and a bright and successful entrepreneur who loves his specialty publishing company. Two years ago Roger turned down an attractive buyout offer for eight times annual cashflow. Of his three kids, one son and one daughter are working in the business. His daughter comes in only part time and is busy raising her own young children. His son seems more interested in sales and playing golf than in running the company. His third child is finishing college with an accounting degree. Roger asked my firm to explore options for him. After much discussion and soul searching, we arrived at the following options:

- Sell the company in five to eight years to a third party. Begin to position the company now for a sale; develop a management team that would stay on after the sale. Provide nonvoting stock options or phantom stock as an incentive. Manage the company to maximize cashflow, and don't make risky investments in acquisitions or expand to new locations unless absolutely imperative. Reduce corporate and personal debt.

- Sell 30 percent of the company to an ESOP (employee stock ownership plan) to qualify for the tax-free rollover provision. The proceeds would diversify Roger's personal estate and allow him to keep his options open for the remaining 70 percent.

- Sell the company to the kids—perhaps the son finishing his accounting degree will come in as an "inside" financial person. But Roger is concerned (rightfully) that "the kids" don't seem to be passionately interested in the business.

Roger should begin setting aside a portion of the company's annual earnings to protect the options he has today. If he sets aside $100,000 of after-tax earnings each year for the next eight years, at 8 percent interest he will have $1 million in cold cash, regardless of which option he ultimately chooses. Roger's existing assets in a pension and profit-sharing plan will continue to grow as well.

The point is, with a little planning, often 50 percent to 100 percent (depending on how much time there is to plan, and how much money can be set aside) of the value of the business can be prefunded! (See Figure 22-1.)

Prefunding provides tremendous advantages to the business owner who reaches age 65 and considers (1) gifting stock—*and can do so* because financial security has been preestablished; (2) selling to kids or key employees—*and can do so* by holding an installment note because financial security was prefunded (in this case, a rabbi trust, private pension plan, or secular trust might have been used to "escrow" the funds); or (3) selling to a third party—*and can do so.* The prefunded cash becomes a premium over the fair market value of the business. Because Roger will have an existing cash "cushion," he will be a "better seller." That is, when he decides to sell, Roger will be in a better position to negotiate terms and contracts. He won't be totally dependent on an "all cash" deal, and can therefore be more flexible in negotiating with interested buyers.

Business Owner's Age	Deposit Needed at 6%	Deposit Needed at 8%	Deposit Needed at 10%
50	$23,589	$18,363	$14,204
53	$30,525	$24,724	$19,937
55	$36,747	$30,534	$25,288
58	$49,962	$43,076	$37,071
60	$63,012	$55,626	$49,057

Figure 22-1. *Prefunding business value.* For every $1 million of business value, here's the annual deposit needed to "prefund" a business owner's interest at age 70.

Partnering in the 1990s

The strategic alliance, or strategic partnering, has been around for a long time. In the 1990s, however, I predict that more and more manufacturers and suppliers will understand how important the family business distribution network is to them. This realization may create unique options for family business owners who are unsure about their succession plans. Consider these existing programs:

- Anheuser-Busch, itself a family business, runs regular training programs on succession planning for its family business beer distributors.

- Waste Management, a billion-dollar public company, has for many years offered a "partners" program to independent waste haulers as a succession-planning alternative. Waste Management cashes out the existing owner's interest, leaving children running the family business while it infuses the company with new capital. A series of options gives the children the ability over time to then buy out Waste Management, or to sell their interests to Waste Management as well.

- Service Corporation, a 500-location, NYSE funeral home acquisition company, created a lending subsidiary to provide financing to independent funeral home operators for expansion and for financing interfamily and intrafamily succession plans.

- Fleming Foods, one of the largest wholesale food distributors in the United States ($12 billion in annual revenues in 1990), understands that almost 65 percent of its sales come from family business retail grocery chains. Fleming provides accounting services, business valuation services, and financing to its family business customers. In some cases, Fleming will invest directly in stores (its "equity stores") as part of an overall succession game plan.

These unusual alliances represent farsighted, win-win arrangements for both parties. The sponsoring partner may gain competitive advantages in ensuring that existing distribution systems are maintained, and the family business owner gains options that may prove beneficial for the family and the business.

The key element in successful partnering is a climate of trust; relationships have to be emphasized along with contracts. When strategic alliances fail, in all cases, the climate of trust has failed as well. Too often suppliers use "partnering" in their own self-interest without realizing that their responsibilities to the "distributor-partner" must change as well.

The Distributor Supplier Council, a group of building material distributors and their manufacturers, has mutually established a list of expectations as a first step toward creating a partnership mentality. (See Figure 22-2.) As one CEO stated, "It's no longer business as usual."

In the past, manufacturers or suppliers viewed family business distributors as potential acquisition targets. These acquisitions didn't always perform as expected, resulting in unfortunate erosion of the value of family business goodwill, heritage, and customer service. In addition, the acquisitions created

Distributor Expectations of Manufacturers	Manufacturer Expectations of Distributors
1. Manufacture defect-free, quality products and deliver them on time.	1. Deliver an agreed-upon market share. Stock an adequate representation of the manufacturer's product line in order to maintain a good service position.
2. Provide effective well-trained field representatives.	2. Pay invoices promptly.
3. Assign the distributor reasonable geographical sales territories without unreasonable interference from national buying situations or excessive distribution.	3. Give top management support to the line.
4. Understand the trading area of the distributor (i.e., urban-suburban).	4. Provide a well-informed inside and outside sales force.
5. Recognizes the distributor's need for a reasonable profit margin.	5. Call on and service key customers on a regular basis, including independents, chains, and industrial accounts.
6. Consistently offer a mix of programs that will pull products through channels of distribution for each product line.	6. Extend a "sell-through" service to key customers, including assistance in advertising, training, and merchandising.
7. Establish a mutually satisfying policy to respond quickly to customer complaints.	7. Consider specialized sales coverage according to the supplier need.
8. Provide training for all distributor personnel.	8. Assume responsibility for in-house service (display and merchandising), for all customers, including direct bill accounts which provide other than products liability claims.
9. Promote the services of the distributors to all customers.	9. Represent the supplier in all matters with customers other than product liability claims.
10. Encourage feedback from distributors through an annual meeting.	10. Aggressively participate in all major promotions sponsored by the supplier.
11. Hold the distributor accountable for implementing a mutually established marketing plan.	11. Implement a mutually developed marketing plan and review the results periodically.
12. Recognize the need to modify national promotions to meet the needs of regional markets.	

Figure 22-2. Clear expectations are critical in fostering a partnership mentality. (*Source: National Building Material Distributors Association*, The Journal, *vol. 4, no. 5 (October-November 1991)*

ill will and a competitive relationship with the remaining independent distributors, who then viewed the supplier as a predator and competitor.

Partnering is an option with exciting possibilities; managed properly, and carefully, it represents a symbiotic alliance. Mismanaged, it forecloses options for all participants.

Other Options

Even if the "best" option seems like a sale to a third party, don't overlook the key employee group as potential buyers. Install a phantom stock plan now to give them financial incentives. Give them an ability in five to ten years to "cash in" their phantom stock shares and use the proceeds as a down payment to purchase real stock from the owner as the first phase of a leveraged buyout.

Additional options that should be considered include:

1. *Diversify assets.* If the business value is not the primary asset in the estate, the survivors have the option of keeping the business as an income-producing asset or selling it.

2. *Plan for retirement.* For basic planning, maximize opportunities with qualified and nonqualified retirement plans from the company.

3. *Consider an S election to withdraw corporate cash.* For income tax purposes, electing S corporation status results in the business being taxed as a pass-through entity, like a partnership. Earnings and profits pass through and are taxed to the shareholders. Also, earnings and profits can be withdrawn, thereby "freezing" the business value and providing a method of using company profits in other ways for personal diversification. The S election must be carefully coordinated with estate planning, as discussed in Chapter 26. And the fact that an S corporation can have voting and nonvoting shares is helpful to the business owner who wants to shift value but not control.

4. *Use a voting trust.* The family business owner can create a revocable trust and place his or her stock in the trust. After the owner's death, or at some earlier, preestablished date (e.g., the owner's age 75), the successor trustee would vote the shares.

For example, if members of the next generation are not sufficiently mature or experienced to run the business, the stock could go into a revocable voting trust and avoid probate on death. The company could be run by professional managers for an interim period. The owner will need to develop a layer of professional management and educate family members on finding and evaluating professional managers who can be hired to run the company. Company board representation should include objective "outsiders" who can maintain continuity, represent the family's interests, and evaluate the professional managers' performance.

In essence, this strategy buys some time. Although a decision may still be made to sell the company, other alternatives can be evaluated without pressure to make a premature decision. During the time it takes family members to gain experience, the owner can retain key employees by giving them financial incentives based on company profitability or earnings. In addition, the supplemental executive retirement plan (SERP), described in Chapter 10, can create golden handcuffs to retain nonfamily key employees during this critical period. Finally, the owner should consider transferring a minority interest in the company to key nonfamily employees with a redemption formula tied to the increased value they bring to the stock while they are running the business on the family's behalf.

23
Equalization Provisions

One of the most difficult issues related to transferring business interests arises when one or more children are active in the family business and other children are inactive. The issue is compounded when the family business constitutes the majority of value in the business owner's estate. It is important to create assets outside the business in order to diversify and create value for inactive children. Often that diversification doesn't occur sufficiently for the parents to feel a sense of fairness to their inactive children.

Lifetime gifting of stock to an active child can lower the value of the business in the estate; at the same time, it can compound the problem of equalization. The dilemma often focuses on how, and from where, additional assets of equal value can be transferred to inactive children. Often such nonbusiness assets will be needed for parents' retirement. Some parents avoid transferring the business because they believe there is no solution to the equalization dilemma. As a result, parents often wind up leaving the business to all the children equally, hoping the children will work it out.

Timing can confuse the equalization issue further. If stock is transferred to an active son today, with the intent to equalize with the other children at some future time, what is the value of the transfer to the son? Is it the value of the stock today or on the date of the parents' death? If a son or daughter has worked hard to enhance the business's value, why should the value for the inactive children include the increased future value created by the active child?

On the other hand, if the value of stock transferred today is equal to the value of other assets to be transferred to other children, a timing dilemma exists: One child receives stock currently, while the other children have to wait a number of years before they receive anything of equal value.

Often the value transferred to an active child is a minority interest in the business. As discussed earlier, the real value of a minority interest is severely limited. Therefore, transferring a minority interest to an active family member perhaps should not require a transfer of equal value to inactive members. If the estate has sufficient assets to ensure the parents' long-term financial stability, however, parents may elect to do so. Furthermore, if properly discounted, the present value of a minority interest would be lower, so the value of other assets transferred to inactive family members should be equally reduced.

Case Study

George Lincoln emphasized equality among his 11 grown children, 5 of whom were active in the business. A number of years ago he and his wife, Martha, began a gifting program, using their annual exclusion to gift $20,000 worth of shares to each of the 11 children. The 5 active children were concerned about the 6 inactive children ultimately having majority control. The inactive children had concerns of their own.

Like many family-run businesses, George's company does not pay dividends; earnings are retained for corporate growth. The company has a substantial amount of inventory. (LIFO reserves were the main reason the company did not make an S election.)

After consulting with outside financial advisers, George decided to recapitalize the company's common stock into voting and nonvoting shares. Having two classes of common stock enabled the parents to continue to allocate value equitably among all 11 children, but to give the active children voting control and prevent the inactive children from disputing management decisions of their active siblings. (See Figure 23-1.)

The 11 children then entered into a comprehensive shareholder agreement with the company, covering the standard provisions of death, disability, and withdrawal for the active children and death only for the inactives.

In addition, "puts" and "calls" enable the company to "call" the inactive children's stock beginning in two years—first to the eldest inactive child, and then each year to the next eldest. If, after six years, the corporation doesn't call the stock, the inactives get an automatic "put" that can require the corporation to buy their shares.

One consideration relating to the call provision is an existing covenant the company has with its local bank regarding working-capital ratios and debt-to-equity ratios. If the debt created from buying in inactive shares causes those ratios to exceed the bank's requirements, the bank would probably call the company's working-capital loan. Therefore, the ability to buy in the shares has to be managed from a balance sheet standpoint. Also, the active shareholders will need to decide each year whether available capital should be used to buy out a sibling or should be reinvested for business growth.

A valuation clause in the agreement stipulates the buyout price: the *higher* of fair market value, determined by an outside appraisal, or $4000 per share. With the shares currently worth approximately $2500 each, the potential built-in premium for inactive shareholders will affect the timing of the active shareholders' repurchase decision. There is no economic reason for the corporation to buy the stock back as long as the current value per share is less than $4000. However, the active siblings have an incentive to buy out their inactive siblings as soon as the stock is equal to or worth more than $4000 a share. Establishing the floor (the ceiling is fair market value) addressed George's concern about equalizing future growth in value (the

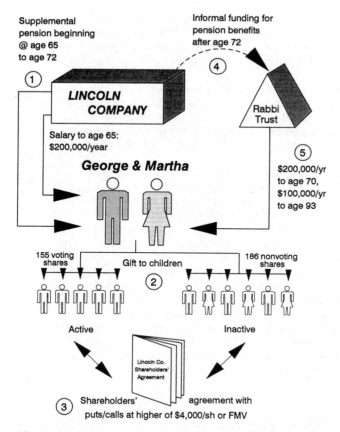

Figure 23-1.

deemed upside potential) without penalizing those who were making it happen. The active children have an incentive to build the company, and a mechanism to buy out the siblings on a prospective basis as the value of the company increases.

The inactive siblings are satisfied with the transaction because their nonvoting shares actually represent estate proceeds that they would have inherited from their parents. The parents are protected with financial security from a newly established nonqualified retirement benefit from the company that will be paid by the company with pretax dollars.

For the next seven years, the company will make deposits into a newly created rabbi trust established for George's benefit. After the trust is fully funded, in seven years, it will begin to distribute a retirement benefit to George and Martha. The benefit will be paid for twenty years and should provide a comfortable retirement income. The trust has both "springing" and "call-down" provisions to protect George and Martha. The springing provision provides for an acceleration of deposits and the call-down aspect provides for a lump-sum distribution; these devices are triggered if the company does not maintain its equity or historical cashflow.

There is one other important factor here. That is, the $4000-per-share valuation was George's determination of what the true fair market value of the stock was worth if the company were sold to an outside third party. George's advisers had discouraged gifting because of the "strings" usually associated with that process.

As you can imagine, the active children don't look at the arrangement as a gift. They have to buy out their siblings (with corporate dollars) and, in addition, provide a retirement benefit to their parents. However, the stock deal (at $4000 per share) plus the present value of the retirement plan (after taxes) cost a total $2 million—a 30 percent discount from what the company is really worth.

It took eighteen months to resolve all of the complex issues. When the documents were finally signed, one (active) son commented that it seemed like "the deal from Hell," because of the time it took to build consensus among the 13 family members, and 2 key nonfamily managers.

All family members feel the price of the deal is fair. The active children and the parents believe the inactive siblings are being treated equitably. The active shareholders do not have to put any money down or sign personal guarantees. They are simply "buying" a successful, stable family business for a discount from its true value. George is pleased at the commitment the active children are making in the transaction.

A windfall provision in the shareholder agreement says that if active children sell the company within the six-year buyback program, a portion of any excess over the buyback price will be shared with inactive siblings. This provision makes sure the active children don't profit unfairly if they sell the company immediately to an outside party.

Don't Let "Equality" Slow You Down

One advantage of having a business partner, says Kathleen Wiseman, a consultant in Washington, D.C., is that two or more people can move an idea forward more quickly. In addition, different life experiences and skills that partners bring to an enterprise "add richness to a firm." But Wiseman believes that "a company, in order to flourish, needs one leader."[1]

Partnerships often get snarled by the notion that everyone is equal. "I have seen a number of firms where there are three or four partners, and they can't get off the dime because they keep working for consensus," says Wiseman. "They keep thinking everybody is equal, that they all bring equal skills, and they can run things equally. That's not true."

Business owners will find tension between needing one leader and managing a partnership. "It's almost as though one partner has to agree to let there be some leadership by another," adds Wiseman. Partners who get locked into this equality business, she warns, get bogged down by spending too much time trying to build consensus.

Partners in some businesses maintain that the equality of their relationship—with equal control and an equal say in everything—is more important than the business. The notion of equality is a very important value in U.S. culture. But how can partners keep their company from being "mired" in equality?

To begin with, they must be clear about who will lead. One person will probably emerge as the leader—ideally, the partner who can carry the business vision forward. It's easy to fall into the trap of letting the most recalcitrant partner lead by default. The one who is most against innovation and who says "I don't want to do this" can stop a company from moving forward. A partnership will function better when its leader knows how to achieve a balance between building consensus around some issues and leading on others.

Partners must be clear about what each person brings to a partnership and what each wants from it. Then they will see the inequalities and can determine what tradeoffs it makes sense to make. The partner who wants to work less, for example, may settle for less financial reward. Or, if the partners choose, they can retain an equal division of financial interest in the company. "I've seen companies where somebody has taken the major leadership responsibility but insisted that everybody share equally in the profits and in the salaries," says Wiseman.

It is possible to switch leadership at different times or over different issues. When one woman in charge of a company took time off to have a baby, for example, someone else in the firm took the leadership responsibility. Striving too hard for equality can keep partners in what Wiseman calls a "no-action mode." Leadership is the key, she says. "In my opinion, that's not a consensus game."

Is Equalization Healthy for Everyone?

Sometimes an equalization attempt is the product of dysfunctional relationships. A differentiated, healthy family can recognize individual differences in its members. In that case, being fair probably means being *unequal*, since the differentiated family members are *not* identical and do not need the same treatment.

Consider the String family's problem. Roy and June had raised their three children to be independent thinkers, competitive, and strong-willed—all qualities needed for success today. The children had developed different management styles, yet each was successful in running a different division of this medium-size family business. The crown-jewel of the company was a subsidiary, Sapphire, Inc., run by a nonfamily professional manager. Sapphire generated a substantial part of the earnings and cashflow that drove the three company divisions managed by the children.

Each child wanted to head the board at Sapphire. In the children's competitive view, the head of Sapphire would be the family "leader." The three politicked, negotiated, and maneuvered for the job, according to their own style. At 72, Roy knew it was time to turn over the board chief's job, but he couldn't decide who should get it. Choosing one child over the other was, in his mind, tantamount to claiming that he loved that child more than the other two. The children began to argue as time went on, and the squabbles only caused Roy to procrastinate more. One family business consultant tried for several years to resolve the problem by suggesting the children take turns in the top spot, five years each. The children couldn't agree on who would be first, so the consultant was fired. The stakes were high because Roy had delayed his estate planning until this issue was resolved.

As discussed in Chapter 5, the real problem was that the children were triangling Roy to give them the Sapphire leadership. At this point my firm was called in.

My associates and I suggested bringing in an outside person to run Sapphire (the stock would be held in a dynasty or Megatrust™ for the benefit of multigenerations), coupled with a spin-off of the three divisions. Sapphire would be retained as a subsidiary of a family holding company, Family Enterprises. Family Enterprises would function for the benefit of *all* family members while the spun-off divisions would be managed and owned as separate profit centers by the three children. After the spin-off, the three divisions would be recapitalized with voting and nonvoting shares; each managing sibling would have the voting shares of his or her company. Puts and calls in three shareholder agreements provided each sibling (in each company) with a way to stay in or be bought out of the three spun-off divisions.

This approach satisfied Roy and June's objective to be fair and equal but also to preserve their second-generation business. It also satisfied the three children, whose careers were already involved in managing their divisions. Preserving Sapphire was everyone's goal. As it turned out, for all three children, becoming board chief of Sapphire was less important than knowing that another sibling would not become chief. "Not losing" was the dominant theme here; the outsider brought in to run Sapphire was acceptable to all.

Equalization Through a Buy-Sell Agreement

An alternative to the timing and equalization dilemma is to gift or sell a few shares of voting common to the active child or children to establish a minority ownership position. A binding stock purchase agreement at fair market value can then be entered into between the majority and minority owners, and the corporation. In exchange for a note, the stock of the majority owner would be sold back to the corporation at his or her death. The note could be divided equally among all children on either the first or second parent's death. The company, now controlled by the surviving shareholder(s), would "buy" the business pro rata from each of the inactive children, providing income and fair value to them.

At the same time, voting control and future growth are protected for the active participants. One way to protect active minority shareholders against a change of heart is for the parent (the original majority shareholder) to convert all of his or her shares to nonvoting stock at retirement. In this way, voting control remains in the active children's hands, while equalization of value exists for all children.

Having active children or the corporation buy stock from the estate on behalf of inactive children eliminates the difficult emotional issues associated with gifting and equalization. The transfer is accomplished at fair market value and no favoritism has been shown to any child. Alternatively, the corporation could recapitalize into common and preferred shares at death, with common (growth) shares bequeathed to active kids and dividend-paying preferred (no-growth) shares bequeathed to inactive children.

If gifts of stock are made to inactive family members, repurchase agreements requiring the business to buy their shares at a certain time (death or retirement of the current owner, for example) offer value for inactive children.

Equalization Through a Will or Trust

If parents gift stock to active children during their lifetime, an equalization provision may be included in the will or the trust of the parents to ensure that each inactive child will receive assets from the parents' estate that equal the value of those gifts before the remainder of assets are divided among everyone. This arrangement ensures equal treatment before distribution is made to *all* family members.

In the following example, John and Paula have seven children. Three are active in the family business; four are not active. During their lifetime, John and Paula have made substantial gifts of stock in J&P Manufacturing Company to the three active children: Frank, Sherlock, and Lee.

John and Paula want to be sure that all their children share equally in the total estate. In order to do so, they have included an equalization provision in their marital trust agreement, granting the remaining four children—Robert, Andrew, Matthew, and Sue—an amount equal to the value of gifts made during John and Paula's lifetime to Frank, Sherlock, and Lee. Upon the death of the surviving parent, the trustee will allocate the remaining trust estate as follows:

The value of all shares of stock from J&P Manufacturing Company that has been gifted to Frank, Sherlock, and Lee will be added into the remaining trust estate at the second death. The value of those shares will be calculated as of the date of transfer to the child.

The total value of the surviving parent's estate, which has increased with the added-in value of the gifted stock, is then divided equally so as to provide equal shares to each of the seven children. Frank, Sherlock, and Lee's portion of their parents' estate is then decreased by an amount equal to the value of the stock gifted to them during their parents' lifetime.

For example, the stock that Frank, Sherlock, and Lee received via gift was valued at $60,000 for each. John and Paula's estate was worth $3 million. The gifts were added back ($180,000) so that each child's share was rounded to $455,000 ($3,180,000 divided by 7). Frank, Sherlock, and Lee would each receive $395,000; their siblings would receive the full $455,000.

Other Solutions

Making a Subchapter S election and then gifting shares is a way to distribute a company's earnings to all shareholders until (or if) a redemption occurs. Stock in an S corporation can be left in trusts (qualifying Subchapter S trusts or grantor trusts) for the benefit of all children, providing equalization as well as a mechanism for distributing company earnings to all children, active or inactive. Here too, using nonvoting stock is a good idea.

Another equalization mechanism is to have the business buy "split-dollar" insurance on the life of the owner. That is, the inactive children are the beneficiaries of the proceeds, and upon death the business recovers all of the premium it paid. The death benefit is actually "split" between the corporation, which paid for the coverage, and the named beneficiaries. Inactive children receive an income-tax-free death benefit and the business is made "whole" because it recovers its cost of funding the program. Or the death benefit can be used to fund the repurchase of stock held by inactive family members at Dad's or Mom's death. Finally, if pension or profit-sharing proceeds are available, they can be distributed at death to inactive children as another equalization provision.

Equalization should not be a reason to avoid ownership succession planning. If everyone is committed to the health of the family business and active children are involved, then owners should plan now to provide for children who are not active in the business. With proper planning, owners can eliminate potentially warring camps while providing fairly *and* equally to all children.

References

1. Kathleen Wiseman, "Don't Let Equality Bog You Down," *Nation's Business*, December 1990.

PART 6

Estate Planning and Wealth Transfer

24
Essentials of Estate Planning

Every taxpayer already has one estate plan. Created by the taxpayer's state government, it is designed to impose the maximum amount in taxes and transfer costs. This statutory plan clearly lays out the way property will be distributed at death if the decedent dies without a valid will. These state laws, called intestate succession statutes, are based on spousal and blood relationships and specify who will own how much of a decedent's property. If there are no relatives, the state keeps it all.

Alternatively, individuals can contract around this plan and distribute property according to their intentions and desires. Most people today still believe that having a properly drawn will and a bypass or credit shelter trust is sufficient to give them maximum estate tax benefits.

Unfortunately, they are sorely mistaken. The result of such inadequate planning, and the attitude that "it's already taken care of" sow the seeds for unnecessary transfer costs at death, lack of liquidity in the estate to pay the transfer costs, and family disputes surrounding the estate's major asset: the family business.

Impact of Estate Taxes

The gross estate includes the value of all property in which a decedent had an interest at the time of death. Therefore, the gross estate includes business interests, real estate, securities, bank accounts, and personal property *as well as* property interests which pass directly to a beneficiary without becoming part of the estate. This includes life insurance proceeds, retirement plan accounts, jointly owned property, and any property over which the decedent had a general power of appointment.

Property is included in the gross estate at its *fair market value at the date of death*. Fair market value, as discussed earlier, means the price at which a property would change hands between a willing buyer and a willing seller.

There is currently an unlimited marital deduction, which means that a person can leave a surviving spouse his or her entire estate free of the federal estate tax, regardless of the amount involved. Property must qualify for the marital deduction; the executor makes this election on the federal estate tax return. Unfortunately, many business owners believe that because estate taxes can be avoided on the first death, additional estate planning is unnecessary.

Sophisticated planning techniques abound and are available to anyone who is concerned about future family wealth. Estate-planning techniques fall into three categories: freezing the estate, creating tax-exempt wealth, and disposing of wealth already accumulated in a tax-efficient manner.

Estate freezing keeps future growth of an individual's wealth free of tax by diverting that growth to the next generation. It combines income, gift, and estate tax planning, and must be coordinated with family dynamics, coupled with good timing. Creating tax-exempt wealth takes advantage of special provisions in the tax code that exempt certain assets such as life insurance benefits from being taxed. Reducing tax on existing assets can be accomplished through a combination of techniques for gift giving, using charitable deductions and engineering valuations.

Regardless of which combination of techniques business owners employ, they need to remain flexible, as tax laws are likely to continue changing.

As shown in Figure 24-1, the federal estate tax is graduated, beginning at 18 percent and increasing to 55 percent on estates over $3 million. Most family business owners mistakenly look at Figure 24-1 from a current estate perspective, and evaluate the need for estate planning in terms of estate taxes due in the near future.

In fact, planning should be done with a view to saving future as well as current estate taxes. It's important to realize that reasonable appreciation of assets (from inflation as well as real growth) will usually lead to an increased estate tax liability. Between $10 million and $21.04 million, the estate tax is 60

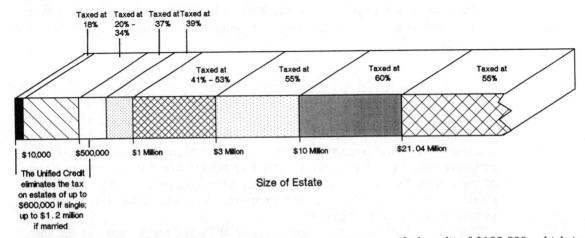

Figure 24-1. *Federal estate tax rates.* Every person receives a unified credit of $192,800, which is the amount of estate tax that would be due on a $600,000 estate. This is also known as the federal estate tax equivalent exemption.

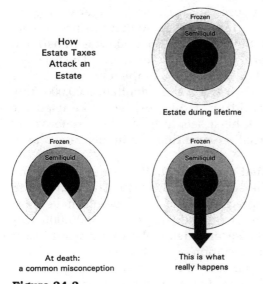

Figure 24-2.

percent through the end of 1992; amounts in excess are taxed at 55 percent. As Figure 24-2 shows, estate taxes primarily drain an estate's liquid assets. They do not—as many people mistakenly believe—"attack" all assets equally.

The primary problem then changes from how much will be due to how it will be paid. Normally the federal estate tax must be paid in full nine months after the date of death. However, the IRS may grant extensions for paying the tax. Installment methods (examined in Chapter 27) offer another option, but they may not be as good "a deal" as they initially seem.

Every person receives a unified credit of $192,800, which is the amount of estate tax that would be due on a gross estate of $600,000. A married couple can therefore leave the first $1.2 million in assets estate-tax-free to their heirs. If annual gifts in excess of $10,000 were made during a lifetime (discussed in Chapter 13), even if gift tax returns were filed but no gift tax was paid, then the excess of $10,000 is deducted from the $600,000 unified credit (per individual).

If a business owner "owns" the family business when he or she dies, the special valuation rules—the fair market value—will determine value in the estate for tax purposes. If ownership has been transferred, then the consideration received (cash, installment notes, and so on) will be subject to estate tax—at least whatever's left that hasn't been spent or given away.

Bypass Trusts

With an unlimited marital deduction, many people still do not understand that leaving everything directly to a spouse is not the most efficient way to transfer assets. The unlimited marital deduction avoids any estate tax on the transfer when all assets are left to a spouse. But it doesn't take advantage of the unified credit at the first death. For example, assume that business owner Jake Jones made no gifts during his lifetime. At death $600,000 was transferred in trust for his children, and the balance went to his wife, Jenny. The $600,000 was subject to an estate tax of $192,800, which was completely offset by the estate tax *credit* of the same amount. When Jenny dies, another $600,000 from the estate can pass tax-free to the children. However, had Jake used the unlimited marital deduction and left all his assets to Jenny, her estate would be larger—by $600,000 plus any appreciation, resulting in a higher estate tax at her death.

On a $5 million estate, if the unlimited marital deduction is used to transfer the entire estate to the spouse, at the second death (assuming that the $5 million has neither been spent nor appreciated), the estate would have a tax liability of $2.198 million. However, if on the first death $600,000 was transferred to a "bypass" trust, on the second death the estate would save $192,800 as well as taxes due on any appreciation of those assets.

Referring back to Figure 24-1, note that estates are subject to progressively higher marginal estate tax rates. That is, there are *lower* marginal rates available to each separate estate. For example, a $5 million estate taxed as one estate would pay $2,198,000 in estate taxes. However, dividing the estate into two, each valued at $2.5 million, would mean estate taxes of $1,666,000—a saving of $532,000! This results from each spouse using a bypass trust *and* having each estate taxed in a lower marginal bracket.

Deferring income tax to the future is usually smart planning. That does not apply to estate tax. Whether an estate grows through asset appreciation or by accumulating income (i.e., earnings on assets which were "saved" and not consumed) the estate tax will be levied on the total value. Therefore, electing to pay taxes earlier—on the first death—should be considered. It makes economic sense to direct up to $2.5 million to the bypass trust on the first death (up to $2.5 million, the estate's top bracket is 49 percent; after $2.5 million, the estate is in a 53 percent bracket). Assets in the bypass trust, plus appreciation, would pass to heirs tax-free at the second death.

If the bypass trust has more than one beneficiary, then it should not be used to receive S corporation stock, since having multiple beneficiaries of the trust could invalidate the S corporation election. An alternative is to have separate bypass trusts, each with a single beneficiary, as long as the trusts' beneficiaries, considered shareholders, do not bring the total number of shareholders to more than the 35 permitted for S corporations.

Marital Deduction Trusts

The Economic Recovery Tax Act of 1981 allows married people to give during their lifetime or to leave at death an unlimited amount of their assets to the other spouse.

In order to qualify for the marital deduction, an owner must transfer property to a spouse in one of three ways: outright, by specific bequests in a will; by having jointly held property pass automatically to the surviving spouse; or by leaving assets in a trust from which the surviving spouse receives all the income at least annually, and over which the spouse has the unrestricted right to control the principal during his or her lifetime or at death (or both if so desired by the original owner).

As discussed above, it is advisable to transfer most of the estate to the other spouse at death (less $600,000 that goes to the bypass trust for kids). By using the unified credit amount and then the marital deduction, an owner can structure the estate plan so that the $600,000 exemptive amount is set aside in a bypass trust. The remaining assets go into a marital trust or outright to the surviving spouse, ensuring that the $600,000 in assets held in the bypass trust will not be taxed at the death of either the first or surviving spouse.

If the family business is to be sold after the death of the current owner, the stock should transfer through the estate as part of the marital deduction. A subsequent sale of the stock might avoid income taxes—if sold at the same value claimed on the estate tax return. At the least, income taxes on the sale should be reduced, by the estate having a stepped-up basis. Keep in mind that the proceeds of the sale (at least, whatever is not spent or gifted) will still be in the spouse's estate for estate tax purposes.

An important factor in deciding to use the marital deduction or the bypass trust is the estate's tax bracket. If the estate is in a 55 percent estate tax bracket, and capital gains taxes are 28 percent, using the bypass trust—that is, going with the taxpayer in the lower tax bracket—might make more sense. Other issues involve the appreciation rate on the asset (whether it is retained or sold) and the time frame being considered for ultimately selling an asset.

Qualified Terminable Interest Property (Q-tip Trusts)

The Q-tip trust can also be used for the marital deduction and offers a major advantage in not requiring a "power of appointment." The power of appointment benefits an owner who might opt to forfeit the marital deduction because of concerns about giving a surviving spouse the freedom to decide who will ultimately inherit the property (e.g., children from a previous marriage). Trusts with a general power of appointment allow the surviving spouse to direct the property to whomever he or she wishes.

The nickname "Q-tip" derives from tax laws that require qualifications for the marital deduction; for example, the property left to the survivor must not be a "terminable interest." This type of marital deduction allowance is called "qualifying terminable interest property."

The terms of a Q-tip trust must specify that the surviving spouse will receive all the annual income and that during the surviving spouse's lifetime, no one can appoint any part of the property to anyone other than the surviving spouse. An executor must make this election on the decedent spouse's estate tax return. To use this trust with the exempt amount plan, the exempt amount goes into a standard bypass trust so that it won't be taxed at the survivor's death. The balance of the marital property goes into the Q-tip trust. (See Figure 24-3.)

Properly structured, the Q-tip trust can hold S corporation stock by having it qualify as a subchapter S trust.

In both the bypass trust and the Q-tip trust, the decedent spouse can name the remainder beneficiaries upon the surviving spouse's death. The power-of-appointment trust would be used primarily by a couple wanting the survivor to reassess the estate in order to select or change the beneficiaries.

One planning opportunity, when a family is charitably inclined, is to use the Q-tip trust in conjunction with a charitable gift at the survivor's death as an alternative to a charitable remainder trust (charitable trusts are discussed in detail in Chapter 26). The survivor would receive all income from the Q-tip, as he or she would from a two-life charitable trust, but would lose the current income tax deductions available with the charitable remainder trust. However, the degree of control over assets retained with the Q-tip trust may make it advantageous over the charitable trust.

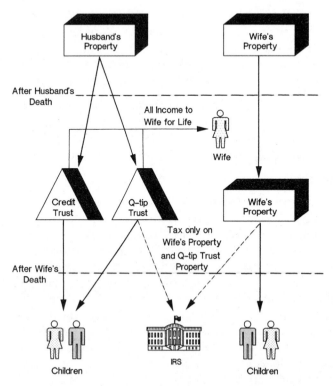

Figure 24-3. Estate distribution using a credit trust and a qualified terminable interest property (Q-tip) trust.

The estate would receive a deduction for the assets being distributed from the Q-tip to charity, thus reducing or eliminating estate taxes. When this arrangement is used in conjunction with an irrevocable life insurance trust (described below), the value of assets distributed to charity can be "replaced" for family members through insurance proceeds. Properly structured, the insurance proceeds would pass income- and estate-tax-free to heirs. *Potentially, estate taxes could be eliminated entirely and the entire value of the estate could be transferred tax-free to family members.*

Revocable Living Trusts

The two major types of trusts are *testamentary* and *living* (or *inter vivos*). Testamentary trusts become effective upon death and are created by will. The governing provisions are included in the trustor's will rather than in a separate trust document. When probate is concluded, property is distributed to the newly created trust, not to the individual heirs.

Living trusts are created during one's lifetime, but may continue after death. The advantage of living over testamentary trusts is that the former are not subject to probate, since the trustee, rather than the decedent, is the legal owner of the property. Even if the decedent were also the trustee, there would be no probate, because the trusteeship is considered an office that outlives the current occupant. Should a trustee die, a successor trustee assumes the office, and the trusteeship continues uninterrupted.

Statutory laws and the terms of the trust agreement dictate what the trust does and how it will operate. These laws vary from state to state, but generally apply various limitations on the powers of the trustee and on the length of time the property can be held in trust. No state will allow a trust to operate indefinitely (except in the cases of charitable or employee trusts).

The person who creates the trust, the trustor, can determine how the trust will operate within the guidelines set up by the state in which it will be effective. The trustor determines the purpose of the trust, the amount and type of property it will contain, the length of time it will last, the beneficiaries, how much they will receive, and when they will receive it. The trustor can also specify conditions that a beneficiary must meet in order to receive income or principal from the trust.

The principal advantage of the revocable living trust is an avoidance of probate. Since probate is a public record, an important aspect of avoiding probate is privacy: Family assets are not disclosed in courthouse records. Property transferred into a living trust belongs to the trustee rather than the trustor, so it is not considered part of the probate estate. To avoid probate, property must be legally transferred into the ownership of the trustee, that is, *the living trust must be funded.* The trustee is usually the grantor of the trust as well.

Revocable living trusts have other advantages. Trustors can:

- Avoid publicity and interruption of income to family members as the trust continues operating the day following the trustor's death

- Provide for future incapacity of the grantor and thus eliminate the need for a court-controlled conservatorship

- Place property beyond the reach of creditors, in some states

If stock is placed into a revocable trust, that transaction should be coordinated with any stock repurchase agreements.

A trustor can always change a revocable trust, either wholly or in part, during the remainder of his or her life. An irrevocable trust is an irreversible step; neither the trust nor any of its terms can be changed in any way or form—except by operation of law.

Transferring Wealth: An Opportunity or a Burden?

Before delving into estate-freezing opportunities and estate-planning techniques, let us pause for a moment to consider the human side of wealth transfer. The use of trusts is an important tool in any effective tax minimization estate plan. Trusts generally can effectively help avoid unnecessary taxes and preserve assets until children can handle them wisely.

Trusts should be established only after factoring in family issues. John Levy, a consultant on inherited wealth, has looked at "the human side" of trust planning and identified five common motives for establishing trusts—and the pitfalls associated with each.

1. *Provide for the children until they are adequately mature.* This laudable motive can sometimes backfire. Seeing and treating young people as immature often serves as a self-fulfilling prophecy—they don't grow up.

2. *Prevent the children from making costly mistakes.* Being overprotected and guarded generally delays maturation. Risk is an essential element of growing up. We all learn from our mistakes, often painfully, but most of us won't learn any other way.

3. *Guard children from the dangers in the world.* Here again, the motivation is usually praiseworthy but the effects can be dubious. Certainly the world is a dangerous place. Inheritors can and often do get involved with manipulative people and dubious causes. But this can be a valuable part of their learning and maturing process. When children are too protected against making their own errors, they may grow up lacking self-confidence and self-esteem—and they may resent their parents.

Wealthy parents usually provide their children with the best academic educations they can find, but too often they seem not to be aware of the importance of other kinds of education, mainly from life experience and making mistakes.

4. *Maintain control over children's lives.* Most parents want their children to be and to behave as the parents would wish. (Too often this is translated as

being as much like the parents as possible.) Many inheritors have described, with sadness and anger, how their parents' promises of inheritance and threats of disinheritance make them feel controlled and coerced. And trusts are often used with distributions contingent on adult heirs' behavior satisfying their parents or trustees.

One way in which parents keep in control through trusts and other such documents is by setting up poor reporting systems which are so intricate that it is nearly impossible for the inheritors to know where they stand. A surprising number of wealthy young adults are in the dark about the extent of the family fortune, how much will come to them, in what form, and when. The response to this sort of ignorance is sadness and anger toward parents, which hurts everyone.

One especially damaging form of control is forcing children to work in the family business, without taking into account their talents and inclinations. There are occasions when such work is right, when it's an opportunity for the inheritor. But many heirs spend their working lives in occupations which really do not suit them. Inheriting wealth should provide beneficiaries with freedom and opportunities, enabling them to choose their work and their lives. But too often parental coercion changes this potential blessing into a burden.

5. *Establish and maintain a dynasty.* Wealthy people can become quite captivated by the prospect of their name and their progeny going on through time as important and famous—the American equivalent of European aristocracy.

Although the stated (and perhaps even real) purpose for setting up the fortune in this way is usually to provide for the security and comfort of the grandchildren and great-grandchildren, too often it seems rather to be a form of self-aggrandizement. Perhaps a clue to the "dynasty" motive is that such trust instruments are usually named after the donors, not the beneficiaries. A much more satisfactory form of immortality is healthy, well-functioning children.[1]

Common Mistakes in Basic Estate Planning

Before we examine the "bells and whistles" (discussed in Chapters 25 and 26), it is important to review common mistakes made by many family business owners.

1. *Improper titling of assets.* Often assets are improperly titled. Asset owners may not realize that the manner in which the asset is titled may take precedence over how their will describes the transfer of that asset in the estate. For example, assume a wife's will directs her assets to go in trust for her current spouse, and after her spouse's death, to the children of her first marriage. If in fact the asset is titled as joint tenants with rights of survivorship, the wife's assets will pass directly to her husband and bypass any trust arrangements she had created. Sometimes life insurance trusts are established but the beneficiary designations are never changed on the policy. One client was surprised to find that an old life insurance policy named his first wife as beneficiary—even though they had been divorced for 10 years.

When the transfer of business interests is coordinated, it is important to check stock certificates, since they are often issued differently than the way the owner remembers. In one example, a business owner assumed that business real estate was titled in the corporate name. However, in checking records, he found that when he had incorporated his business 10 years earlier, the real estate had never been transferred into the corporation. From a planning standpoint, he was happy to learn that the real estate was outside the company, but the accountant was extremely upset because he had been treating the real estate as a corporate asset and depreciating it on the corporate books. Furthermore, the company had never paid rent to the owner because everyone thought the real estate was in the corporation.

2. *Making no provision for the income beneficiary (the spouse) to change trustees.* The local bank that acts as sole trustee probably has known the family for years; bank officers know the family business owner from the local business network and through community involvement. However, do not expect the bank to provide the same services to the spouse that it provides to the family business. The banker may not even know the spouse.

It is important, therefore, to afford the spouse as much flexibility as possible in changing the institutional trustee. Giving the spouse the right in the trust document to change the trustee, however, may keep the bank "on its toes," but may also result in the IRS claiming the spouse had a general power of appointment over the trust assets and therefore including those assets in the spouse's estate for tax purposes.

Some attorneys solve this with a "Trust Protector" clause, which gives someone a power to remove and replace an independent trustee with another independent trustee. The Trust Protector has no other interest in the trust (a sibling of the grantor or a close family friend), and would act to represent the family's interests.

3. *Having disappointed heirs contest the will.*   There are six grounds on which a will may be contested:

- *Improper execution.*   An essential ingredient is missing, such as the proper number of witnesses signing the document.
- *Incompetence.*   Testator was not legally competent to make a will.
- *Duress.*   Testator was under duress or unduly influenced by another to make the will as he or she did.
- *Fraud.*   Someone defrauded the testator into making a will by lying or misleading the individual.
- *Forgery.*   The will is not the true will or the signature is not the testator's.
- *Revocation.*   Someone claims the will had been revoked by the testator before death.

4. *Improperly drafted or nonexistent stock purchase agreements for business interests.*   Often there is no agreement at all. Therefore, the fair market value of a

business will remain an asset of the estate subject to estate tax and will also be subject to probate. Without an agreement, there is no guarantee that the intended heirs will actually receive the business. If the stock goes in trust during the spouse's lifetime (after the decedent's death), what happens if the trustee disagrees with the way the children run the business? What if the spouse remarries? What ability do "active" children have to acquire real estate assets that are used in the operation of the business?

Unrealistic valuation methodology often fails to take advantage of valuation discounts or offset transfer methods. Overinflated valuations may require excessive cash to transfer assets or generate unnecessary estate taxation.

5. *Leaving stock to all children equally, regardless of their involvement in the business.* Those who are active in the business and those who are not active will have different interests. For example, inactive children will want to derive economic value from that asset. If they do not receive compensation from the business, they will probably press for dividends. This directly opposes the interests of the active children, who often want to retain earnings in the company to help the business grow.

The payment of dividends to inactive family members is an inefficient way of transferring earnings out of the company. As an alternative, the active children may attempt to buy out the inactive children, but rarely do the two sides agree on value. The only recourse may be to sell the business. The compensation of active family members may be subject to the control of those who are not active. Again, disagreements often arise as to what constitutes "fair" compensation.

6. *Gifts not substantiated with third-party valuations.* Whether or not a gift tax return has been filed, the ability to substantiate value is important in order to avoid the inclusion of previously transferred assets in the estate.

7. *Improper ownership of life insurance.* Although life insurance proceeds are free of income tax to the beneficiary, those proceeds are often inadvertently included in the estate for estate tax purposes. Or worse, if paid to a corporation, they may also be subject to a 20 percent corporate alternative minimum income tax. An insurance policy purchased to provide liquidity to an estate may contribute to the problem it was designed to solve! If the insurance is included in the estate, its proceeds may inflate the estate, requiring additional estate taxes.

Properly structuring the ownership of insurance can remove the value of the policy from the estate. This can result in the policy providing both an income- and estate-tax-free benefit.

8. *Having the wrong insurance beneficiary.* When insurance proceeds are paid to the corporation, to a spouse, or to others, they may inadvertently be included in the estate. For example, if John Smith held a 51 percent ownership interest in a $2 million business, the value of his stake is $1.02 million. If insurance proceeds of $1 million at his death are paid to the business, the value of his business interest will increase to $1.53 million and the value in the estate will also increase.

An irrevocable life insurance trust can name the spouse as owner and beneficiary of the insurance to provide income and avoid having the proceeds in the spouse's taxable estate. Ultimately, the remainder will go to the children at the second death.

With proper planning, a substantial amount of estate tax liability can be either eliminated or significantly reduced.

Commonly Used Trusts

Type	Major identifying characteristic
Pour-over trust	A living trust designed to receive property to be "poured over" from the trustor's will via his or her probate estate.
Life insurance trust	A living trust designed to receive the proceeds of life insurance; sometimes also to own life insurance.
Bypass trust	A trust that gives a surviving spouse or beneficiary a lifetime interest, to avoid estate taxes on second death.
Marital deduction trust	A trust that takes advantage of the ERTA marital deduction by placing assests in trust, so that the survivor has control of both income and principal.
Q-tip trust	A trust, also qualifying for the marital deduction, in which the spouse has rights to income from the trust until his or her death but has no control over the property within the trust.
Charitable trust	A trust that has a charity as its beneficiary.
Support trust	A trust designed to provide the funds necessary to support a beneficiary.
Accumulation trust	A trust that retains, rather than distributes, all the income it earns.
Discretionary or Sprinkling trust	A trust in which the trustee has the power to retain or pay the income earned in whatever proportions deemed best.
Spendthrift trust	A trust in which the principal is protected from a beneficiary's creditors.

References

1. John L. Levy, Presentation originally given to Bar Association of Santa Clara, California, Estate Planning Division. Revised May 1991.

25

Freezing Taxable Value and Shifting Wealth

With the 1990 Tax Act, the IRS took steps to create a level playing field: Planning transactions will now *begin* with a fair market value determination, although the concept of fair market value will still stimulate diverse opinions. In addition, discounts (for minority interest or lack of marketability) and premiums (for control) are still subjective, even though 50 years of court cases have helped narrow the spread of opinion.

Two sound planning techniques that incorporate the fair market valuation approach have survived IRS challenges: (1) the use of irrevocable trusts and (2) the ability to split and separately value an asset into its income components and a remainder interest.

These two planning techniques, discussed at length in the following chapters, enable family business owners to reduce or eliminate estate taxes while preserving family wealth for future generations. The brief overview of historical planning strategies and IRS attacks presented in this chapter should help create a perspective on where we are today.

Freezes, Anti-freezes, and Refreezes

In years gone by, family business owners and their attorneys would conceive an estate plan that was, in essence, an attempt to freeze the value of Mom or Dad's family business stock from appreciating for estate tax purposes. If the stock value could be "frozen," then the future estate taxes on that value would also be frozen. The common method used was a preferred-stock recapitalization. All current value would be packaged into a new class of preferred stock owned by Mom or Dad. All future value was attributed to a newly created class of (unfrozen) common stock. Because the newly created common didn't have any current value, it could be given away to family members with no gift taxes.

As the family business grew, the common stock appreciated, as planned. The preferred stock retained its frozen value. Estate taxes could be projected on the nonmoving preferred stock; the family had time to create liquid assets to pay estate taxes due on the preferred.

Some of the important rights that many attorneys assigned to the preferred shares included retained voting rights, conversion rights, and noncumulative dividend rights, which fueled the IRS's claim, during its estate tax audit after Mom or Dad died, that the frozen preferred was merely a disguised form of common stock. In fact, the IRS claimed that it shouldn't be frozen at all, and that gift taxes should be paid whenever the rights were not exercised and estate taxes paid as if the preferred shares were garden-variety common stock.

Despite the outcry from family business owners, my own view is that the IRS clampdown under the 1987 Tax Act was a blessing in disguise. Preserving control in the hands of aging owners until they died might be what aging owners (or their aging advisers) wanted, but it wasn't particularly good for the family business. The preferred recaps allowed owners to ignore reality during succession planning. But letting go is, in fact, a good idea if the business is to survive.

In Section 2036(c) of the 1987 Tax Act the IRS employed the now-(in)famous anti-freeze devices. Many claimed the IRS was using a sledgehammer to kill a fly. Throughout 1987 and 1988, the IRS issued new rules, clarified others, and confused everyone, including its own people. In essence a "string" was deemed to be attached to most transactions—whether gift or sale—involving family businesses. This string allowed the IRS to pull all transactions back into the parents' estate for estate tax purposes. Suddenly it made more tax sense to transfer the family business to a stranger than to a family member working in the company. All transactions, whether tax-motivated or not, were suspect.

However, Section 2036(c) inadvertently encouraged aging business owners to let go of their companies. One technique permitted by the IRS allowed owners to exchange their controlling interests for qualified debt, which enabled the kids finally to get control, and the parents to implement an IRS-blessed, legitimate freeze.

Succession plans, however, weren't thought out any better than before. Aging owners were motivated more by fear of estate taxes than by the need to perpetuate the family business. Even with qualified-debt transactions, valuation disputes with the IRS increased. Public outcries of "foul" turned up the heat in Washington, and late in 1990 Congress repealed Section 2036(c) of the IRS Code retroactively to 1987. In its place came a new chapter of the Internal Revenue Code (IRC): Chapter 14.

Chapter 14 goes to the heart of the family transfer: Any transfer must be fairly valued (and possibly taxed) at the time of transfer. The provision created special valuation rules for transfers of stock in family business corporations. The rules also apply to transfers of interest in trusts and to buy-sell (shareholder) agreements. An important exception is that Chapter 14 preserved the use of valuation discounts—for minority interests or lack of marketability—in family transfers.

The special valuation rules are (no surprise) more complex. Estate freezes through preferred-stock recapitalizations are still discussed, but not implemented very often. Outside valuation opinions are more important than ever. As we'll see below, there are still planning opportunities. But as one business owner advised: "Don't die yet."

Family Transfer Strategies

Strategy 1: Give Early and Give Often, but Cut All Strings Attached to Gifts

Under this strategy, each parent can give an annual gift of $10,000 to each child. Each spouse can gift his or her full $600,000 unified credit to heirs without tax. However, there is serious talk in Congress about reducing or eliminating this credit in the future.

Gifts in trust can be useful when the donor business owner does not want to make an outright gift. A trust as receptacle for gifts can be a flexible device and can be structured to give broad discretionary powers to the trustee. In addition, trusts can provide a flexible plan of distribution to take into account the needs of beneficiaries.

From a tax point of view, the trust to which gifts are made must be irrevocable; otherwise, the gifts will be disregarded for tax purposes. In order to maximize tax benefits, the gift should qualify for the annual gift tax exclusion discussed in Chapter 13. In addition, if the donor retains certain prohibited rights, the value of the gift may be brought back into the donor's estate. These prohibited rights include the right to alter, amend, revoke, or terminate the transfer.

One 79-year-old client, who wanted to retain an interest in his business but was also concerned about future estate taxes, understood that it would be beneficial to reduce his ownership below 50 percent so that his estate, at his death, could avail itself of minority-interest discounts. At the same time, he was concerned that his three daughters, who were not active in the business, might get divorced. Since the family business was in a community property state, his concern was well founded. Outright gifts, at the time they are made, are treated as "sole and separate" property, not community property. However, the increase in the value of the gift may be a community property interest.

Let's assume stock in the family business is gifted to a child and valued at $100,000. The sole and separate value is $100,000. The stock value grows to $600,000 and then a divorce occurs. Depending on the state, the courts may find that the $500,000 increase is a community property asset, especially if the increase occurred because one or both spouses were active in the business during the tenure of marriage.

The 79-year-old client chose to recapitalize the company's stock into voting and nonvoting shares and use three irrevocable living trusts. One trust was established for each daughter; each was gifted nonvoting shares. By gifting 17 percent of the value of the business to each of the trusts, the client removed 51 percent of the value from his and his wife's estate, using the unified credit and electing to pay some gift tax on the transfer.

The trusts were established to distribute the stock (or the value, if the stock was sold by the trustees) to each of the daughters one year after Dad's death. The original gifts and growth in their value (including the proceeds of a sale) would be sole and separate until one year after Dad's death. The trustees would distribute the proceeds of a sale to the daughters at that time. Since the daughters were not active, and had no plans to come into the business, Dad instructed the trustees to sell the business after his death. Therefore, Dad protected the sole and separate nature of the gift *and* a potential windfall (if the business were sold within a year of Dad's death) from becoming a community property interest.

Strategy 2: Create a Grantor-Retained Annuity Trust

Gifts can be made, and value transferred, on a discounted basis by transferring income-producing assets to a grantor-retained annuity trust (GRAT). A discount is realized, since only a portion of the gift is valued for gift tax purposes.

The donor transfers income-producing assets (appraised at fair market value) to an irrevocable trust, which pays a fixed annuity (determined at the time of the transfer) to the donor for a fixed period. At the end of the period, the trust terminates, and trust assets are distributed to the trust's beneficiaries (e.g., the donor's children).

The value, if any, of the remainder interest in the trust constitutes a taxable gift, which is considered a gift of a future interest and is therefore not eligible for the $10,000 annual exclusion. However, the unified credit can be used to offset any gift tax due (up to $1.2 million of gift value). The fair market value of the gift is reduced by the present value of the donor's annuity payments. Hypothetically, if annuity payments are high enough and last long enough, the present value of the annuity may equal the value of the assets transferred, resulting in a gift tax value of zero. To obtain maximum benefit, though, business owners should increase the amount transferred to the GRAT by $1.2 million, the unified credit amount. The increased value of assets transferred still results in a zero gift tax.

However, if the donor dies before the expiration of the trust term, trust assets are included in the donor's estate as if he or she did no planning. If the donor outlives the term of the trust, the asset passes to the beneficiaries at the termination of the trust and avoids estate inclusion.

Owners should consider using S corporation stock with a GRAT as a means of retaining income (the S dividends) while shifting future value. One client recapitalized his company, an S corporation, into voting and nonvoting shares and then transferred the nonvoting shares to three separate GRATs for his children.

Another example is Lee, a 60-year-old client who wanted to transfer property to her son, Jake. The property was a debt-free warehouse building leased to her family business. The appraised fair market value of the warehouse was $3,050,000. The applicable 10.4 percent federal interest rate at the time provided an annual income of $317,200 for Lee and her spouse for the 10-year term of the GRAT (also the length of the lease). The business had already decided not to use the warehouse after the expiration of the lease, which provided sufficient rent to cover the trust payments to Lee.

The present value of this 10-year annuity is $1,916,010, which resulted in a taxable gift of $1,133,990. As shown in Figure 25-1, Lee and her spouse used their unified credits to offset the gift tax due. Alternatively, Lee could have chosen a different trust term, illustrated in Figure 25-2, and elected to pay some gift tax.

Assuming the property appreciates at 4 percent a year, the warehouse building in 10 years will be worth more than $4.5 million. If Lee and her spouse live beyond the 10-year trust term, the warehouse building, after the 10 years, will be owned by Jake. There were no gift taxes (they used their unified credit) and there will be no additional transfer taxes. If Lee and her husband had retained the warehouse building in their estate (or if they die before the 10-year trust expires), the property and the appreciation could be taxed at a 55 percent estate tax rate, resulting in almost $2.5 million in estate taxes.

Lee's objective was to transfer an asset to Jake during her lifetime. Because the business would no longer use the warehouse after the lease expired, Jake would own the warehouse free and clear and could sell it at that time. After

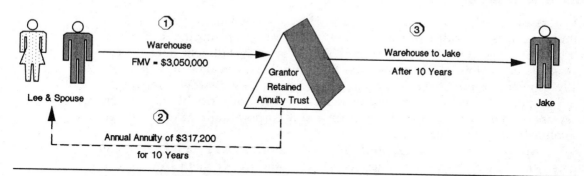

1.) Lee transfers the warehouse to the trust. The value of the gift for gift tax purposes is $1,133,990 (the fair market value of the property transferred less the present value of the income interest retained). Lee and her spouse use their unified credit to eliminate the gift tax.

2.) Lee and her spouse receive an annuity income of $317,200 from the trust for 10 years.

3.) At the end of the term, the warehouse passes to Jake.

RESULTS:

- Removes a valuable asset from the estate at a reduced transfer tax cost.
- Transfers future appreciation of the warehouse to Jake.
- Maximizes the use of the unified credit.
- Provides Lee and her spouse with the present use and enjoyment of the warehouse.

Figure 25-1. Grantor-retained annuity trust (GRAT).

(A)	(B)	(C)	(D)	(E)	(F)	(G)
Term of Annuity	Warehouse FMV	P.V. of Annuity (at 10.4%)	Value of Gift (B – C)	Unified Credits Used	Remaining Unified Credits	Gift Tax Payable
5	$3,050,000	$1,190,250	$1,859,750	$1,200,000	$0	$659,750
10	$3,050,000	$1,916,010	$1,133,990	$1,133,990	$66,010	$0
15	$3,050,000	$2,358,545	$691,455	$691,455	$508,545	$0
20	$3,050,000	$2,628,383	$421,617	$421,617	$778,383	$0
25	$3,050,000	$3,050,000	$0	$0	$1,200,000	$0

(E) Assumes that both Lee and her spouse use their unified credits.

Figure 25-2. How the term of the GRAT annuity affects the value of the gift and the gift tax payable.

paying income taxes on the sale, Jake can use the proceeds to buy his uncle's interest in the family business.

Strategy 3: Coordinate a SERP with a Business Transfer

Owners can shift business ownership to their children tax efficiently. The family reduces the value of the company by creating an unfunded liability with a SERP and sells the business to the kids for an installment note. Or the owner defers selling stock to the kids for a number of years, until they are fully groomed to take over. Meanwhile, the owner converts this company to an S corporation and receives dividend income without a double tax. When they are deemed ready, the children form a new corporation that will manage the old company for a fee.

This works like a recapitalization. Children are protected by a management agreement, which provides business continuity, and they benefit from future growth in the business by having the management agreement include a performance-based compensation clause.

In early 1991 media coverage of preferred-stock recapitalizations following the 1990 Tax Act focused on a central point: There are better ways to skin the cat. One of the major difficulties in using preferred-stock recaps is the requirement to use high (nondeductible) dividend payments. Additional problems are created because of special valuation rules that apply to the preferred shares (which may not agree with normal valuation practices), and restrictions on distribution and conversion rights. Ultimately, unexpected gift taxes may be due as a result of an incorrect preferred-stock recap.

On the other hand, if a stockholder's objective is to freeze value, there are additional, simpler methods to accomplish the same result—methods that are probably more beneficial from the standpoint of perpetuating the business.

Nonqualified plans are one substitute method of deriving income from the business instead of preferred stock dividends. They have two significant advantages as well:

1. The nonqualified plan (e.g., a SERP) is paid with pretax corporate dollars; dividends are paid with after-tax dollars. Because of the corporate taxes saved, the company's ability to make the promised payments is enhanced.

2. A finite-life SERP (e.g., benefits paid for 20 years) can be a way of making value disappear. The value of the SERP in the estate of the participant is the present value of the future payments that haven't been received. If the participant dies in the nineteenth year, the value in the estate is the one year of benefit payments remaining. If the unlimited marital deduction is used, the balance of payments due would go to the spouse estate-tax-free.

Alternatively, if there's a concern for spousal income, the SERP could be designed to terminate at the participant's death. The company's tax savings (realized from the SERP) could be used to fund a split-dollar insurance program on the life of the SERP participant with an irrevocable trust as beneficiary. At the participant's death, the insurance proceeds (in excess of premiums paid) would go to the irrevocable trust established to provide spousal income. The insurance proceeds paid to the trust would provide the spouse a lifetime income at the same level as the participant. And the funds would be available for the children, estate-tax-free, at the spouse's death, since they would be sheltered inside the irrevocable trust.

Strategy 4: Create a Family Limited Partnership

A family partnership can be formed to segregate the three components of ownership: income, equity, and control. By using a family partnership, a parent can maintain control of the asset and continue to receive some of the income. Future appreciation may be passed through to the children by gifting limited partnership interests. Or the limited partnership interests can be transferred to a GRAT to increase the leverage of the gift. If planned properly, the value of the limited partnership interests transferred can be reduced by valuation discounts.

Strategy 5: Sell Rapidly Appreciating Assets to Children

By selling or spinning off rapidly appreciating assets to the next generation, the parents can effectively freeze their estate. There are several ways to accomplish this, including a sale for cash or a redemption of stock by the corporation using installment notes.

Strategy 6: Consider Disclaiming Inheritances

If the next-generation business owners are wealthy, they might wish to disclaim any inheritance they are entitled to receive. By passing the assets on to their kids, they avoid any taxation in their own estate. This may seem simple, but too often it is never considered as an opportunity to pass wealth to a lower bracket.

Summary

The key to effective planning is the integration of objectives and tax vehicles. Combining the proper tools with right reasons will also give the family an alternative to paying high taxes. Flexibility and simplicity are desirable goals. Unfortunately, many of today's estate tax strategies are complex, but are well worth the time and effort invested in understanding them.

26

Using Irrevocable Trusts to Explode Asset Value or Make Taxable Value Disappear

Irrevocable trusts have become *the* planning tool for value shifting and for reducing (or eliminating) estate taxes. This tool is rapidly becoming the cornerstone for gifting (in community property states), for creating tax-free wealth for multiple generations, for making value disappear, and for creating lifetime income.

Figure 26-1 illustrates the fact that many trusts already discussed in this book use the irrevocable trust as the common vehicle. Rabbi and secular trusts (Chapter 10) use irrevocable trusts to provide retirement security. Voting and divorce trusts (Chapter 25) use irrevocable trusts as a means of retaining control over family business stock. Dynasty trusts, charitable remainder annuity trusts (CRATs), charitable remainder unitrusts (CRUTs), and wealth replacement trusts—all discussed in this chapter—use irrevocable trusts as a way to make value disappear, explode tax-free, or replace assets transferred out of the estate. Grantor-retained annuity trusts (GRATs) and their "cousins," grantor-retained unitrusts (GRUTs), use irrevocable trusts to provide income for a period of time and then move assets out of an estate at a discount. Qualified personal residence trusts (QPRTs) and grantor-retained income trusts (GRITs) use irrevocable trusts to transfer valuable personal residences to the next generation. Q-tip and bypass trusts (Chapter 24) use irrevocable trusts as a basic estate-planning vehicle.

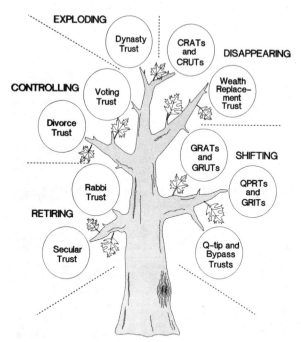

Figure 26-1. The irrevocable trust can explode asset value tax-free and/or make taxable value disappear.

Life Insurance Trusts

Trusts that own a life insurance policy, or that are the beneficiary of a life insurance policy, are called life insurance trusts. If these trusts are revocable (meaning the grantor can change the policy or the trust at any time), the proceeds will be included in the estate for estate tax purposes.

By contrast, the irrevocable life insurance trust can shelter insurance proceeds from the insured's gross estate (meaning the proceeds would not be subject to estate tax) as well as from the probate estate of the beneficiary *and* from the gross estate of the spouse. The irrevocable trust also permits income tax planning for the future earnings of the insurance proceeds, since proceeds may be distributed to income beneficiaries or retained inside the trust. In addition, the trust offers the advantages of property management and flexibility with respect to the benefits and eventual disposition of the property.

As shown in Figure 26-2, the irrevocable life insurance trust provides lifetime income to the spouse, but eliminates the value of the insurance proceeds in the spouse's estate. This saves estate taxes (on the second death) and increases the amount the children will eventually receive as an inheritance.

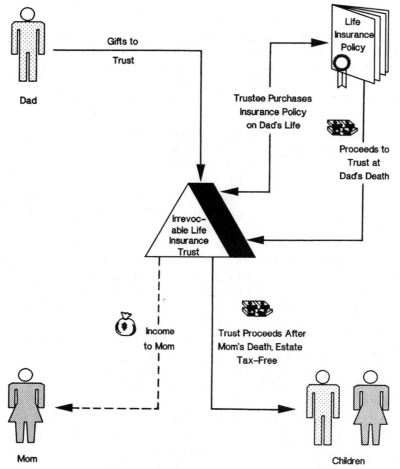

Figure 26-2. The irrevocable life insurance trust.

Irrevocable Life Insurance Trusts

After a string of unsuccessful court challenges, the IRS announced late in 1991 that it would no longer litigate the issue of whether the proceeds of a life insurance policy are includable in an individual's gross estate when an irrevocable trust is the applicant, original owner, and beneficiary of the insurance contract. This announcement lends an extra degree of certainty to the fact that the irrevocable life insurance trust is one of the most beneficial estate-planning techniques available.

In a typical irrevocable life insurance trust, an individual empowers the trustee to buy a new policy on his or her life and contributes enough cash to enable the trustee to pay the premiums. Assignment of an existing policy would be considered a gift for gift tax purposes. Upon the insured individual's death, the policy proceeds paid to the trust would generally be excluded from the individual's taxable estate. The result: a significant reduction in the effective rate of federal and state transfer taxes, since the face amount of the insurance has been removed from the taxable estate. The insured must not retain or transfer within three years of death, any "incidents of ownership" in the policy. Incidents of ownership include changing a beneficiary, surrendering or canceling the policy, assigning the policy, revoking an assignment, pledging the policy for a loan, and obtaining a policy loan against the policy's surrender value.

Before 1991, the IRS had consistently maintained that in paying the premiums on a policy within an irrevocable life insurance trust, the insured individual was making a "constructive transfer" of an ownership interest in the policy and thus retained an incident of ownership in the policy—a "string" to the asset which required that the proceeds be included in the estate. However, the courts had just as consistently ruled that payment of premiums is irrelevant in determining whether an individual has retained any incidents of ownership. In making the announcement that it will no longer litigate this issue, the IRS pointed out that its decision was based solely on those adverse court decisions, and not on any change in its position. In the view of the IRS, the proceeds of these policies should be included in the taxpayer's estate.

Establishing an irrevocable life insurance trust can provide a tremendous transfer tax saving. For example, the federal transfer tax saving that can result from the exclusion of a $1 million policy on the life of an individual with a $3 million taxable estate is $550,000. Moreover, if the arrangement is properly structured, the proceeds can be transferred to the insured's grandchildren without being subject to the 55 percent generation-skipping tax.

Additional benefits are that the magnitude of the estate can be increased on a tax-free basis for heirs. When the irrevocable life insurance trust is modified into a dynasty trust or Megatrust™ (described below), opportunities can be created for establishing a family bank for multiple generations. Probate expenses and publicity regarding assets can be avoided, and the grantor of the trust can control the dispositive provisions through the design of the trust terms.

As with all plans, there are cautions and pitfalls as well:

- The trust cannot be a simple off-the-shelf document. Unskilled attorneys can mistakenly draft provisions that can cause tax problems later on.

- The trust is truly irrevocable, which means the grantor can't change the trust in any way later on. Stable family relationships are a real plus here.

- The grantor, who is often the insured, should not act as trustee of the irrevocable trust. Nor should the insured be able to change the trustee in the future. (The grantor may act as trustee of a revocable trust.)

Gifts to the trust, usually sufficient in amount to pay insurance premiums as they come due, can avoid gift tax as a present-interest gift as long as the irrevocable trust has "Crummey" powers (discussed in Chapter 13). That is, each time a contribution to the trust is made, the beneficiary has a temporary right to demand withdrawal of the funds. If the demand right is not exercised, the annual transfer for that year stays in the trust and is available to the trustee to pay insurance premiums.

In some cases, the grantor may elect *not* to use the Crummey powers and subject the transfer to gift taxes, or may use a portion of the unified credit. This can occur when the grantor is concerned about the spendthrift nature of children or grandchildren (who might withdraw funds during the 45-day notice period) and yet wants to provide a managed income stream to those same children (estate-tax-free) after the grantor's death.

Creating a Family Bank

An irrevocable life insurance trust can be used to create a family bank that spans several generations.

Technically known as a dynasty trust or Megatrust™, a family bank provides income to the grantor's children for their lifetime, and the proceeds pass tax-free to grandchildren and unborn great grandchildren. The dynasty trust avoids estate taxes as well as generation-skipping transfer taxes. The trust could conceivably be drafted to last 120 years!

Property held in conventional trusts is subject to a generation-skipping tax of 55 percent when assets "skip" a generation. The tax is imposed at the time of the skip. However, there is a $1 million exemption for an individual; $2 million for a married couple. The 1988 Tax Act changed many generation-skipping rules that made family wealth retention almost an impossible task beyond the $2 million generation-skipping exemption.

The dynasty trust avoids the generation-skipping tax by shielding assets inside a custom-designed irrevocable trust. When life insurance is acquired inside the trust, it creates an asset that mushrooms in value at death. The premiums deposited to the trust are often leveraged five to ten times in value at the death of the insured. The growth pattern is depicted in Figure 26-3. Assume a married couple, both age 55, transfers $100,000 a year to a dynasty trust for 12 years. Using their combined unified credit (ignoring the annual exclusion for this example), no gift taxes would be due. The trust uses the deposit to acquire a $10 million survivor life policy on the couple and pays the premium each year for 12 years. The policy is constructed so that future premiums are not projected to be due after the twelfth year.

The initial insurance face amount is $10 million; that is, at the death of the second spouse, the trust assets would "mushroom" into $10 million of income- and estate-tax-free cash.

Assume the trustees (perhaps children of the insured) are allowed to loan (or distribute) 70 percent of the trust's annual *earnings* to family members as venture capital, or start-up seed money, for future family enterprises. If the $10 million earns 7 percent (tax-free), and 2 percent is always reinvested (5 percent is loaned or distributed each year to family members), the fund would

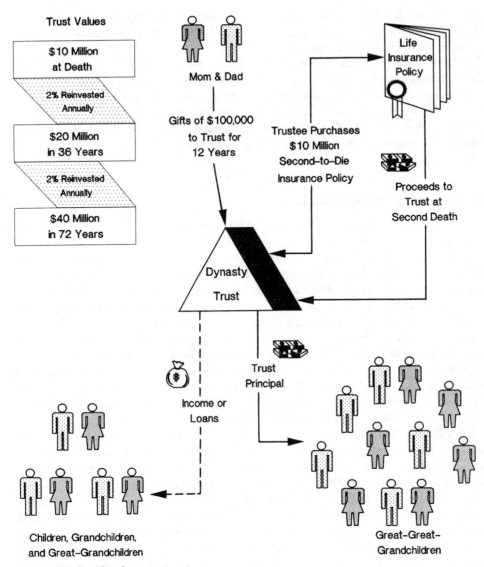

Trust Values

| $10 Million at Death |
| 2% Reinvested Annually |
| $20 Million in 36 Years |
| 2% Reinvested Annually |
| $40 Million in 72 Years |

Mom & Dad

Gifts of $100,000 to Trust for 12 Years

Life Insurance Policy

Trustee Purchases $10 Million Second-to-Die Insurance Policy

Proceeds to Trust at Second Death

Dynasty Trust

Income or Loans

Trust Principal

Children, Grandchildren, and Great-Grandchildren

Great-Great-Grandchildren

Figure 26-3. The dynasty trust.

grow tax-free to $20 million in 36 years, approximately when the children die. In another 36 years, the trust would have grown to $40 million! The initial tax-free gift of $1.2 million ($100,000 annually for 12 years) has become a $40 million fund within three generations. Meanwhile the second and third generations benefit annually from the family bank.

A dynasty trust can be used in conjunction with a split-dollar life insurance plan (discussed below) whereby the family business pays the insurance premiums even though the policy is owned by the trust. The business can recover its premiums at the first death of the insureds. Or the dynasty trust can be coordinated with the marital deduction Q-tip trust. The Q-tip trust can provide income to the spouse, with proceeds at death of the spouse going to charity. At the spouse's death, the companion dynasty trust mushrooms in value when insurance proceeds are collected. The entire estate avoids taxation while wealth is preserved for future generations.

Making Taxable Value Disappear (and Replacing It Tax-Free)

Family business owners have often been active in their community while building the family business. Charitable activities and community support often go hand in hand with the family business's success. Typically, owners are involved as board members with their local hospitals, economic development councils, or chambers of commerce. As discussed earlier, increasing involvement of an aging owner with outside organizations may present an opportunity for successors to raise the issue of management and ownership transfer.

Genuine concern by an owner for community and charitable causes can often be coordinated with extraordinary planning opportunities. These planning opportunities have significant income and estate tax benefits for the family business owner, but they will likely backfire if they are not supported by a truly charitable intent.

Again, the cornerstone is the irrevocable trust, and the planning technique involves splitting an asset into an income stream and a remainder interest. In this case, the beneficiary of the remainder interest is a "qualified" charity. The beneficiary of the income interest is the grantor-donor and/or the spouse. The income can be paid for life, for both spouses.

Examples of qualified charities are nonprofit schools and hospitals, churches and synagogues, United Way, YMCA, YMHA, American Red Cross, Heart Association, American Cancer Society, Boy Scouts, and Girl Scouts. The IRS publishes a list of qualified charities; local community foundation organizations are often good contacts for information on local charitable organizations.

Figure 26-4 shows the steps involved in setting up a charitable remainder trust. A donor establishes an irrevocable trust and contributes property to it. The property may be cash or securities, closely held stock in the family business, or a piece of (debt-free) real estate. The property must be appraised by an independent valuation firm.

Because the ultimate beneficiary of the trust is a charitable organization, the donor may take a current income tax deduction equal to the value of the remainder interest that will go to the charity after the donor receives income for a specified period, such as during the life of the donor and spouse.

If the property in the trust at any point fails to provide sufficient income to satisfy payments to the donor, the trustee will sell the property and invest the

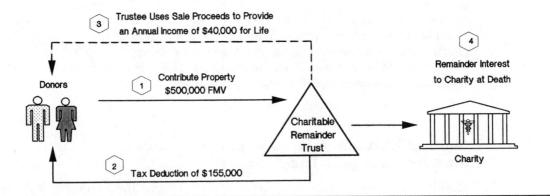

1.) Donors transfer asset worth $500,000 to the trust. The trust sells the asset and invests the proceeds.

2.) Donors receive a current year income tax deduction of $155,000 for the transfer of property to the trust.

3.) Donors receive an annual fixed income (annuity payment) of $40,000 from the trust for life.

4.) Remaining trust assets pass to the named charity at the second death.

RESULTS:

- Removes a valuable appreciating asset from the estate.

- A non-income-producing asset is converted to provide the donors with a lifetime fixed income.

- Income taxes are saved currently and estate taxes are saved at death.

Figure 26-4. The charitable remainder trust.

proceeds in something that will produce the required income. For example, closely held family business stock normally will not pay dividends; yet if the donor contributed family business stock to a trust that was obligated to pay income to the donor, the trustee would need to sell the stock quickly and reinvest the proceeds.

The logical buyer for the stock is the family business itself! A landmark court case, which set a precedent for this technique, is described below.

Mr. Palmer had voting control of both a corporation and a private foundation. He contributed his stock to the foundation and took a charitable contribution deduction. He then directed the corporation to purchase the shares from the foundation for cash. Neither Palmer nor his foundation recognized taxable income on the transaction. The IRS argued that, in substance, the corporation had redeemed the shares directly from Palmer (a taxable event), followed by a contribution of the proceeds to the foundation.

The Tax Court supported Palmer. The IRS lost.

The trust has the right to keep the stock. In practice, however, trustees do not prefer to invest in nonmarketable securities, and the corporation does not want its stock in the hands of outsiders. Therefore, the corporation offers to redeem the stock at the established value for cash. When stock is placed back in the corporate treasury, a donor who is the sole stockholder has fewer shares, but still owns 100 percent of equity in the company.

Private foundations are generally funded with cash or marketable securities, not closely held stock in a family business. When a private foundation is funded with closely held stock, the income tax deduction is equal to the donor's basis in the stock, not its current market value. However, the income tax deduction with a charitable remainder trust (having one or more public charities as beneficiaries) is equal to the full market value of the closely held stock, minus the present value of the income paid to the grantor.

There are a number of additional advantages to using charitable remainder trusts:

- When the trustee sells the asset, no taxes are paid on the capital gains.
- Proceeds can be reinvested in income-producing assets that grow tax-free.
- For the rest of the donor's and spouse's life, a secure income stream is guaranteed.
- Future estate taxes are reduced, since the property conveyed to the trust (and the future growth) is not included in the estate for tax purposes.

Variations on the Theme

Charitable remainder trusts, more recently called wealth accumulation trusts (WATs), allow the donor to choose how the income will be paid: When paid as a percentage of the trust assets, it is called a charitable remainder unitrust (CRUT); when paid as a fixed payment, it becomes a charitable remainder annuity trust (CRAT). The payout in both cases must be at least 5 percent.

Assume $500,000 in property was contributed to a CRUT, the property yields 10 percent, and the CRUT percentage is 8 percent, or $40,000 the first year. As the other 2 percent compounds each year in the CRUT, the actual dollar amount distributed in the second year will be $40,480, and will continue to increase each year. If the same $500,000 in property were contributed to a CRAT, with the same 10 percent yield, the CRAT annuity would be $40,000. Although this also equals an 8 percent payout the first year, the dollar amount remains constant while trust assets appreciate.

Which is better, CRUT or CRAT? The decision is complex, but one consideration is that IRS annuity tables used to determine the remainder interest of the CRAT often result in a much larger *current* income tax deduction for the donor than does the CRUT. Therefore, current income tax planning must be coordinated with the choice of CRUT or CRAT. Another determination relates to the type of property transferred, its current yield, and opportunities (if any) for the trustee to sell the asset and replace it with a higher-yielding investment.

Using Real Estate

The charitable remainder trust can be an effective tool for selling appreciated real estate that has a low cost basis, has no debt, and provides little or no income.

Assume that Bill and Sandra have an office building worth $600,000 with a cost basis of $25,000. With no debt on the building, it nets $24,000, or 4 percent per year. The charitable remainder trust can sell the building and invest the proceeds at 8 percent to provide Bill and Sandra with an income of $48,000 per year. Bill and Sandra can avoid the tax on selling the building, increase their cashflow, and leave more of an estate to their children if they elect to create the companion wealth replacement trust (discussed below).

There are several cautions to bear in mind before making charitable gifts of real property:

1. Have a qualified appraisal.
2. Avoid having a sale of the property already arranged.
3. Determine whether accelerated depreciation taken in prior years will result in taxable income to the donor.
4. Make sure the property is not still encumbered by a mortgage.
5. Determine if the alternative minimum tax will be a factor.

Wealth Replacement Trusts

At the death of the donor (or the donor and spouse in a two-life trust), the property in a charitable remainder trust will be distributed to a qualified charity. In certain cases, the donor may want to *replace* for the family the value of the assets going to charity. The irrevocable life insurance trust can be established as a companion trust to accomplish replacement, usually *with no cost to the donor.*

This is also referred to as a wealth replacement trust (WRT), for several reasons.

- The income tax saving generated from the charitable trust can be gifted to the companion wealth replacement trust.
- The wealth replacement trust uses the funds to acquire second-to-die or survivor life insurance on the life of the donor and spouse.
- The wealth replacement trust is the owner and beneficiary of the life insurance contract.
- At the second death (of the donor and spouse) the insurance proceeds are paid to the properly drafted wealth replacement trust, free of both income and estate tax.
- The beneficiaries of the wealth replacement trust can be the donor's children, who then receive tax-free cash, to replace the asset that went to charity.

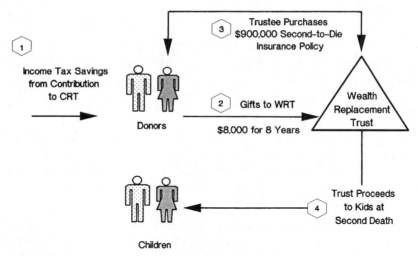

Figure 26-5. The wealth replacement trust.

Figure 26-5 shows the operation of a wealth replacement trust tied to a second-to-die life insurance policy. For example, Roy had an offer to sell his business to a large acquisition company. As part of the proposed transaction, Roy would receive $900,000 cash for his stock along with noncompete covenants and consulting contracts.

Roy's basis if he sold his stock was low, so the entire $900,000 would be subject to capital gains tax. The projected tax due was approximately $250,000. Roy intended to invest the remaining $650,000 in tax-exempt securities and expected a tax-free income of about $45,000 per year for himself and his wife.

Roy wanted to protect the $650,000 for his two children but was surprised to learn that, in his estate tax bracket of 55 percent, almost $360,000 in estate taxes would be due after his and his wife's death. He was frustrated and angry when he realized that, of the original amount of the cash, his family would keep only about 32 cents of each dollar.

At my suggestion that he give the stock to charity, Roy balked. He felt that at least he was keeping about $300,000! If he gave it away, he wouldn't even have that. He had already made plenty of charitable gifts while in business. Now he was interested in taking care of himself and his wife and kids. "Give it to charity? No thanks."

I asked him to listen to my rationale for giving it away. Within an hour, he was on the phone to his attorney instructing him to prepare documents to gift the entire $900,000 in stock to a local children's hospital.

Here's why. Roy would contribute the stock to a charitable remainder trust. The trustee would sell the stock to the acquisition company and receive the $900,000 sale proceeds. The trust is a tax-exempt entity, so no taxes would be due. The trustee would invest the sale proceeds in income-producing vehicles and pay Roy and his wife an income for the rest of their lives. The hospital will own the remainder interest. Roy's contribution to the trust qualifies for a charitable contribution deduction.

The present value of the remainder interest can be determined from IRS tables. In Roy's case, the present value of the remainder interest, $180,000, was taken as a charitable contribution deduction on his tax return. Again, because the trust is a tax-exempt entity, it didn't owe one nickel in income taxes on the entire $900,000 collected.

Result 1.   In a 31 percent bracket, Roy *saved* over $55,000 in taxes instead of paying $250,000 in capital gains taxes. By investing in high-quality bonds and government securities, the trustee felt the trust could achieve a 9 percent yield, providing Roy and his wife with an income of $81,000 per year. After taxes, they would net about $56,000.

Result 2.   Giving the stock to charity resulted in $10,000 *more* annual net income than keeping the proceeds, paying taxes, and investing the net proceeds.

To make sure that his children realize some value from the note after he and his wife die, Roy used his tax saving from the contribution of the stock to fund a wealth replacement trust. The trust is the owner and beneficiary of an insurance policy covering both Roy and his wife. This type of life insurance is called a second-to-die contract, since the insurance company covers two lives in one policy and pays the death benefit on the second death. Because the joint life expectancy for two lives is greater than that for one life, the cost to acquire the coverage is often substantially less than the cost to acquire single coverage.

The wealth replacement trust is not subject to estate tax on either Roy's or his wife's death. The insurance proceeds for the children will be free of both income tax and estate tax.

Result 3.   The children will receive the full amount of the stock, $900,000, on the death of their parents (in the form of life insurance proceeds). The $360,000 in potential estate taxes is eliminated. Roy will gift $8000 annually to the trust, for eight years, so the trust will have sufficient funds to pay the insurance premium. After eight years, no further premium is required. Roy is still ahead, in terms of annual cashflow.

Result 4.   There's a new wing being dedicated at the hospital. Guess who it's named after?

To summarize the results of this transaction, Roy and his wife: (1) saved more than $600,000 in income and estate taxes, (2) preserved a $900,000 asset intact for the next generation, (3) created a new $900,000 gift for charity, and (4) enhanced their personal cashflow by over 20 percent.

The benefits of charitable giving to solve business transfer problems are unique. Current tax savings can be realized by the donor, and appreciated property can be sold by the trust with no tax liability to the donor. In addition to the personal benefit to donor and family is the value of the charitable gift and the community benefit it will provide.

The Charitable Lead Trust Alternative

A variation on the above is used when the income stream is directed to a charitable organization for a period of years, and the remainder interest goes to a family member, usually children or grandchildren. This is called a charitable lead trust and it also provides some extraordinary planning opportunities, using our old friend, the irrevocable trust.

A charitable lead trust can reduce current income taxes, reduce or eliminate estate and transfer taxes, and provide for a contribution to charity. However, the lead trust is not for someone who needs current income. Here's an example of how a charitable lead trust works:

Jack and Jill together own all the stock of Health Services, Inc., which is valued at $3 million. Their estate is currently worth $5 million, and Jack and Jill are concerned about the increasing value and increasing estate tax liability of Health Services, Inc., a regular C corporation.

Their 26-year-old son, Jack, Jr., works in the family business. Jack and Jill regularly and generously contribute to charity. The company is currently providing the three of them with maximum salaries and benefits, yet the increasing retained earnings concern them. They therefore plan to begin paying dividends.

Jack and Jill create a charitable lead trust with a 15-year term. The income is directed to a public charity that Jack and Jill support. The trust is funded with all the stock of Health Services, Inc., which begins to pay dividends to the trust in amounts sufficient to satisfy the annual amount the trust pays to charity. At the end of the 15-year term, the trust will terminate and the stock will be distributed to Jack, Jr., with no additional tax consequences.

Jack and Jill use their unified credit today in transferring the stock; the value of the stock transferred is reduced by the income stream paid to the charity ($3 million stock value minus $1.8 million present value of the charity's income stream, or a $1.2 million gift).

Jack and Jill remove an appreciating-in-value asset from their estate, saving more than $1.5 million in current estate taxes, at a 55 percent estate tax bracket. The money saved in estate taxes will almost cover the trust's payments to the charity ($1.8 million was the present value of the charity's 15 years of income). The business and all future growth was transferred to Jack, Jr.—the "cost" was the use of Jack and Jill's unified credit.

Combining a prefunded, nonqualified retirement plan (SERP) with a charitable lead trust gives donors an opportunity to create an income stream for themselves while transferring ownership to the next generation.

The Gift Annuity

There may be times when a gift annuity should be considered. For example, stock in the family business is to be transferred to a charitable trust, but the family business doesn't have *cash* to purchase the stock outright from the trust.

An installment note cannot be used between the family business and the charitable trust because the IRS could view the installment note transaction as self-dealing. The penalties for self-dealing are harsh: loss of the income tax deduction, possible inclusion in the estate at death of the asset transferred, and penalties for trustees. The solution may be a gift annuity, since an installment note between the family business and a public charity is not subject to the self-dealing rules.

With a gift annuity, the donor receives a guaranteed income for life, in exchange for making a direct gift (closely held stock, real estate, or other property) to a charity. The income is paid in the form of an annuity; part of each payment is a return of principal so only a portion is taxed as ordinary income. The income can begin immediately or can be deferred until a later date. If deferred, the annuity payments will be higher because the original investment will have had time to grow. Regardless of when the income begins, the donor takes a charitable income tax deduction at the time the gift is made. At death, the charity keeps whatever value remains.

As a planning technique, consider the following: Mom wants to retire and sell the business to her two active children. Rather than sell the 1000 shares (100 percent ownership) back to the company or to the kids, Mom elects to give each child one share and then contribute 998 shares to a gift annuity. The charity sells the 998 shares to the company for a long-term installment note. This transaction, properly structured at fair market value, avoids the self-dealing problems. It should provide Mom with both a charitable income tax deduction and a guaranteed income stream. The family business avoids having to use its valuable cash for the redemption; and the one share held by each child gives each 50 percent ownership. Mom believes the kids' commitment is represented in their willingness to repay the company's obligation to the charity.

Planning Strategies

When an existing charitable interest can be combined with irrevocable trusts—in their many different forms—exciting planning possibilities occur. Valuation methodology using discounts (minority and/or marketability) heightens those opportunities. Nonqualified plans can create a tax-favored income stream from the business and add one more planning arrow in the quiver of the family business owner.

These tools, when properly combined, can provide every family business owner with sufficient means to transfer the family business in a tax-efficient manner while reducing (or eliminating) estate taxes on the business and for the survivors.

27

Funding for Liquidity Needs

One of the biggest estate-planning mistakes is not providing sufficient liquid assets (cash or cash equivalents) to pay estate taxes. Without sufficient liquid assets, heirs may have to sell the family business to raise enough cash for estate taxes.

There are seven ways to pay estate taxes:

1. Self-insure, maintaining sufficient liquid assets to cover taxes due.

2. Liquidate assets to raise cash.

3. Borrow from the government, if the estate qualifies.

4. Borrow from a bank or other financial institution.

5. Redeem stock in the family business for cash, if the estate qualifies for a 303 redemption.

6. Carry life insurance on one individual.

7. Carry second-to-die or survivor life insurance.

Self-Insurance

Self-insurance requires a systematic savings plan, with funds set aside on a periodic basis in a securities account or bank account.

Some owners intend to use retirement plan accounts (such as pensions, profit-sharing plans, and IRAs) to provide estate liquidity. These accounts, however, may be subject to *triple taxes*—an income tax on withdrawal, an excess retirement accumulations tax, and an estate tax at death—and may not provide sufficient funds to cover future liabilities.

Other owners believe that real estate provides a better rate of return than traditional securities. Even during boom cycles, though, real estate portfolios are highly illiquid. They may be severely discounted in a forced sale, and their value can fluctuate unpredictably along with local economic conditions.

Liquidation of Assets

Real estate, or other assets, may need to be sold quickly at death to raise cash. Depending on the timing of the sale, discounts from fair market value may be 20 to 30 percent; fortunately, estate taxes would probably also be lower, reflecting the liquidation price in the estate of the assets sold. Unfortunately, if a cash-poor business is the primary asset in the estate, it may have to be sold to satisfy Uncle Sam.

Borrowing from the Government

If the value of the closely held family business constitutes 35 percent or more of the adjusted gross estate, the executor may "borrow" the estate taxes due from the government by using the 6166 election. Section 6166 of the Internal Revenue Code describes how taxpayers can qualify for an installment payment of estate taxes. Interest-only payments are made for the first five years; beginning in the fifth year, principal and interest on the unpaid balance is then amortized over a maximum of 10 more years. Yes, there is a "doubling up" in the fifth year.

These provisions, however, offer relatively little benefit. In substance, except for a bargain interest rate on a portion of the tax, the provisions simply give the estate the right to borrow money from the federal government at a market rate of interest. In addition, numerous technical requirements must be met to qualify for the tax deferral. Accordingly, the deferral provisions are generally viewed as a fallback solution, and do not replace a carefully considered plan for financing transfer tax liabilities. Finally, many states do not permit the deferral of inheritance taxes and require prompt payment in order to close probate.

For purposes of the 35 percent rule, interests in two or more businesses are treated as one business if 20 percent or more of the value of each business was in the decedent's estate and the combined values aggregate 35 percent or more of the adjusted gross estate. Also, ownership by family members (brothers, sisters, spouse, children, parents) may be combined in order to meet the 35 percent rule.

There are some pitfalls in using the 6166 election that should be carefully considered:

1. If nonbusiness assets in the estate appreciate faster than business assets, the estate may not qualify for the 6166 provision.

2. A 4 percent interest rate is payable on the first $1 million in value of a closely held business; the rate of interest on the excess is adjusted quarterly

by the Treasury Department in accordance with changes in the short-term federal rate. It is impossible to predict in advance how much interest will be paid on the government's variable-rate loan.

3. The deferral is available only for a *proportionate* amount of the tax, not the entire amount. If the business makes up 80 percent of the estate, then the deferral is 80 percent of the total tax. Additional borrowing or other sources of liquidity will be required.

4. The election to defer the tax is automatically terminated if more than 50 percent of the decedent's interest in the business is sold (or assets representing more than 50 percent of the business value are withdrawn). Therefore, the family could not sell the business for a small cash down payment with the balance in an installment note, because the deferred estate tax would become due and payable. The illiquid installment note could not satisfy the family's needs for cash.

5. Depending on state probate procedures, the estate may have to remain open until the final installment payment of tax is made.

Borrowing from a Bank

Borrowing from a financial institution may be a viable option depending on interest rates charged, term of the loan, and collateral to be pledged.

Often, though, the collateral may be the stock in the family business. The additional financing may severely restrict the company's ability to expand, grow, renovate, or make needed equipment upgrades. The result of new indebtedness may deter the company from competing, resulting in lost market share and a reduced business value just when the value needs to be maintained to provide sufficient collateral to cover the new loan. Selling the business may be the unplanned, but only feasible alternative.

The business may be able to afford a portion of the estate tax debt through recovery of the deceased's salary and perks. The compensation recovered can be redirected for principal and interest payments; the tax deduction of the interest paid may provide some slight tax relief. However, leveraging the estate in this manner when bank terms, interest rates, and economic conditions are an unknown seems a high-risk gambit for the future of the family business.

Stock Redemption Under the 303 Election

Estates comprised largely of close corporation stock may have a liquidity problem in the event of death. Congress enacted Section 303 of the Internal Revenue Code expressly to aid estates in solving this problem, and to protect small businesses from forced liquidation or merger because of the heavy impact of death taxes. Within the limits of Section 303, corporate surplus can be withdrawn from the business free of income tax.

Section 303 provides that under certain conditions, the corporation can redeem part of a deceased stockholder's shares without the redemption being treated as a dividend. Instead, the redemption price is treated as payment in exchange for stock (a capital transaction). The capital gains tax is then offset by the fact that the shareholder's basis in the stock gets "stepped up" to the date of death value. Therefore, no gain is recognized by the estate.

The 303 redemption can safely be used in connection with a partial redemption of stock of a family owned corporation because it avoids the attribution rules discussed earlier. The following conditions must be met for the stock redemption to qualify for nondividend treatment under Section 303:

1. The stock that is to be redeemed must be includable in the decedent's gross estate for federal estate tax purposes.

2. The value for estate tax purposes of all the stock of the redeeming corporation which is includable in the decedent's gross estate must comprise *more than 35 percent* of the value of the deceased's adjusted gross estate.

3. The dollar amount that can be paid out by the corporation under Section 303 is limited to an amount equal to the sum of (a) all estate and inheritance taxes and (b) funeral and administrative expenses. Any excess over this amount will be taxed as a dividend to the seller (i.e., the estate).

If the 303 election is to be used to provide liquid assets to the estate, the business must have sufficient cash, or access to it, to satisfy the 303 redemption requirement. If life insurance payable to the business is to be used

Value of Corporate Stock in Gross Estate...(1)	**$2,000,000**
Gross Estate Less Allowable Deductions...(2)	**$3,000,000**
35% of Gross Estate Less Allowable Deductions..................................(3)	**$1,050,000**
Qualifies if (1) is Greater Than (3)	

AMOUNT OF REDEMPTION PERMITTED UNDER SECTION 303

Funeral and Administrative Expenses (Including Probate Costs)................................	$120,000
Federal Estate and Generation–Skipping Taxes..	$862,960
State Death Taxes..	$171,440
Maximum Allowable Section 303 Redemption..	**$1,154,400**

Figure 27-1. Determination of whether the estate qualifies for Section 303 stock redemption.

to fund a 303 redemption, the business may have to pay a 20 percent alternative minimum tax on the insurance proceeds. Also, as discussed previously, if the estate plan uses the unlimited marital deduction, the 303 election will not make much sense until the second death, when estate taxes become due. Figure 27-1 illustrates how the 303 limitation provision is calculated.

Planning Tip. It is important to know that the redemption of stock is normally thought of as a means of providing liquidity to the estate for estate tax purposes. However, there are no requirements that the repurchase of the stock by the corporation be in cash. Corporate assets may be paid "in kind" as a means of distributing corporate property to the estate. For example, if the objective was to remove corporate real estate and transfer it to the family, the value of the real estate could be used to redeem stock from a deceased shareholder's estate. The property would be transferred out, subject to gain at the corporate level. This approach can be attractive if the asset removed from the corporation is then leased back to the entity by the shareholder's spouse or other family members.

Life Insurance

Funding for liquidity needs of the family and the business is a critical component of every plan. While insurance is not the only solution, often it's a key part of the overall plan. Insurance is an extremely sophisticated financial instrument. Understanding how it works and what it does can be challenging but rewarding. To avoid purchasing mistakes, take time to understand the options and risks available in the insurance market today.

Choosing Your Insurance Provider

Will you outlive your life insurance company? Until quite recently, the question was rhetorical. Little in life was as secure, stable, and enduring as the insurance industry. In 1981 not a single insurance company went out of business. Between 1983 and 1988, 89 insurers folded; in 1989 alone, 36 more became insolvent. Most of those were relatively small, but the largest firms haven't fared much better. In 1990 and 1991, several major firms went into receivership, others merged, and many had their credit ratings downgraded by independent rating agencies such as Standard & Poor's and Moody's, because of underlying weaknesses.

Monitoring the industry's members—in terms of both short-term performance and long-term survival—begins by checking credit-rating agencies' reports. Outfits such as A. M. Best, Moody's, Standard & Poor's, and Duff & Phelps analyze the finances of hundreds of insurers and pass judgment on the firms' financial health. Figure 27-2 explains the credit ratings.

Rating the Claims-Paying Ability of Life Insurance Companies

To determine whether your insurance company is fiscally fit, review its credit-rating reports.

A. M. Best Company annually examines and rates about 1400 life and health insurance companies. The firm's historical data on insurers is useful for comparative analysis. It rates a variety of important factors and gathers financial information on the basis of companies' annual reports. Individual company reports cost $15. (Ambest Road, Oldwick, NJ 08858; 908-439-2200)

Standard & Poor's Insurance Rating Services rates 135 life insurers through an in-depth analysis of carriers' projected claims-paying ability. Rather than computing ratios from annual statements (A. M. Best's method), S&P examines unpublished historical data, corporate projections, and management battle plans. Individual company reports cost $25. (25 Broadway, New York, NY 10004; 212-208-1592)

Moody's Investors Service rates the financial condition of 60 life insurance companies. The ratings, similar to its bond-rating system, are accompanied by a thorough review of an insurer's financials. Detailed company reports cost $1500 annually; a life handbook summary costs $150. (99 Church Street, New York, NY 10007; 212-553-1658)

Duff & Phelps rates the claims-paying ability of life insurers. It publishes in-depth reports on 100 insurers. D&P provides customized individual company reports for varying fees. Charter subscribers pay $495 per year. (55 E. Monroe Street, Chicago, IL 60603; 312-368-3157)

National Association of Insurance Commissioners publishes the *IRIS Ratio Reports*, which track companies that have fallen outside five measures of risk. The fee is $100 for the report plus $5 shipping. (120 W. 12 Street, Suite 1100, Kansas City, MO 64015; 816-842-3600)

The American Bar Association publishes the *ABA Primer: Life Insurance Products Counselor—Life Insurance Products, Illustrations, and Due Diligence.* (researched by The M Financial Group), which costs $34.95 plus $3.95 for shipping. (750 N. Lakeshore Drive, Chicago, IL 60611; 312-988-5571)

RATING DESCRIPTIONS	A. M. BEST	S&P	DUFF & PHELPS	MOODY'S
SUPERIOR Negligible risk	A +	AAA	AAA	Aaa
EXCELLENT Small, slight variable risk	A A-	AA + AA AA-	AA + AA AA-	Aa1 Aa2 Aa3
GOOD High claims-paying ability for now	B+	A + A A-	A + A A-	A1 A2 A3
ADEQUATE Less protection against risk	B B-	BBB + BBB BBB-	BBB + BBB BBB-	Baa1 Baa2 Baa3
BELOW AVERAGE Below average quality, higher risk factor	C +	BB + BB BB-	BB + BB BB-	Ba1 Ba2 Ba3
FINANCIALLY WEAK High risk factor	C C-	B+ B B-	B+ B B-	B1 B2 B3
NONVIABLE Nonviable or about to be	NA-7 NA-10	CCC CC D	CCC CC D	Caa Ca C

Figure 27-2. What the ratings mean.

Insurance Illustrations—Are They Credible?

Insurance illustrations based on a company's current dividend scale are *not* guarantees about how a policy will perform. *Caveat emptor* applies when attempting to gauge the credibility of an illustration; therefore, this section will outline some pitfalls to beware of and questions to ask an agent or company.

Life insurance illustrations provide year-by-year projections of premiums, cash values, and death benefits for a particular policy. The illustrations can be built with a variety of specified or implicit assumptions about mortality, lapses, investment experience, company expenses, and other factors that affect policy performance. The most credible illustrations are based on assumptions that reflect current levels of actual experience. The policy will therefore perform as illustrated *if* current conditions continue.

Although it is difficult for the lay insurance reviewer to judge these factors, the life insurance company should be able to state that the mortality, persistency, and investment assumptions in its products are fully supported by current experience. A clue to unsupportable assumptions can sometimes be found in the "supplemental interrogatories" of companies' annual statements at state insurance departments. This addresses the key question: Can current illustrations be supported for two years under current conditions? If the answer is no, then the insurance carrier or company should produce illustrations that incorporate supportable assumptions.

Consumers should compare competing life insurance products; the company should be asked for the internal rates of return on both death benefits and surrender value after 10, 20, and 30 years and at the combined life expectancy of both insureds (for a survivorship policy, which is explained later in this chapter).[1] The comparison of internal rates of return upon death and surrender is helpful when evaluating more than one illustration. It can be used to check out how reduced assumptions, such as a more conservative interest rate, would affect policy performance. (See Figure 27-3.)

	Male, Age 60 Female, Age 58		
	Company A	Company B	Company C
Face amount	$1,000,000	$1,000,000	$1,000,000
Annual premium	$17,358	$19,750	$23,692
Current crediting rate	9.00%	8.65%	8.85%
Vanishes after year	10	8	6
Total premiums projected	$173,580	$158,000	$142,152
Year 10			
Cash value	$210,073	$192,084	$189,147
Death benefit	$1,093,094	$1,006,917	$1,000,000
IRR on death	37.90%	29.62%	28.19%
Year 20			
Cash value	$463,921	$395,468	$391,600
Death benefit	$1,011,130	$1,018,171	$1,000,000
IRR on death	12.48%	11.80%	11.68%
Year 30			
Cash value	$859,463	$541,530	$627,782
Death benefit	$1,121,429	$1,031,354	$1,000,000
IRR on death	7.81%	7.33%	7.32%

Figure 27-3. Comparing three survivor life insurance products.

Questions to Ask About Illustrations

1. Does the current illustration project the premiums, cash values, and death benefits that can be expected?

2. Does the interest rate accurately reflect current investment performance? Has another, more conservative rate been illustrated in addition to the company's current rate?

3. Is the mortality assumption underlying the illustration based on current experience or does it include projected improvements? (It should not!)

4. What services exist after the insurance policy is issued to provide re-projections of in-force policies or to administer the pattern of premiums, withdrawals and loans illustrated?

5. Are different rates being credited today to new contracts than to contracts issued in prior years?

6. Are rates being illustrated which exceed the current rate actually being credited?

7. What types of investments (investment grades, maturity durations) currently support the rate? How is the current rate set? Is it tied to investment results of a specific segment of the carrier's portfolio?

8. Are the carrier's new investments today yielding enough to adequately cover the rate being illustrated today and the required interest spread? Given the company's present investment strategy, how does the carrier expect future rates to compare with outside indices such as Moody's or U.S. Treasuries? How closely have they tracked historically?

Questions to Ask About Carriers

1. What are the company's primary lines of business?

2. How large is the company's surplus?

3. What is the company's net portfolio rate of investment return?

4. How do the company's lapse, mortality, and expense ratios compare with the industry average?

5. What is the average policy size?

6. How does the company typically market its products?

7. Is the company backing the product a subsidiary of another insurance company or part of an affiliated group of related companies?

8. How does the company treat its in-force policyholders?

9. What is the company's retention level—that is, how much of the insurance will be reinsured with another carrier?

Individual Life Insurance

Survivor or second-to-die life insurance (discussed below) is often the least expensive way to pay estate taxes, but there are times when life insurance on one life—for the purpose of paying estate taxes—can make good sense. These situations usually occur when one individual is subject to the standard insurance premium and the other is highly "rated." (Because of current impaired health or medical history, the insurance company sometimes tacks on an additional "cost" or "price" to the standard premium for a policy and calls it a "rating.") Similarly, when one spouse is uninsurable and a survivor life policy is not available or is prohibitively expensive, it can make sense to acquire insurance on the healthier spouse. Generally, when insurance to fund estate taxes is being explored, pricing considerations (when other factors such as carrier strength and product design are comparable) will ultimately drive the purchasing decision.

Insurance on one life may also make sense when there is an intent to pay estate taxes at the first death. As noted in Chapter 24, because of graduated estate tax rates, it often makes sense for the bypass trust to receive more than $600,000—sometimes up to $2.5 million—and have the estate pay some estate tax on the first death. Insurance that pays a death benefit on one life can create the funds necessary to pay first-death estate taxes.

Insurance on one life is often appropriate when stepfamilies are created or when assets are intended for children prior to a spouse's death (and, therefore, subject to estate tax). Finally, when one spouse is widowed or divorced, insurance on one life may be the most efficient way to create readily available income-tax-free funds for Uncle Sam without having to liquidate other estate assets.

The type of insurance should either be universal life or whole life coverage—insurance that will be maintained for the rest of one's life. Term insurance policies are not a proper vehicle for estate planning, because they are priced *not* to be in force at the time of death. Term insurance provides protection on a temporary basis, not permanently. Term policies have an increasing premium structure; therefore, they tend to lapse or get canceled at the point when the policyholder believes that the cost (versus benefit to be received) is too expensive.

There are several ways to structure the insurance purchase so that the proceeds will escape estate taxation. If the insured is also the policyowner, the insurance will be subject to estate taxation. Having a third party as original owner of the policy—for example, grown children of the insured who are also the beneficiaries of the insurance—provides a double benefit: The insurance money is received income-tax-free and escapes estate taxes as well.

Survivor Life Insurance

Survivor life insurance, also known as second-to-die life insurance, can be an attractive choice when a significant amount of cash is required at the second of two deaths. Therefore, when an estate plan makes substantial use of the marital deduction or in some other manner defers the need for cash until the second death, survivor insurance may be the most efficient way to create the required funds.

Survivor life is a joint policy insuring two lives. However, the proceeds of a survivor policy are not payable until the second death. Therefore, the policy does not provide cash for a surviving spouse upon the first spouse's death.

Estate taxes on the survivor policy can generally be avoided by placing the policy in an irrevocable trust. The trust should be established *before* the policy is purchased, and should be the applicant, owner, and beneficiary of the policy. Premium payments may be made out of trust income if the trust is funded with income-producing property.

The grantor of the trust may also make gifts to the trust; these qualify for the annual gift tax exclusion of $10,000 for individuals and $20,000 for married couples. The gifts can then be used by the trustee to pay premiums. To minimize the chance that the IRS will consider the insured to have made either an indirect or a constructive transfer of the policy, the gifts should not be in the same amount as the premiums and should not be made too closely to premium due dates.

An additional advantage of a trust is protection of the estate should the surviving spouse remarry an unscrupulous individual.

By insuring both lives together, policyholders are able to purchase substantial estate protection for fewer premium dollars. If there is a divorce or change in estate tax law, the policy can usually be exchanged for two individual policies without having to provide evidence of insurability.

Who should consider survivor insurance?

- Married couples with assets of more than $1.2 million

- Business owners who would like to keep the business in the family rather than have it liquidated to pay death taxes

- Business owners who prefer to pass the business on to one child who is active, yet ensure that other children are treated fairly

- Employers who want to provide an employee benefit by using the split-dollar method (discussed below) to purchase survivor policies for key employees

- Parents of mentally or physically handicapped children who want to establish a sufficient fund to provide income after the second parent's death

- Parents who would like to leave a substantial portion of their estate to a charity or private foundation without depriving their children of family wealth

- Business owners who want to fund a stock redemption agreement at the spouse's death

Survivorship life insurance provides relatively low-cost estate liquidity when it is most needed: at the time of the second death. The amount of property ultimately passed to the decedents' heirs is preserved.

Case Study

John, 60, and Brandy, 58, have a $3 million gross estate. The family business is valued at $2 million. Typical of family business owners, John is asset-rich and cash-poor. The good news is that the estate qualifies for the 6166 deferral (if the family needs to use it) and can also qualify for a 303 redemption. If the unlimited marital deduction is not fully used at the first death, the executor can decide to subject some of the estate to a first-death estate tax in order to create liquid cash via the 303 stock redemption.

The $3 million estate will grow conservatively at 4 percent annually. At the second death, projected at age 85, the estate will be worth over $8 million—and it is assumed the family business is still in the estate, but at 4 percent annual growth, the business value is now $5.7 million.

Figure 27-4 compares the cost of funding for estate taxes, inheritance taxes, probate, and administrative expenses of $4.35 million due at the second death. The federal estate tax due would be $3.2 million. State inheritance taxes are $900,000, and administrative expenses and probate costs of 3 percent would eat up another $250,000. However, assets could be sold; in Figure 27-4 a 10 percent liquidation discount was factored in.

	Male, Age 60 Female, Age 58					
	Forced Liquidation of Assets (A)	Sec 6166 Deferral (B)	Bank Financing (C)	Sec 303 Redemption (D)	Single Life Insurance (E)	Survivor Life Insurance (F)
Cost During Life:	$0	$0	$0	$0	$1,088,444	$679,476
Cost at Death:	4,845,845	2,139,687	0	4,361,260	0	0
Deferred Cost Paid by Estate:	0	3,678,338	7,097,750	0	0	0
Total Costs:	$4,845,845	$5,818,025	$7,097,750	$4,361,260	$1,088,444	$679,476
PV of Total Cost:	$1,135,874	$1,064,114	$1,238,561	$1,022,287	$785,722	$490,498
Cost Per Dollar:	$0.26	$0.25	$0.29	$0.24	$0.18	$0.11

Present value calculated at 8% assuming death at age 85.

(E) 14 premiums of $77,746 paid annually, $4,350,000 face amount of insurance.

(F) 14 premiums of $48,534 paid annually, $4,350,000 face amount of insurance.

Figure 27-4. Comparison of funding alternatives.

The Section 6166 deferral allows for only 50 percent of the estate tax to qualify for installment payments. The payments would be about $200,000 (interest only) the first four years and then would jump in the fifth year to $220,000 of principal payments *plus* interest on the outstanding balance. For example, in the sixth year the family would need about $400,000 to satisfy the installment obligation. The family would still need about $2 million in cash at the second death to pay the other 50 percent of estate taxes due.

Bank financing isn't any more attractive; the $4.35 million debt, amortized over 10 years at 10 percent, would require annual payments of $710,000.

The 303 redemption can also be used at the second death; in this case, the company could redeem enough stock to pay the entire liquidity needed by the family for taxes. The problem is the company will need to distribute $4.35 million of retained earnings. If the company had key employee life insurance, the insurance money paid to the business would be subject to a 20 percent minimum tax.

A $4.35 million life insurance policy on Mom would be about $75,000 of annual premium; 14 premiums would be paid on a vanishing basis (see below). If the policy had been on Dad, the annual premium would have been about $100,000 for 14 years. Survivor life insurance of $4.35 million would also take 14 premiums; the annual cost, however, would be about $48,000 annually.

The taxes will have to be paid; the ultimate question is what's the most efficient and least expensive way of handling it?

The "Vanishing" Premium

Most whole life or universal life policies today can be structured with a "vanishing" premium, so the policyholder can reasonably project how many premiums will need to be paid, can calculate a "rate of return" on proceeds to be received (versus deposits made), and can compare the insurance purchasing decision with other funding alternatives. (See Figure 27-5.)

The premium does not actually vanish. The policy's dividends are used to purchase "paid-up additions"—small increments of additional insurance coverage. The premiums are usually paid for 7 to 10 years by the policyowner; after that, future premiums are paid out of the policy's own values, by an internal (to the insurance company) mechanism that relieves the policyowner of having to make future payments. This "vanishing" mechanism, however, is dependent on the insurance company maintaining its own earnings on investments (which are credited to the policy as dividends) as well as other factors. Any change in the insurance company's own operating profitability will affect the nonguaranteed vanish points in the policy.

For example, in Figure 27-6, the effect of a drop in the interest rate credited to a policy can be seen both in extending the premium-paying period and reducing ultimate values. Therefore, always request alternate illustrations (showing what happens to the policy under different scenarios) when considering an insurance purchase.

Male, Age 50

Year	Age	Annual Premium	End of Year Account Value	Death Benefit	Death Benefit IRR	Cost per Dollar
1	50	$ 23,888	$ 15,459	$1,000,000	4086.20%	0.02
2	51	23,888	31,452	1,000,000	498.94%	0.05
3	52	23,888	49,359	1,000,000	208.22%	0.07
4	53	23,888	68,857	1,000,000	121.19%	0.10
5	54	23,888	90,099	1,000,000	81.74%	0.12
6	55	23,888	117,763	1,000,000	59.83%	0.14
7	56	23,888	147,768	1,000,000	46.10%	0.17
8	57	0	156,755	1,000,000	37.53%	0.17
9	58	0	166,305	1,000,000	31.50%	0.17
10	59	0	183,429	1,000,000	27.06%	0.17
Total		$167,216				
11	60	0	195,666	1,000,000	23.67%	0.17
12	61	0	208,374	1,000,000	21.02%	0.17
13	62	0	221,447	1,000,000	18.88%	0.17
14	63	0	234,757	1,000,000	17.13%	0.17
15	64	0	248,036	1,000,000	15.67%	0.17
16	65	0	260,531	1,000,000	14.43%	0.17
17	66	0	273,182	1,000,000	13.37%	0.17
18	67	0	285,913	1,000,000	12.46%	0.17
19	68	0	298,456	1,000,000	11.66%	0.17
20	69	0	348,751	1,000,000	10.95%	0.17
Total		$167,216				
21	70	0	366,313	1,000,000	10.33%	0.17
22	71	0	384,089	1,000,000	9.77%	0.17
23	72	0	402,036	1,000,000	9.27%	0.17
24	73	0	420,325	1,000,000	8.82%	0.17
25	74	0	438,919	1,000,000	8.40%	0.17
26	75	0	457,755	1,000,000	8.03%	0.17
27	76	0	476,830	1,000,000	7.69%	0.17
28	77	0	496,070	1,000,000	7.37%	0.17
29	78	0	515,437	1,000,000	7.08%	0.17
30	79	0	534,898	1,000,000	6.81%	0.17
Total		$167,216				

Figure 27-5. Vanishing premiums.

Split-Dollar Life Insurance

Split dollar isn't a type of policy, it's a method of paying premiums. The concept can be used whenever one party needs insurance and another party has the ability to pay for it. It's most often used as a fringe benefit for key employees and executives, but it can be valuable in family situations. It is also a cost-effective way for an owner-employee to purchase personal insurance with corporate dollars.

Male, Age 50			
Crediting rate	8.6%	7.6%	6.6%
Face amount	$1,000,000	$1,000,000	$1,000,000
Annual premium	$20,570	$20,570	$20,570
Vanishes after year	10	12	15
Total premiums projected	$205,700	$246,840	$308,550
Year 10			
Cash value	$216,248	$204,398	$193,188
Death benefit	$1,000,000	$1,000,000	$1,000,000
IRR on death	27.72%	27.72%	27.72%
Year 20			
Cash value	$378,381	$411,014	$448,298
Death benefit	$1,000,000	$1,000,000	$1,000,000
IRR on death	10.44%	9.63%	8.74%
Year 30			
Cash value	$545,775	$576,103	$609,334
Death benefit	$1,000,000	$1,000,000	$1,000,000
IRR on death	6.32%	5.71%	5.01%

Figure 27-6. How the interest crediting rate affects product performance.

In effect, split-dollar life insurance is ordinary life insurance that allows a corporation and an employee (or a shareholder) to share the economic burden (premiums) and benefits of the policy. The concept is based on the simple fact that an ordinary life insurance policy has two main features: (1) increasing cash values, and (2) decreasing pure insurance protection. The corporation normally pays the premiums on, and receives the benefit of, the portion of the policy representing the cash value; the employee pays the premiums on the "pure insurance" portion and controls disposition of those proceeds.

The employer is generally named beneficiary of that portion of the death proceeds equal to its total contribution to the plan. The employee, by agreement with the payor, retains the power to name a beneficiary for that portion of the proceeds in excess of those payable to the employer. The employee's designation of a beneficiary for the excess death benefit is a form of compensation, and he or she is required to report the value of this economic benefit as taxable income. Figure 27-7 depicts the arrangement.

In most split-dollar plans, the employee usually has incidents of ownership in the insurance policy and the proceeds paid to his or her beneficiary are includable in the gross estate.

It is possible to avoid this inclusion and the resulting estate tax if the split-dollar plan is arranged between the employer and an irrevocable life insurance trust (or another third party such as children of the insured), rather than with

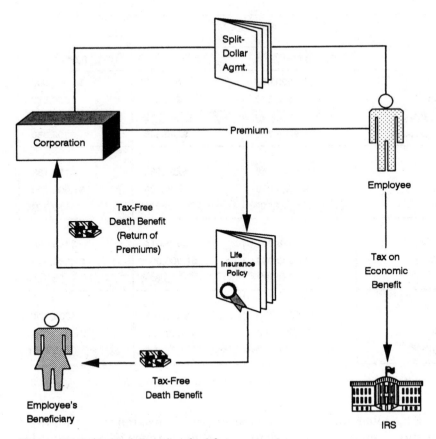

Figure 27-7. Split-dollar plan for life insurance.

the employee directly. The third party should apply for and own the policy and use a collateral assignment (of the policy's cash values) back to the employer.

Special care must be taken if the insured is also a majority shareholder (owning greater than 50 percent) of the corporation. This ownership will cause the corporation's incidents of ownership in the insurance policy, if any, to be attributed to the majority shareholder and therefore include the proceeds in his or her estate. A clear solution is to restrict the corporation's rights as "owner" to (1) borrowing against the policy up to the amount of premium contributions, and (2) designating a beneficiary for its part of the death proceeds. The power the corporation specifically must *not* have is the right to surrender the policy.

References

1. Richard Schwartz, "Due Diligence: Assessing the Survivorship Purchase," *Trusts and Estates,* May 1991.

PART 7
Conclusion

28
Where to Go from Here

David Bork, a well-known family business consultant, examined 250 family businesses in the early 1980s and from that experience derived 10 qualities that healthy and successful family businesses and business families exhibited. He calls these qualities Management Principles for Family Business.[1]

1. *Shared values.* Healthy business families share values about people, work, and money.

2. *Shared power.* Power is shared across generations, between spouses, and among siblings. This is not to be construed as equal power.

3. *Shared activities for maintaining relationships.* Families that maintain their sense of humor, demonstrate an ability to have fun, and play together are putting "relationship currency" into the family bank so there is a reserve to draw upon during times of disagreement.

4. *Traditions.* The healthy business family has traditions that make it special and set it apart from all other families.

5. *Willingness to learn and grow.* The family that is open to new ideas and approaches is one that, as a group, can solve most problems.

6. *Genuine caring.* There is open expression of feelings of concern for other family members.

7. *Mutual respect.* There is a trust between and among family members that is built on a history of keeping one's word.

8. *Mutual assistance and support.* Especially at times of grief, loss, pain, and shame, family members support one another.

9. *Privacy.* Family members respect one another's individual space as well as the private space required in each family unit within the extended family.

10. *Well-defined interpersonal boundaries.*   To keep individuals from getting caught in the middle, well-established boundaries keep conflicts between two family members from involving a third person.

Open discussion of these qualities is a helpful starting point. Understanding how a family's values and ethics translate into behavior can lead a family to a constructive succession path. After all, family values are often represented in the culture of the family business.

Finding that first (or next) step in the succession plan can be daunting. There are a number of possibilities to explore before starting down a particular path. Should family members hold a meeting, call the attorney, find a consultant, or attend one of the dozens of seminars now available for the family business?

There is no "packaged" solution that will work every time out. There are no simple answers. The greatest benefit of using consultants, attending seminars, or reading books is to get in closer touch with personal objectives, dreams, and goals and to encourage important others to freely express *their* dreams and goals as well.

Clearing the path requires getting centered and understanding the different hats people wear at different times. Distinguishing a sense of obligation from what is right for the family and the business is critical. What family members feel they should do may be very different from what each one wants to do. Hopefully, what everyone wants to do will also be the "right" thing to do to protect the business and maintain the family. But most business families find a wide gap between expectations, readiness, commitment, and letting go. Transitions are never easy; getting in touch with dreams and balancing them with a dose of reality is the first step. Sprinkling compassion and acceptance over the process will smooth the bumps in the road.

Family Business Consultants

In 1985 a group of consultants and academicians with a common interest in family businesses organized the Family Firm Institute (FFI). FFI is a professional organization comprised of three groups: professionals who serve family-owned businesses, academic researchers who study such businesses, and family business owners and managers who lead them. FFI's primary mission is to generate, stimulate, and disseminate knowledge about family business issues so that family-owned businesses may function more effectively.

Most family business consultants belong to FFI, since it is the only professional organization that focuses on the family business. But family business consultants come in all stripes, sizes and colors. For example, consultants whose background is therapeutic or clinical (psychiatry, psychotherapy, family counseling) tend to look initially at therapeutic or clinical solutions to problems. Consultants with legal, tax, or financial backgrounds (lawyers, CPAs, financial planners, estate planners) tend to look initially at structural solutions to the same problems. Competent consultants combine these approaches. Even so, the methods of combining the approaches may vary widely with equally variable rates of success.

In *interdisciplinary consulting*, a consultant brings other advisers in at different times (or all at once) to develop a collective view of the family's needs. For example, the therapist who doesn't understand financial statements may network with an accountant to supply that expertise and an attorney to provide a legal perspective. The drawback to interdisciplinary teams is that each professional has his or her own expertise but often lacks an understanding of the other perspectives. Creative solutions that come from synergy may be missing. As a result, the client winds up quarterbacking the consultant as well as existing advisers.

Also, the consultant's "main business"—defined by where the consultant generates most of his or her income—may be in a particular practice area (such as family counseling or organizational consulting) rather than in family businesses per se. In this case, personal income "pressures" may keep the consultant from expanding his or her own knowledge base.

Integrated consulting is a newer approach that requires the consulting "team" to have in-depth knowledge of different disciplines. Required disciplines include family systems and mediation skills, legal (corporate and estate) expertise, tax (individual and corporate) planning, organizational development (strategic planning, team building, leadership development), and business valuation training. When these disciplines are integrated into one consulting team, the client gets promoted from quarterback to coach and the consultants can spearhead the process. Also, the integrated approach is more effective with existing advisers, because the integrated team can fluently speak each adviser's language (legal, tax, organizational development, banking, and so on).

During the first interview, the main client should try to establish the credibility of the consultant. The consultant should meet all the clients—Dad, Mom, active kids (and spouses), inactive kids (and spouses), and nonfamily key employees—along with existing advisers. The consultant's role is to find (or create) a common solution for the family, so everyone needs to be involved in the hiring process. If the consultant is initially hired by one family member, those not involved in the selection process tend to perceive the consultant as an advocate rather than a consensus builder.

An article in *Family Business Review*[2] proposes the following professional and educational criteria for evaluating consultants:

- A master's degree or higher in a recognized professional field relating to either business organizations or the treatment of individuals or families

- Membership in good standing in a national or state organization or association that licenses or sets standards in the chosen professional field

- A minimum of 10 years of professional experience in that field

- Demonstrated mastery of the literature on family-owned businesses

Also, review the consultant's written publications, if any. Journal articles and monographs can provide a good perspective on the consultant's philosophy. Check references. Overall, determine if the "chemistry" is right. The family business consultant's work can significantly influence the future of the family and the business.

Consulting fees range from hourly rates to per diems. Some consultants quote a fixed fee on a project basis. It won't be cheap. On the other hand, it may be only a fraction of what a business broker or investment banker would charge to sell the business—or a miniscule amount compared with the millions in estate tax savings that can be realized.

Seminars

A growing number of universities and colleges are "discovering" family businesses. Kennesaw State College (near Atlanta), Oregon State University (in Corvallis), and the Wharton School (in Philadelphia) were forerunners in developing ongoing family business forums. These membership-based programs bring family business owners together several times a year in an academic setting to discuss relevant topics presented by local or national experts. The programs are for owners, family members, key nonfamily members, and even existing advisers who want to learn more about their family business clients.

Besides exposure to information, the forums provide an opportunity for family businesses to learn that they are not alone—other family businesses also have similar problems. One attendee commented that learning what goes on in other family businesses made him believe that not only were his problems solvable but his family wasn't nearly as "screwed up" as he thought. Several of the other families who were forum members appeared to have more serious problems.

In addition to family business forums, two nationwide organizations that indirectly address family business issues are the Young President's Organization (YPO), which sponsors many programs, and The Executive Committee (TEC), which has 10- to 12-member groups in 35 metropolitan areas in the United States. Membership is exclusively CEO-owners, and each group has a professional facilitator who coordinates the monthly meetings. Local groups or chapters can be reached through the national office.

Family Offices

Family groups who sell the family business to the next generation or to outsiders, or who recapitalize significant family assets, often create a "family office" to centralize the management of assets. Family offices provide investment record keeping, tax planning, and other personal services similar to those provided by support staff in the family business. Often both the business and the family benefit, because the family office continues to provide former owners (and their children) the services that the business owner once enjoyed from the company.

The Family Office Exchange in Chicago recommends setting up family offices for several reasons. To begin with, business owners should establish a fund of marketable securities, outside the operating business, that can be used to pay unexpected financial obligations (disability, divorce, estate taxes, and so on). Having assets inside a family office structure allows investments to be made that are countercyclical to the family business and avoids keeping all the eggs in one basket.

Families can structure the family office as a holding company to coordinate various other businesses owned by the family. The family office then becomes the focal point for all family members, whether or not they work in the family business.

Sometimes it is helpful to develop an important role for family members who are not in the business—a role that elevates them from second-class-shareholder status. The family office can provide continuity beyond the family business, a place to focus on family unity where all siblings or cousins are equal. Often the family office investment of assets can provide an opportunity for some family members to start another successful business.

Finally, the family office provides an appropriate setting to start educating younger family members about financial matters. The family office manager can help teach principles of wealth management and provide an objective financial adviser when needed. Families who establish small funds for children to invest on their own are providing them with a sense of independence and essential lessons that are often learned only through experience. This concept is called "money to grow on."

Boards of Directors

It is difficult for most people to conceive of evaluating a family business owner—and having the owner sit still long enough to listen to a critique of how he or she is doing. The outside board of directors, when properly constructed of respected peers, can provide that service, along with many others.

Much has been written about professionalizing the family business—having professional managers, establishing leadership development programs, installing feedback systems, focusing on team building, and having clear policies, procedures, and overall a strategic plan. Less is written about professionalizing ownership responsibilities. Often this can occur with the "right" board of directors.

Recent research from the Harvard Business School provides important insights into assembling the "right" board.[3] CEOs were asked to rate their board on perceived value. The most prevalent board, comprised entirely of family members, received the lowest value rating. The highest value rating occurred when boards were comprised of five or more outsiders. An outside director was defined as one who was not a member of the controlling family, not an active or retired employee, not a retained professional adviser, and not a close family friend of the CEO. As one business owner noted: "In forming my board, I made the classic mistakes, inviting my attorney, banker, and insurance man....I learned that the worst thing that an owner can do is to have friends and personal advisers on the board. The second worst thing an owner can do is not to have a board at all."[4]

The less family-dominated the board is, the more valuable it is perceived to be by CEOs. Two outsiders on a board provide a crucial demarcation. Boards with only one outsider imply that the CEO may not really want to "open up" the company to outside perspectives. Two or more outside board members create a critical mass.

As summarized in Figure 28-1, CEOs tend to value outside board members more for their business acumen than for their family assistance. General objectivity was valued more than specific technical expertise. People *other than* outside board members were considered to be more useful for mediation, arbitration, and assistance with choice of successor. Interviews with outside directors support this view: They view themselves as silent supporters, not active participants, when it comes to family tensions and conflicts.

A CEO must honestly want an outside board for it to work. The CEO has to be open and must maintain open communication; otherwise, board members will come to feel that their efforts are useless. The selection process for board members can be enhanced if other outside directors are involved. A poorly chosen outsider can actually be a detriment to a board.

Finally, CEOs who use their boards for advice, counsel, and accountability develop their boards into an important resource that fulfills their expectations. Realistic expectations of what a board can do is a critical component of the board's success.

Overall, the Harvard study found that "the sooner the better" was the best advice in putting together a board for the family business. Keeping outsiders off a board can serve the personal purposes of the owner, but possibly at the expense of the business's survival.

Summary

James Conant once remarked, "Behold the turtle. He makes progress only when he sticks his neck out." Family businesses have been created by courageous entrepreneurs who stuck their necks out. Vision and passion are two key components for entrepreneurial success. Developing it, focusing it, maturing it, and making mistakes are all part of the process of empowering successors and developing the succession plan. The most courageous job of all, however, is to perpetuate the family business successfully. Loving, giving, and forgiving is what ties family members together—and is often the true basis for their business's success.

MOST HELP	LEAST HELP
Unbiased, objective views	Day–to–day operations
Accountability of management	Issues of family conflict
Network of contacts	Technical expertise
Asking challenging questions	Very specific matters
Long–term perspective	
Setting executive salaries	

Figure 28-1. The areas where outside directors provide the most help and the least help.

Throughout this book we've explored a number of "how tos": how to transfer a family business, how to maintain and preserve family wealth, how to recognize the obstacles to a transfer. Values and ideas must be consciously shared. Children or successors cannot share the owner's goals through osmosis. They need to talk to one another, share with one another. Owners should explain to successors why they do the things they do and make the decisions they make.

Communication should begin with children at an early age. The family business is a unique environment for children. As they grow up, children can come to feel part of and love that business environment.

The family business is constantly evolving over time, just as its individual members evolve. The evolution of the family business can benefit those who are part of it and stay with it. Continued personal growth that leads to greater fulfillment, family growth that leads to greater harmony, and business growth that leads to economic success are the by-products of passing the torch. Those who see ownership succession as an adventure, a challenging opportunity, and a potentially rewarding experience have the greatest chance of succeeding with their business transfer.

Owners' future, and the future of their children, will be built on the plans they design and implement today. Successors' and owners' ideas and dreams should be part of those plans. Respect and communication among all participants will give everyone the incentive to make the transfer a success. Family business and business families can help each other mature.

There can be a dynamic balance between the present and the future, the aging owner and the younger successors. The plans put in place today will affect the family and the business for years to come. Henry Van Dyke's perspective may help you through the process:

> Be glad of life because it
> Gives you the chance to
> Love and to work and to
> Play and to look up at
> The stars.

References

1. David Bork, Presentation to M Financial Group, Los Angeles, October 1990.

2. Thomas Davidow, and Richard Narva, "Credentials: A Commentary," *Family Business Review*, vol. 3, no. 3 (Fall 1990).

3. Marc A. Schwartz and Louis B. Barnes, "Outside Boards and Family Businesses: Another Look," *Family Business Review*, vol. 4, no. 3 (Fall 1991).

4. Clayton A. Mathile, "A Business Owner's Perspective on Outside Boards," *Family Business Review*, vol. 1, no. 3 (Fall 1988).

Bibliography

Adizes, Ichak. *Corporate Lifecycles: How and Why Corporations Grow and Die.* Englewood Cliffs, NJ: Prentice Hall, 1988.

Alexander, Charles N., and Ellen J. Langer. *Higher Stages of Human Development: Perspectives on Adult Growth.* New York: Oxford University Press, 1990.

Aronoff, Craig E., and John L. Ward. *Family Business Sourcebook.* Detroit: Omnigraphics, 1991.

Bolman, Lee G., and Terrence E. Deal. *Reframing Organizations: Artistry, Choice and Leadership.* San Francisco: Jossey-Bass, 1991.

Bridges, William. *Transitions: Making Sense of Life's Changes.* Reading, MA: Addison-Wesley, 1980.

Bork, David. *Family Business, Risky Business: How to Make It Work.* New York: AMACOM, 1986.

Checkland, Peter. *Systems Thinking, Systems Practice.* New York: John Wiley & Sons, 1981.

Cooper, George. *A Voluntary Tax? New Perspectives on Sophisticated Estate Tax Avoidance.* Washington, DC: The Brookings Institution, 1979.

Danco, Leon. *Beyond Survival: A Business Owner's Guide for Success,* 5th ed. Cleveland: The University Press, Inc., 1979.

———. *Inside the Family Business.* Cleveland: The University Press, Inc., 1980.

DePree, Max. *Leadership Is an Art.* New York: Dell, 1989.

Dychtwald, Ken, and Joe Flower. *Age Wave: The Challenges and Opportunities of an Aging America.* New York: Bantam, 1990.

Dyer, W. Gibb, Jr. *Cultural Change in Family Firms.* San Francisco: Jossey-Bass, 1986.

Edinberg, Mark A. *Talking with Your Aging Parents.* Boston: Shambhala, 1987.

Eliot, Robert S., and Dennis L. Breo. *Is It Worth Dying For?* New York: Bantam, 1984.

Erikson, Erik H. *Childhood and Society.* New York: W. W. Norton, 1963.

Fisher, Robert, and William Ury. *Getting to Yes: Negotiating Agreement Without Giving In.* New York: Penguin, 1983.

Fisher, Roger, and Scott Brown. *Getting Together: Building Relationships As We Negotiate.* New York: Penguin, 1989.

Flamholtz, Eric G. *How to Make the Transition from an Entrepreneurship to a Professionally Managed Firm.* San Francisco: Jossey-Bass, 1986.

Gould, Roger L., M.D. *Transformations: Change and Growth in Adult Life.* New York: Touchstone, 1979.

Heskett, James L., W. Earl Sasser, Jr., and Christopher Hart. *Service Breakthroughs: Changing the Rules of the Game.* New York: The Free Press, 1990.

Hoffman, Lynn. *Foundations of Family Therapy: A Conceptual Framework for Systems Change.* New York: Basic Books, 1981.

Jaffe, Dennis T. *Working with the Ones You Love: Conflict Resolution and Problem Solving Strategies for a Successful Family Business.* Berkeley, CA: Conari Press, 1990.

Jaffe, Dennis T., and Cynthia D. Scott. *Take This Job and Love It.* New York: Simon & Schuster, 1988.

Kolbe, Kathy. *The Conative Connection.* Reading, MA: Addison-Wesley, 1990.

Laing, R. D. *The Politics of the Family and Other Essays.* New York: Vintage Books, 1971.

Laszlo, Ervin. *The Systems View of the World.* New York: George Braziller, 1972.

Leimberg, Stephan R., et al. *Financial Services: Professionals' Guide to the State of the Art, 1989.* Bryn Mawr, PA: The American College, 1989.

Levinson, D. J. *The Seasons of a Man's Life.* New York: Ballantine, 1978.

McQuaig, Jack H. *Your Business, Your Son, and You.* Coral Springs, FL: B. Klein, 1979.

Maccoby, Michael. *Why Work: Motivating and Leading the New Generation.* New York: Touchstone, 1988.

Marlin, Emily. *Genograms.* Chicago: Contemporary Books, 1989.

Maslow, A. H. *Eupsychian Management.* Homewood, IL: Richard D. Irwin, 1965.

————. *The Farther Reaches of Human Nature.* New York: Viking, 1971.

————. *Toward a Psychology of Being.* New York: Van Nostrand Reinhold, 1968.

Millman, Marcia. *Warm Hearts and Cold Cash: The Intimate Dynamics of Families and Money.* New York: Free Press, 1991.

Myers, Albert, and Christopher P. Andersen. *Success over Sixty.* New York: Summit, 1984.

Nair, Keshavan. *Beyond Winning: The Handbook for the Leadership Revolution.* Phoenix, AZ: Paradox, 1990.

Naisbitt, John. *Megatrends: Ten New Directions Transforming Our Lives.* New York: Warner, 1982.

Peters, Tom. *Thriving on Chaos.* New York: Alfred A. Knopf, 1988.

Peters, T. J., and R. H. Waterman, Jr. *In Search of Excellence.* New York: Harper & Row, 1982.

Poza, Ernesto J. *Smart Growth.* San Francisco: Jossey-Bass, 1989.

Pratt, Shannon P. *Valuing A Business.* 2d ed. Homewood, IL: Dow Jones–Irwin, 1989.

Rosenblatt, P. C., et al. *The Family in Business.* San Francisco: Jossey-Bass, 1985.

Russell, G. Hugh, and Kenneth Black, Jr. *Human Behavior in Business.* Englewood Cliffs, NJ: Prentice Hall, 1972.

Scarf, Maggie. *Intimate Partners.* New York: Ballantine, 1987.

Senge, Peter M. *The Fifth Discipline: The Art and Practice of the Learning Organization.* New York: Doubleday, 1990.

Sheehy, Gail. *Passages: Predictable Crises of Adult Life.* New York: Bantam, 1977.

Tichy, Noel M., and Mary Anne Devanna. *The Transformational Leader.* New York: John Wiley & Sons, 1986.

Toffler, Alvin. *Powershift: Knowledge, Wealth and Violence at the Edge of the 21st Century.* New York: Bantam, 1990.

Ward, John. *Keeping the Family Business Healthy.* San Francisco: Jossey-Bass, 1987.

Waterman, Robert H., Jr. *The Renewal Factor.* New York: Bantam, 1987.

Weisbord, Marvin R. *Productive Workplaces.* San Francisco: Jossey-Bass, 1990.

Wright, Jeffrey P. *What Is a Business Worth?* Scottsdale, AZ: EVS Publications, 1990.

Index

Note: An *f.* after a page number refers to a figure.

About the Author

Mike Cohn is president of The Cohn Financial Group, Inc., a Phoenix, Arizona-based firm specializing in the design and implementation of ownership succession and wealth transfer plans for family-owned businesses throughout the United States. He is a nationally recognized family business consultant and lecturer, who is a workshop leader for national and regional trade associations, and serves on the board of directors for the Family Firm Institute.

In addition to being a business owner himself, Mr. Cohn grew up in a family-owned business and has personal experience with many of the issues covered in this book. His unique ability to discuss business issues, as well as valuation, legal, and tax issues, in light of family dynamics provides a fresh perspective to families who are attempting to transfer financial, cultural, and psychological assets from one generation to the next. Mr. Cohn holds a B.A. and M.A. in psychology.